Know Your
Parenting Personality

April '03.

To Jeanette —
best wishes,
Janet Lewis

Also by Janet Levine

*The Enneagram Intelligences: Understanding Personality
for Effective Teaching and Learning*

*Inside Apartheid: One Woman's Struggle
in South Africa*

Know Your Parenting Personality

How to Use the Enneagram to Become the Best Parent You Can Be

JANET LEVINE

WILEY

John Wiley & Sons, Inc

Published by John Wiley & Sons, Inc., Hoboken, New Jersey
Published simultaneously in Canada

Design and production by Navta Associates, Inc.

The majority of the material in the appendix appeared previously in chapter 1 of *The Enneagram Intelligences: Understanding Personality for Effective Teaching and Learning* by the author and published by Greenwood Publishing Group. Used here with permission.

For general information about our other products and services, please contact our Customer Care Department within the United States at (800) 762-2974, outside the United States at (317) 572-3993 or fax (317) 572-4002.

Wiley also publishes its books in a variety of electronic formats. Some content that appears in print may not be available in electronic books. For more information about Wiley products, visit our web site at www.wiley.com.

ISBN: 0-471-25061-9

Printed in the United States of America

10 9 8 7 6 5 4 3 2 1

To my parents,
Solly and Eileen Berman

CONTENTS

Acknowledgments   ix

Introduction   1

1. Discovering Your Parenting Personality   9
    What's Your Type?

2. The Helper   33
    Meeting the Needs of Others

3. The Organizer   55
    Loving through Doing

4. The Dreamer   79
    Connection Is Everything

5. The Observer   101
    Let's Step Back and See

6. The Questioner   125
    "Be Prepared"—That's My Motto

7. The Entertainer   149
    Let's Have Fun! Let's Play!

8. The Protector   171
   I Am Your Sanctuary: Nothing Threatens You Here

9. The Peacekeeper   195
   Living Life through Others

10. The Moralizer   221
    Always Striving for Perfection

Epilogue   245
   Taking the Next Step

Appendix   251
   History, Research, and Theory on Personality Studies

References   268

Topics for Discussion   269

Index   273

ACKNOWLEDGMENTS

Thanks to Bob, Dave, Donna, Franklin, Heather, Jody, Katherine, Larry, and Terry for sharing their wisdom and experience, and to Guy and Louise for their input.

Thanks to Roger for his staunch support in all ways to do with this book.

Thanks to Kay for her patient listening and tireless interest.

Thanks to Wendy for her loyalty and for giving me space in her home in which to write part of the book.

Thanks to my persistent agent, Cullen Stanley, and to Carole Hall and Kimberly Monroe-Hill, my admirable editors at John Wiley.

Thanks to my many colleagues and friends in our Enneagram community for their interest in and enthusiasm for this project.

Introduction

This book, in matter-of-fact, straightforward language, describes the personalities of ordinary people and how they function as parents. While the book is based on Enneagram (E-model) theory, the material encompasses the latest ideas and trends in the field of personality studies as a whole.

The Enneagram is a model of personality that describes nine worldviews or strategies—nine intelligences. In Greek *ennea* means "nine" and *gram* means "graph" or "model." Fully accounting for individual differences—race, sex, age, ethnicity, socio-economic status, intelligence—the E-model allows for an infinite variety of individual expression within its nine strategies. The model is based on nine patterns of thoughts, feelings, motivations, and perceptions. Each encompasses a distinctive way of perceiving the world. No E-strategy is better than any other; they are all equally valid.

I believe that the E-model is an invaluable path to one's inner growth as a parent. This dynamic system can be your best guide to becoming the parent you want to be.

The aim and purpose of this book is to help you put this groundbreaking understanding of personality to work for yourself and your family. When you first uncover the motivations underpinning your personality, some aspects may seem strange and unfamiliar. But as you become more comfortable with knowing yourself, the strangeness fades. Soon you'll wear your new knowledge like a pair of glasses that allow you to see not only your own worldview clearly but also the worldviews of the others with whom you share your life. I look forward to showing you how to use this vision to achieve your parenting goals. Let's start by looking at what some of those goals might be.

Establishing Strong Connections with Your Child

Imagine parent-child interactions in which you're aware of how your personality affects the way you behave as a parent and how the personality of your child interacts with your own. In such a situation you are both winners. No one feels alienated because of personality differences. Being aware of your personality patterns provides insight to help you mobilize good parenting strategies. In this way you can reconcile the differences between yourself and your child.

It's important to recognize that all personalities are equally valid; none is better than another. Recognizing that there are alternate worldviews helps you nurture your child's self-esteem and allows you to connect in ways you never knew were possible.

Changing Self-Defeating Behavior Patterns

We all know that personality differences exist in the world. How often have you caught yourself being reactive in response to someone else and sighed, "Here I go again"? When you know your own personality strategy, you are freed from habitual patterns of behavior and a perspective with a narrow focus. This knowledge improves interactions with your child (and others). Such knowledge leads you out of the cage created by your habitual patterns of behavior and unlocks for you an accurate understanding of the attributes of personality.

When you grow to be aware of your personality strategy, you realize that it is both your greatest strength as a parent (parenting by personal example) and your greatest weakness (alienating for your child, whose motivations for his or her behavior are quite unlike your own). This knowledge can free you to become a true guide. By being less dominant as a parent and finding ways to encourage your child to be him- or herself, you cease to be at the center of your parenting stage and become a facilitator for your child's growth and development.

At first this behavioral shift can feel counterintuitive. But allow time for the dynamic to develop, and the results can be affirming for you and your child.

Deepening Communication with Your Child

Communication is your essential tool as a parent. It's evident that our personality disposition is all too present in the way we communicate. What if, inadvertently, the way you communicate is the primary reason you do *and do not* connect with your child? For instance, let's take a situation in which you try to explain to your child that he or she has to bear the consequences for certain actions, like carelessly throwing a softball and breaking a neighbor's window. The child with the same personality as your own will understand what you're saying, because your minds work the same way. But what about the child with a different personality? *The very way you communicate* can be alienating in and of itself.

Some parents, whom I name *Moralizers,* communicate through a message that focuses on details, analysis, and morals. In another parenting style, that of the *Helper,* the primary motivation is to meet the child's need and forgo the consequences of his actions. It's hard for these parents to hold a line. Parents who are *Organizers* want to work with the child and create a schedule of tasks that will help redress the situation. *Dreamers* strive to connect emotionally with the child in reference to the circumstances and find a creative solution together. Whatever else transpires, they want their child to be happy. *Observer* parents look for the big picture, sit down with the child, and try to bring objectivity and perspective to the table. Parents who are *Questioners* create a mental argument and go back and forth with questions, doubts, and worst-case-scenario imagining until they're convinced that the child has a sure, logical base for understanding the situation. *Entertainers* prefer a more laid-back style and shoot the breeze with their child. They like anecdotes and leave conclusions open-ended and multioptional: the child can make a choice as to the consequences he or she prefers. The natural bent of *Protectors* is to take charge in a protective way, to yell at the child but then to go to bat for him or her against all comers. *Peacekeepers* are driven by their personality to avoid conflict, so this situation is a catch-22. These parents tend to procrastinate in speaking about the situation, and then they broaden the parameters of the discussion as a way of deflating the intensity and potential for confrontation. They smudge the lines so as to be able to be more inclusive of all points of view.

A personal example illustrates the difficulty with communication. My mother's personality style is that of the Questioner, one who questions, doubts, and spins worst-case scenarios as a way of establishing safety and certainty. My personality, the Organizer, is to be efficient and make things work. I chart a course and forge ahead. This is foolish behavior to her. We love one another, *and* we've had many personality clashes; our worldviews are so different. When I was a child, her way of communicating with me often simply did not make sense. I couldn't understand the basis of her questioning. We could have existed on different planets.

For instance, in South Africa, where I grew up, from an early age I was an antiapartheid activist. My mother questioned all my activism, constantly regaled me with worst-case scenarios, and voiced severe doubts about my motivations for being so involved. *Now* I realize fully that from her point of view she was being protective and (justifiably) concerned for my safety. What I heard *then* was nagging, lack of support, and no understanding of my idealism. It took me years to make time to listen to her doubts and questions. Now I know she's not targeting me personally, but simply questioning the way I'm thinking, or a belief system, or whether the world has to be the way it appears.

Reducing Stress

Certain parent-child interactions are always going to push your buttons and be stressful; the interpersonal chemistry is simply "wrong" or "off." If this situation builds over the years, you can experience parental burnout. Yet other interactions with your child are always pleasurable and enjoyable and induce a natural high. How can you optimize these situations and minimize those that are stressful? In coming to know yourself as a parent, you learn to recognize the internal shift between when you're stressed and when you feel relaxed (secure). In either of these situations you can come across as almost a different parent. This is invaluable information in protecting yourself and your child from the repetitive ravages of stressful situations.

Gaining New Self-Awareness

Thinking about how your personality affects the way you parent can be a whole new way for you to understand yourself. This is true for many thousands of people who've been introduced to this material.

Since the time of ancient Greece, and probably for several thousand years before that, our parenting skills, without in-depth knowledge of our personalities, have been practiced, metaphorically speaking, in the dark. Until now we've not had the technology and the tools to be precise in understanding ourselves and those we love more dearly than life itself—our children. Once we follow the injunction handed down to us from those ancient times and come to know ourselves, we can make adjustments and shifts in our behavior as parents and bring a new passion and awareness based on the understanding of how our personalities work.

Identifying Your Gifts, Enhancing Your Relationships

Our effectiveness as parents is greatly enhanced when we learn about our qualities and gifts and can apply them positively. It is a truism that people have low and high sides to their personalities; we say, "This brings out the best (or worst) in me." Your gifts come to the fore when you feel secure within yourself and manage your anxiety threshold. When you are not feeling down on yourself, you are in a sense more whole, more able to utilize the positive energy of your personality traits. You can also help develop the gifts of your children and others.

Becoming a Facilitator, Helping Support the Flowering of Your Child's Personality

How to become a facilitator? When you become aware of your personality and understand what motivates you and why you behave the way you do, usually compassion for yourself arises with this new knowledge. But you also know now that there are other personality types with whom you share the world, and they are as deeply ingrained in the cages of their habitual thinking as you are in yours. This leads you to feel compassion for them, too. From this new perspective you see your child with different eyes. "Maybe," you think, "he always reacts in *that* way because I'm always coming at him in *this* way." If you can learn to use the parenting strategies in this book, you can change your behavior (mainly by getting yourself out of the way and respecting the fact that your child may be of a different personality from you) and be a better facilitator of your child's progress.

This process may take time; don't be discouraged if at first nothing changes. Constantly think about yourself and others in a paradigm of personality. This lens allows you to see with clarity the rich and complex patterns of human behavior.

Getting Started

In 1990 I started working intensively with the E-model. I've studied it, continue to use it myself, and teach it to others. I wrote a book about it for educators. I've written articles, taught workshops internationally, and conducted panels on it. I've listened to many hundreds of people on panels, most of them parents and teachers, share their understanding of how their inner motivations and behaviors work in the world.

For the illustrations and examples in this book, I draw on the comments and observations of these panelists. I'm grateful to them for their self-observation skills and their willingness to share their stories, insights, and wisdom.

Even though every family is different, you will resonate with these parents' strengths and weaknesses, successes and failures, feats and foibles. Their stories highlight their key motivations, followed by a strategy and action program that enables other parents of that particular personality pattern to use it to their best advantage.

I strongly believe that once you determine your own personality pattern, you will become more interested in how other people—especially those you love—tend to see the world. To that end, I encourage you to read the entire book, including the epilogue and topics for discussion in the back. But, please try to resist the temptation to type other people. Let them enjoy taking the journey themselves.

Let's get started on yours.

CHAPTER 1

Discovering Your Parenting Personality
What's Your Type?

Recognizing What Motivates You

Let's begin with nine simple questions. There are no right or wrong responses to this well-tried methodology for identifying the foundation of your personality, your dominant motivational mode. Once you understand what motivates you, you'll be prepared to discover whether you tend to be a Helper, Organizer, Dreamer, Observer, Questioner, Entertainer, Protector, Peacekeeper, or Moralizer. Following each question are three statements. Choose the one that fits you most closely.

1. **When you reflect on your own approach to parenting, which of the following statements best describes your style?**

    a. My parenting style has to do with interaction and energy, with connecting to my children. I ask myself, "Am I getting through on an emotional level?" I try to feel where they are coming from. Do they understand where *I'm* coming from?

9

How am I coming across to them? How do they see me? It's important that we connect in a meaningful way.

b. My parenting style is intuitive; I have a gut sense about what's right and wrong, fair and unfair. I'm ambivalent about conflict, but when I have something to say, I have a great need to say it and to be heeded. I don't like being encumbered by extraneous demands or the social expectations of others.

c. My parental style is intellectual, no question. I'm interested in how children think, process information, work with ideas. I live in my head—conceptualizing, fantasizing, thinking things through, researching, and proving—that's what's important to me. "Rationality" is a big word with me.

2. **How do you assess the way you communicate with your family?**

a. What you see is what you get. I don't use guile or fancy gimmicks. I talk about things the way I understand them; I give it my best shot. My family gets my honest sense of how it is.

b. I like to present things in the best light possible, not being dishonest but finding ways to connect, to make sure I get a response—the medium is the message, that kind of thing. So I try to put on a show in a way, highlight my ideas, find the nuances of expression that will help me get through to them. I use emotion and some dramatics, anything that will help them better understand what I'm saying.

c. I try to keep things as conceptual, uncluttered, and intellectually pure as I can. I love to ask questions, to practice skepticism, to be a discerning thinker. I try to probe below the surface. I want my children to learn to think this way, too. If we can stick with what's rational and logical, we're on solid ground.

3. **You try to teach your children how to solve problems and make decisions, to encourage their positive personal growth.**

What is most important to you about facilitating your children's growth? Choose one:

    a. I facilitate their growth through mental activity, finding answers, the excitement that comes from seeing their minds open to new possibilities, to big-picture connections, to new conclusions. Their mental energy stimulates my own thinking. I like that.

    b. I facilitate their growth through valuing them as people. I teach them the possibilities of all sorts of human contact and connection: the emotional highs and lows, the feeling of togetherness when we all click and experience some profound interconnection in the moment. My family is a small world complete unto itself; we play out our lives together—unity built on empathy and human understanding, little else.

    c. I facilitate their growth by trying to steer them in a direction where they can make a difference and lead fulfilled lives. People need a sense of themselves, of where they stand. The world is difficult to understand—you can lose your way all too easily. Teaching them, for me, is giving them some skills, some tools, some road maps to take on their journey.

4. Although you get along with your children most of the time, every so often you clash. What would *they* say about *you* in those moments?

    a. I come on too emotionally when I'm talking to them; they often feel as if I'm trying to manipulate them into interacting with me. Why can't I just say things out straight? I try to shine it on; it's almost as though I need their approval.

    b. I'm too abstract, too theoretical, too detached. They need more emotional, personal interaction from me. We're talking, I'm listening, but they have this sense that I'm not really there, that I've moved to somewhere in my head. The harder they try to know where they are with me, the more I distance myself. They question whether anything gets through to me emotionally.

c. I can come across as an immovable force, solid, implacable, although I'm not usually aware of this. I know that I can dig in, and nothing people say or do will shift me. I've been accused of being overly defensive, stubborn, critical. I'm not usually aware of my impact on people.

5. **Your child is in serious trouble in school because of a grave offense. How do you try to help in this difficult moment?**

a. I try to help by being rational and not getting caught up in emotions. I explain the inevitability of the disciplinary decision based on school rules. I can support her best by being logical. Then we can have a rational discussion, and I can help her see all the reasons for this outcome. She knows how strongly I love her; this has nothing to do with that—school rules are school rules.

b. I try to help by being straightforward and down-to-earth, having a face-to-face talk. We know where we stand, how solidly I love her. This in no way affects that relationship—that doesn't even come into the picture; it's the way things are. She made a mistake. We all do. Face-to-face, saying it straight without any extraneous talk, that's always the best way to handle these interactions.

c. I try to help by letting her know how much I care. I don't like handling these situations. When my children are in trouble, it strikes at my heart. I'm more anxious about this than I want to admit—emotional upsets really get to me. I know her so well that I know what she's feeling as if it were myself. Although she's in the wrong—and we all know that—I'll try to get through to her how much I love her.

6. At the last minute your child tells you that he wants to spend his birthday with friends, knowing full well the plans you've made together for the day. What is your first reaction?

    a. Disbelief—I can't accept this at all. I know he has to grow and become independent, but why now, why on his birthday? We've planned this day for months. He knows how much I love birthdays. I'm so disappointed; it's a heart-wrenching feeling. I'll never get over this one.

    b. I guess I should have seen this coming. He made noises about this last year. He's growing up—all the signs are there—I just didn't think they would come down on this day. If you think about it rationally and logically, it's a perfectly legitimate request—shows healthy growth. I allowed myself to be blindsided by my own expectations. I'll learn other good lessons from this. Of course he wants to be with his friends, have his own experiences and memories. I won't take this personally.

    c. I'm upset and angry about this. It's about honoring commitments. It's that simple, you don't let people down at the last moment. He should have given me an inkling, a clue, not gone along making plans without saying a word. You get slammed in this world, one way or the other, even by your own children. The anger is overwhelming; I feel it in my whole body. I'll count to ten, but he must know how unfair this is.

7. You want to be a great parent—your dreams reflect the deepest parts of yourself. Your passion for your vision stems from:

    a. A feeling that I have something my children can relate to. I believe I've got what it takes to put across my vision in a way that's honest, good, and effective. It's all about people. I can get through to people, I'm in tune, and I understand people. I want my children to have this, too. In my heart I know this is true.

b. A hunch, an instinct that I'm in the right place at the right time doing what I'm meant to be doing. When my head, heart, and gut are aligned behind something, I can trust that sense. I can put my full force behind it. I would never commit to being a parent if I didn't feel 100 percent about it. I'm a 110 percent parent.

c. The knowledge that I have first-rate ideas about parenting that will benefit my children. I wouldn't be involved in anything if I weren't convinced of the validity of my ideas, hadn't thought things through, and that includes being a parent. If I weren't absolutely sure of my thinking, I wouldn't be putting myself on the line.

8. You want to run for an open slot on the PTA. You feel confident you can handle the job and make a contribution to the life of your child's school because:

a. Of my proven record as an idea person. No one can question that what I do is conceptually sound. My references attest to my theoretical ability and know-how. I'm as intellectually solid as anyone on the PTA.

b. Of my track record for getting through to people. Whether it's coaching Little League, attending a meeting of the choral-society committee, or volunteering at the community center, I've always been able to put across what I believe so that people will want to be part of it. I know people; people are my life. I can get the world on board.

c. Of the fact that I just know this is right for me now. I can fit right in to the PTA. I have reliable instincts. I've proven it to myself and others time and again. Lots of people have benefited from my instincts. Only something that I believe in absolutely would get me into running in this election. People know where they stand with me, and that makes them feel safe.

9. Your child writes a paper for class on why you are the best parent in the world. It's published in the school magazine. What's your response?

    a. This is wonderful—it validates my parenting style. It's great that my child appreciates the way I think through what I do and my intellectual energy. She's picked up on the highly mental approach I bring to all my activities; it's something she can measure and write about. I'm pleased.

    b. It's gratifying, but her paper isn't about me. I'm not what I do. It's about her, how perceptive and a good writer she is. This paper's being published won't change things one way or the other: it won't make me a better person, or bring more meaning to my life, or change my relationship with her. I'll just go on being the same parent I've always been.

    c. I know I'm a good parent, so I deserve this validation, but there are lots of good parents. What's important is that my child wrote about *me*. That means the world to me. That she knows me so well, values me, is connected to me, and wants to acknowledge me this way. That really pleases me.

How Do I Think? How Do I Feel?

Now that you've completed the exercise, locate your choices on the chart below. Your dominant mode is reflected by the area with the most choices. You may find you have made some choices that do not indicate this mode. There are sound reasons for this that have to do with the shifts you make from your dominant mode when you are under stress or in a particularly secure situation. *Nonetheless, your dominant mode is the one that shows the most circled choices.*

Feeling Mode (Attacher)
    1a, 2b, 3b, 4a, 5c, 6a, 7a, 8b, 9c

Mental Mode (Detacher)
    1c, 2c, 3a, 4b, 5a, 6b, 7c, 8a, 9a

Instinctual Mode (Defender)
    1b, 2a, 3c, 4c, 5b, 6c, 7b, 8c, 9b

Research on personality shows that we make our way in the world primarily as *Attachers, Detachers,* or *Defenders.* My nomenclature—Attacher, Detacher, Defender—is based on the respected work of the pioneering psychologist Karen Horney who, in her book *Our Inner Conflicts,* describes three broad personality patterns as those of *moving toward people, moving away from people,* and *moving against people.* I developed the terminology *Attachers* (who move toward people), *Detachers* (who move away from people), and *Defenders* (who move against people) by aligning my work with hers. People are a complex fusion of these three ways of being, but one is always dominant.

Are You an Attacher?

If your predominant mode of being is emotional, you are activated by your feelings, and these moods and emotions you feel each day affect all that you do. They're the inner triggers that direct your behavior. The Attacher motivation can be described as outer-directed behavior, *moving toward people,* a way of making sense of and operating in the world through connection to people and relationships. The emotional context is the Attachers' environment.

You are aware of the feelings of others and how you are coming across. Therefore, issues of image are important. Some Attachers take pride in denying to themselves that they have feelings. Others suspend their feelings, so they don't interfere with getting the job done. Yet others are constantly aware of feelings and can lose their agenda if they allow their feelings to overwhelm them. All use feelings to open their hearts to others and to the deepest parts of themselves.

Attachers are centrally preoccupied with where they stand emotionally in relation to others. *Do they like me?* The major issue is *approval*. They enjoy *recognition*. They are aware of the *feelings* of others and of how they are coming across to others. Their defenses are marshaled around feelings: to make their way in the world, they have to learn to deal with feelings.

> ## Key Issues for Attachers
>
> *Image:* "How am I coming across? What image am I conveying? How are people responding to me?"
>
> *Connection:* "Am I reaching out? Am I getting through? Am I making contact?"
>
> *Approval:* "Do they approve of me? Do they like me?"

There are three types of parenting personalities most commonly found among Attachers: the Helper, the Organizer, and the Dreamer.

The Helper Parent

Helpers connect with others by being helpful. They can feel the needs of others because they are acutely sensitive to other people's feelings. What motivates them at work and at home is knowing what others need and being of help. Helpers convey feelings of warmth, understanding, and genuine concern. Sometimes they feel frustrated because they're not able to do as much for others as they would like.

To feel comfortable with others, Helpers align by being sincere and quietly empathic, firm and plain-talking, or whatever works for the person with whom they are interacting. Their conversation is based on personal appeal. The underlying message is "Look what I can do for you. You need my help. I'm here to serve you." They pitch their conversations to elicit approval. Approval is the bottom line.

Helpers pick protégés or champion persons of consequence. They attend to the needs of the group as a whole, but they monitor the progress of several favorites. The selected person is wrapped in a cloak of largesse and service. Helpers work long hours to open doors—and hold them open—with expectations of gratitude and heightened emotional responsiveness in return. They can keep a mental tab running on different individuals' schedules and agendas, and they provide unexpected, but appreciated, behind-the-scenes support.

Helpers project a positive persona and turn on stellar performances day after day. They develop a gracious environment, whether at home or at work. They are usually popular. Their excellent communication skills, together with the special care and attention they turn on those they deem significant, elicit admiration, popularity, and love.

Helpers will give unstintingly of themselves for their family or on behalf of the organization for which they work. They will volunteer to do the additional assignment or spend extra, unforeseen hours on a project. They devote time to developing potential among their peers, work for their welfare, and take pride in others' accomplishments. In the process they're often thinking, "They couldn't have done that without me." They work hard at making relationships happen. The allure of someone else's needs always seems more important than the Helpers' own needs.

Helpers can feel misunderstood if others think they are trying to manipulate them. They want to be perceived as warmhearted and sensitive, and they don't like their efforts to appear self-serving. Helpers can feel harried by their constant need for approval and acceptance. Often Helpers recognize that they have a need to give, but far more subtle insight is required if they are to see that their subtext in giving is a need to be admired. If they feel underappreciated, they can become emotional and demanding. Helpers appear to be independent, but internally they know how much time they spend attending to others.

The Organizer Parent

Organizer parents connect with others by fulfilling expectations. They literally perform, both in the sense of getting the job done and in seeking recognition. Organizers like to think of themselves as role models—as parents or in their professions—the image of confidence, brisk efficiency, solid skills, and leadership. They believe that who they are as people is tied up with what they accomplish. Coming first, being a winner, is strong motivation for Organizers, who get a great deal of recognition and reward for what they do.

Organizers play a central role in their undertakings; they are unmistakably present. They create the environment, set tasks, direct interactions, and achieve goals. They communicate by persuasion: "This model works for me, it'll work for you." They get a lot done, most of it successfully. Organizers play to their family and peers, basking in the applause and approval. They work their audience with skill and a finely tuned ability to pick up on pockets of resistance to their message. They adjust their voice, vocabulary, emotional range, and body language until they feel they have their "audience" (even if it's one other person) in the palm of their hand.

Organizers are goal-directed: they drive themselves and expect the same commitment from others. Get the job done, efficiently, without fuss or fretting, because the results are what count. Organizers see the overall goal as getting from point A to point Z. This goal is sorted into various tasks, prioritized, and assigned a time frame—two hours, within a week, this quarter. The larger goal is made manageable in sequential blocks of time. Organizers can juggle several tasks at once, so that time is never wasted. Organizers think in terms of deadlines, an objective measure of progress at any given moment. They are impatient with people who waste their time through bad planning and inefficiency. They hate being held up—by illness, by incompetence, by equipment that doesn't work—and would rather complete the task themselves than wait for someone else to do it.

Natural leaders, they are also team players when they respect the leader.

Organizers sweep others up in their forward-driving energy. They move directly from idea to action with little time lag to accommodate the hesitancy of those who are more skeptical or cautious. They know from experience how hard it is for others to resist their goal-directed momentum. Organizers thrive on the energy and excitement generated by their interactions. They will not be bothered with their own or others' feelings or emotional responses, especially if these reactions stand in the way of completing the task at hand. They feel an illusion of control through constant activity.

In the downtime after attaining a goal, Organizers often can be at a loss as to what to do with themselves. There is then time and space to regard others as people with their own priorities, problems, and responses rather than units to fulfill the Organizer's agenda. This is when Organizers experience feelings and become aware of their exhaustion, accompanied by an unwelcome insecurity. Doubts can arise that affect the Organizers' overarching self-confidence. Organizers then have an opportunity to reflect on their tendency to glib superficiality and quick-fix answers.

The Dreamer Parent

Dreamer parents connect with others by seeking emotionally meaningful connections. These parents live in a rich emotional world, and they feel their own uniqueness.

Dreamers bring the gift of themselves—unique creative talent and depth—both to what they do and to the people with whom they interact. They're extremely resourceful, intensely inventive, and they care deeply about people. They take pride in their own and others' achievements and experience a fulfilling emotional connection at being part of meaningful creativity: "something special." Yet, paradoxically, Dreamers focus not on what they have but on what's missing. They think of themselves as different from others and can often feel lonely and misunderstood.

Dreamers embody emotionality, artistry, and insight; a dramatic tone imbues their relationships. They regard themselves as sensitive, with the ability to experience feelings deeply. Their emotional depth makes them gifted at empathizing with the suffering of others. Yet they are aware of a push/pull in relationships; they can come across either as aloof and self-absorbed or as vitally interested. This inconsistency is often bewildering to others.

Dreamers often violate boundaries in other people because they yearn for connection to both deep feelings and relationships. They can overdramatize their feelings, to the discomfort of others. Yet they are authentic, and they appreciate authenticity in others. They like to be liked and to have their efforts appreciated. However, when praise comes their way, Dreamers often deflect it—the glass is half empty. They experience a cycle of expectation and then regret. Dreamers feel the onset of a high with any new venture they're close to, but regret invariably follows as thoughts turn to what is missing.

Dreamers live with passion and idealism. The daily passage of time, with its routine tasks, is of little consequence to them. They live for the grand-scale occurrences that color what they often feel is the dull oblivion of the rest of their lives. The time when deep feelings emerge in interactions or on projects is memorable, yet Dreamers cannot recall the ordinary matters of everyday life. It's hard for Dreamers to stay in the present moment. *Now* is filled with nostalgia and memories of options not exercised and "if only" thinking. This year's highlights are seen in the rosy-hued, mythic light of significant moments of the past. Dreamers live their lives through dramatic interpersonal events beyond the passage of time.

Dreamers devalue themselves in comparison to others who seem to have more or better. This self-denigration can manifest as competitive envy. Growth occurs when they begin to value the flat, ordinary moments in all undertakings and take their attention off the dramatic high/low extremes. The unavailability of emotional connection (sustenance) may lead to melancholy, even depression.

Are You a Detacher?

Detachers are primarily consumed with *mental activity.* They seek to make sense of the world through mental processes: the realm of the mind is where they feel most comfortable. Living in the imagination, conceptualizing, fantasizing, analyzing, forming contexts, and synthesizing are all based on mental activity. Even when they're with other people, Detachers tend to feel most secure when they're operating in their minds for planning other options, running other scenarios, looking for new concepts to lock ideas together.

Some Detachers in this motivational format live with an investigative mind-set. They seek knowledge to build interconnections among ideas and come to new understandings. Others question everything and voice their doubts. They like to think through the hard questions to build a fail-safe argument. Yet others escape into the imagination, where ideas swing freely—a state of mind called monkey-mind.

Key Issues for Detachers

Interconnections: "I cruise along in my own mind gathering ideas and knowledge, synthesizing and connecting until I make sense out of things."

Mental argument: "I depend on logic and rational thinking. At any moment life can pull the rug out from under you. You have to be careful you don't lose all you've worked so hard for."

Imagination: "I like fantasizing, creating pleasant options, with a major emphasis on planning. Take away my options and you take away my life."

There are three basic personality patterns among parents who are Detachers: the Observer, the Questioner, and the Entertainer.

The Observer Parent

Observers detach from people and the outer world by concentrating instead on their thoughts and emotions in a rich inner life. Minimizing participation is a way of keeping themselves intact and secure. They need more privacy and private time than most people do, which is used to relive experiences and get in touch with feelings that didn't initially surface.

Observers are interested in finding answers and making connections. They seek radical approaches to problem solving that go beyond traditional ways of thinking. Gaining knowledge is finding pieces of the puzzle. Although each piece might be incomplete in itself, it locks together with other pieces to create the whole, the larger picture. Observers look for a new or particular way to put across a complex idea. They appreciate working with others who also struggle to create and to synthesize ideas. They admire those who step outside the bounds of packaged, conventional thinking.

Observers like to watch events rather than be involved in the thick of things. Their interpersonal style is to play it "close to the vest." They are not emotionally expansive and forthcoming in their interactions. They value privacy and respect the privacy of others.

Observers prefer to communicate in closely worded notes, conveying their feedback and appreciation via comments on papers or in private correspondence. They prefer to work in an almost silent environment; silence signals evidence of real thought.

Observers connect with others through an exchange of ideas. They try to be impassive and objective—stony-faced in meetings—to convey that everyone's ideas are equally valid. Often accused of being unresponsive, Observers maintain that by not talking unnecessarily, they empower others who need to be listened to. They may respond that all ideas are heard without value judgments. From the Observers' point of view, detachment shows respect for peers and boundaries. Yet others may interpret their noninvolvement as lack of interest. As a result, Observers may miss opportunities to connect and to do things with others.

Observers are careful about how they spend their time and energy. They apportion time to anticipated demands—shopping for the family, preparing a meal, reading bedtime stories, or being in the office, attending a meeting, traveling to a client. Unexpected demands and spontaneous invitations are jarring. They assess the demand with a reactive response: "What will I get for my time?" Time spent in mental pursuits is time well spent: Observers hold dear the notion that knowledge is power. Knowledge, however, is never given away wholesale. People have to earn access to the Observers' hard-won storehouse of treasures through diligent effort and evidence of real thinking.

The Questioner Parent

Questioners detach by putting their mental energy into logic and rational thinking. They regard the world as inherently unsafe, and their attention is focused on potential threats. Seeking certainty and safety, they use their active imaginations to lock on to what is potentially, as well as actually, dangerous. They either run away from danger or meet it full force.

To feel secure with people, Questioners want evidence that they can interact with their own thinking. Doubting people's intentions, they generate an interrogative climate around themselves, where argument and counterargument are welcomed. In this way everyone ends up with clear conclusions, though drawn from different perspectives. If something is thought through in a logical way, the conclusion is reliable.

Questioners are ambivalent about themselves in positions of leadership. They alternate between being rigidly authoritarian and being nonauthoritarian. Their own inner doubt causes the swing. When they're afraid of being challenged, they exert control; when they're filled with inner conviction, they relax and become permissive. Seeking predictability, they view authority with skepticism. Periods of blind allegiance alternate with ones of rebellious insurrection.

Questioners are constantly vigilant, and they use their inner radar system to seek out the hidden intentions of others. This wariness is often perceived as reactive negativism. Unanswered questions or unexpressed anger undermines the basis of trust they've built with others. Procrastination sets in until doubts are resolved or until the Questioner can separate negative feedback from a personal attack.

Questioners see danger in acting openly, but they often fail to see that inaction and procrastination can be equally dangerous. They experience time as an authority looming over them. In fact, most of the people and circumstances in their lives become the authority with which they must wrestle. They perceive themselves as constantly on the rack of responsibility to satisfy "the authority," whatever form it takes.

Questioners can put aside personal doubts in the service of a cause. They can also be loyal to their family, to a company, to an idea, and to others. Once established, their inner conviction lets them feel certain in promoting their cause. Objective data, they believe, is far more reliable than personal assurances. Yet Questioners can act on behalf of others and rally the troops behind a person or ideal in which they believe. When they're committed, they are generally loyal, extremely trustworthy, even protective. They take responsibility and commitments seriously. When Questioners trust themselves, they can be insightful and creative. They can also be witty, can laugh at themselves, and, in a climate of trust, can be open and sensitive to others.

The Entertainer Parent

The Entertainer parent is an optimist. When reality bites, he or she will detach by mentally focusing on plans and new and exciting options. Entertainers escape into an inner world of upbeat ideas where there are no limits. High-energy Entertainers have many balls in the air, and they focus on keeping them up there. They are fascinated by ideas and interesting options. They dislike doing the same thing the same way twice. New input, new ideas, new problems present exciting directions to try.

Entertainers are process people, planners. The plan's the thing; the execution of it is left to lesser beings. They can spend hours at their desks thinking through how to present material or promote a plan. Entertainers never feel they've exhausted the possibilities of their subject—the layers, the variety, and the complexity are fascinating. Entertainers are imbued with positive mental energy and alertness; their minds race with myriad ideas and responses. Their mental leaps to creative conclusions are often too fast for others to follow. People need to tell them to slow down their thinking. Others can feel swept away by the Entertainers' mental intensity.

Entertainers are fluid, multioptional thinkers. They assume that others are comfortable, too, with shifts in direction, choosing between options, and moving among ideas. Entertainers reformat concepts in ways that baffle other thinkers. There's always another way to present the material. To the Entertainer, on-the-spot ideas, as they arise, seem brilliant and important to throw into the mix—now. It's hard to pinpoint an Entertainer's position. Entertainers' ideas and concepts intersect and connect, while options change as new information is acquired and processed.

Entertainers try to grasp the pattern of another person's thinking: "How does that person see himself? What are the components of his thinking? What issues fascinate her? Is she a detail or a big-picture thinker? Is he open to new possibilities, or is he conservative?" Entertainers subconsciously classify people by thinking style. Discovering how others think allows Entertainers to get along with them by mirroring a perspective or framing an approach. The ability to form patterns and make mental connections is a basic concern.

Entertainers can come across as having a sense of personal entitlement. They believe they're entitled to a pleasant life, and your time, effort, and attention are at their disposal. They'll charm and disarm you. Yet Entertainers can have difficulty coping with the overload of experiencing all that life offers. Planning for the future keeps them from experiencing the present, and furthering all their talents can keep them from deepening just one. Living on the surface can prevent Entertainers from appreciating their own profound feelings (especially emotional pain) or the feelings and concerns of others.

Are You a Defender?

If your predominant mode of being is instinctual, you are aware of boundaries around yourself, your issue is protecting your *autonomy*. You need to establish your space: "Here I am. Period." Intuition, gut feelings, and nonverbal information are important. You have an *intuitive* information-gathering system. The body is where you sense your relationship to others and to the world. Defenders say, "I sense it in my body. . . . I have a gut feel for that." You have a belly laugh. It's easy for you to lose your sense of self, a state of mind called self-forgetting *(acedia)*. Sometimes you can feel like a mouse rattling around in a great suit of armor. The Defender motivation can be described as self-protective behavior, *moving against people,* a way of making sense of and operating in the world with an awareness of intrapersonal space and boundaries.

Some Defenders make their presence felt by being confrontational and combative. Others, by taking a passive-aggressive stance, show stubbornness and signal that they won't be pushed around. Yet others establish their self-identity and protect their autonomy through being critical and judgmental.

> ## Key Issues for Defenders
>
> *Instinct:* "I trust my intuitive sense. This is the only way I feel comfortable."
>
> *Being heard:* "It's important that people listen to me. When I speak, I have something to say."
>
> *Feeling respected:* "If you respect me, I can be present for you."

There are three basic personality patterns among parents who are Defenders: the Protector, the Peacekeeper, and the Moralizer.

The Protector Parent

Protectors defend their autonomy by being confrontational and combative. They live with an innate sense of power and control. Confrontation for the Protector is a means of reading the world, of establishing where the power is, and of knowing who has control. Exerting control is a way of moving through an inherently unjust world. Protectors use confrontation to connect with others. They assume that confrontation is part of interactions; those who stand up for themselves are most able and most open.

Honesty and genuineness are important to Protectors. If Protectors sense that someone is not being honest, they will push and push to provoke a response. When they connect with someone who stands up for his or her beliefs, Protectors will do everything to support that person. Protectors empower those under their protection with a mixture of challenge and support. They do not tolerate weakness in people unless they see where it's coming from. Their anger can be devastating.

Protectors commit themselves with passionate conviction to what they do. Their anger often arises in defense of a belief system, but they come across as personally confrontational. Protectors spend a lot of time mending fences.

Protectors make their own rules. They believe that rules are made to be broken. This often causes a dilemma: how to hold the structure of the organization while believing that its rules and regulations are not always productive or beneficial. Protectors take charge and often do not realize their own force. Control is a survival strategy: peers (and family) either fall in line or resist.

Protectors want to know how people operate under pressure. They're invested in finding out where people stand. Cower, defy, resist, comply—this information is vital to people who are constantly judging if it's safe to lower their guard and be vulnerable. Vulnerability means exposure, feeling fragile, being open to people's coming after them. Protectors seem to be powerful. It's difficult for others to know that the flip side of the bombastic Protector is all soft sentimentality.

As with rules, Protectors control time. If the Protector shows up at your meeting late that's okay, but *you* don't be late for *his* meeting. Dominant Protectors like to be center stage. When they're in charge, people know their impact. During periods of lower intensity, time is of little consequence and can be forgotten, fudged, ignored. Protectors think they own time. That delusion of control often blindsides them when they're caught in the consequences of their power rushes—deadlines missed, angry or anguished family members or coworkers knocking at the door requiring an explanation.

The Peacekeeper Parent

Peacekeepers defend their autonomy by avoiding conflict. They find conflict—and dealing with conflict—distracting and exhausting.

Yet they're natural mediators who can see everyone's point of view. As an antidote to having to deal with conflict, they try to create a climate of harmony wherever they are: "Don't rock the boat. There are many sides to every story." Their energy and motivation come from others. A satisfactory day at work is more about working together with others than with a feeling of self-achievement.

Peacekeepers easily establish rapport and laid-back comfort. They take pride in getting along with others and can be attentive to others' needs. People respond to the warmth, concern, and noncompetitive nature of Peacekeeper relations. They find it diffi-cult to motivate themselves but are easily motivated by the agen-das of others. It is the expectations of others or of the job that gets them moving, and they can be steadfast and accountable. They plan, process, initiate, execute, and perform to meet outside expectations and to avoid the consequences of inaction.

Peacekeepers are easily distracted and can lose their agenda. They need to be kept on track. On the other hand, they are adaptable and don't mind changing their course of action when necessary.

Peacekeepers believe in the concept of a level playing field. It's hard to establish objectives and priorities when every person, every idea, every project gets equal time. Having to set priorities and make timely decisions can therefore be stressful. It's much easier to attend to less essential and more comfortable items than to ones that are more urgent and controversial. When the demands of others are too pressing, the Peacekeeper becomes obstinate rather than display overt anger. Because they believe that expressing anger is damaging, Peacekeepers rarely allow themselves to be overtly angry; hence others don't always take their anger seriously. Anger usually assumes the form of passive-aggressive behavior—a go-slow attitude toward work deadlines and procrastination in getting things done.

Peacekeepers like to maintain structure and routine so that life will be predictable. They like tranquillity and quiet and things that are familiar. Their worldview is uniform and even, with few peaks and valleys. The idea of highs and lows or periods of greater and lesser intensity is not part of the inner framework. Instead there's a sense of wanting to level out the world, smooth it, keep it flat.

Peacekeepers believe that everything happens in its own time. Priorities, choices, and decisions will eventually sort themselves out. Time sets its own course and carries Peacekeepers to where they're going to end up, anyway.

The Moralizer Parent

Moralizers defend their autonomy by setting standards, making judgments, and being self-critical. A sense of inner direction drives them to achieve—seeking perfection in an imperfect world. They have an innate sense of what's right, and they think they know what's wrong—and how to fix it. Things must be done the right way.

Moralizers believe in what they say and do. They feel they owe it to themselves and others to be competent to handle any details, whether in the context of a presentation or a process. They focus on the details and facts. Ideas and materials model precision, ethics, and responsibility. They have a convincing way of communicating, underscored with "right-thinking" messages. Others can feel judged if they disagree with Moralizers. Yet their moralistic energy, which may sometimes be overzealous, is largely appreciated as authentic and inspiring.

When they're committed, Moralizers are uplifting parents, leaders, and team members, imbuing others with the force of their own inner conviction. Moralizers are obsessively self-critical. They spend hours preparing material, deliberately building a model from intricate details. They struggle to make complex notions orderly. They are uncomfortable with open-ended options and do not like changing gears halfway through a process. Nonetheless plans B, C, and D, while not written out, are at their fingertips to help them cope with the unexpected.

Moralizers have to deal with a severe inner critic that produces an unrelenting commentary on their lives. They realize that the critic is a feature of their own consciousness but find it extremely difficult to ignore such familiar thinking. Paying attention to the inner critic is a major drain of time and energy. Any activity is monitored against the critic's measure of perfection: "Do it right, or don't do it at all." Deadlines are a struggle, because the inner pressure to produce a perfect piece of work also has to be perfectly timed. They can resent others who don't do things properly, although they try not to show open anger.

Moralizers live under the whip of time. The inner critic drives them to account for themselves. Their work schedules mirror their preoccupation with correctness—good people work hard and play later—*maybe*. Procrastination arises with fear of making mistakes. Time is siphoned away from a project by a Moralizer who pays too much attention to time-consuming details. Work schedules reflect time well spent, such as with meetings, appointments, preparation, and other "must-do's." There's no leeway to schedule "time off" for pleasure and fun.

The chapters that follow present in-depth profiles of parents representing each of these patterns.

CHAPTER 2

The Helper
Meeting the Needs of Others

Eric—Never Saying No

Eric knew that as normal teenagers his sons would challenge authority, his own included. They would test him, test the boundaries of his professed unconditional love. In a curious way he took pride in their initiative, their rebellion. One night they drove a teacher's car into the main hallway of the school and parked it outside the principal's office. Eventually they owned up to it and were suspended from school for a week. Eric felt that it took ingenuity and resourcefulness to pull off such an escapade. Although he agreed with their punishment, his sons knew he secretly admired their exploit.

As a teenager Eric had been meek and mild. He would never court the disapproval of his parents, friends, teachers, never take risks; that way he wouldn't do anything to bring disapproval down on himself. Eric knew that if he didn't do what his parents and teachers wanted, he would lose their approval and no longer be so liked and loved.

In the classroom, when he was a student, Eric gave back to teachers exactly what they gave to him. They were pleased with themselves and him: "Eric's gotten the entire point of my lesson. He's a model student." Eric used the intelligence inherent in his Helper strategy to root out what teachers needed. But his sons were so unlike him. Nothing that motivated his behavior seemed to be the same for them. Eric loved them unconditionally but often found it hard to understand them.

In their latter years of high school, his sons' behavior became more and more outrageous. There was the usual experimentation with alcohol, fast driving, and defying curfews. Common parental wisdom says that adolescents need boundaries, but Eric found it almost impossible to say no to them. It was simply not his style, not part of his personality. His wife tried to enforce rules and other considerations, and he backed her up (he couldn't say no to her either), but both the boys and their mother knew that there was little conviction behind his words.

Part of Eric's lack of conviction arises from the fact that disapproval and dislike are devastating to Helpers. The Helper's self-defense mechanism is to give to others and to keep giving and giving and giving—a feedback loop to ensure that they are loved, have approval, are liked and validated. The relief of gaining approval and therefore feeling good about oneself reassures Helpers that they have a self.

One morning Eric's wife found both their sons' beds not slept in when she went to rouse them for school. Her apprehension and righteous indignation struck such an empathic chord in Eric that he was galvanized to take firm action. That day turned their family life around. Their sons responded positively to his newfound strength of will.

It was a stressful situation for Eric, being caught between his wife's insistence that he place strictures on their sons' behavior and their overt acting out. Under circumstances of stress, Helpers can access assertive energy, anger, resolve; they can be confrontational. Eric had responded to his wife's need for reassurance (and his own inner conviction that his sons had seriously over-stepped the mark). He felt they were putting themselves in danger and needed him to be firm. Eric helped his sons with his positive use of forceful energy.

Under normal circumstances aggression, anger, and con-frontation are difficult for Helpers. They deny the need for what they regard as these dangerous weapons (people they confront could be angry or disapproving of them) and often fall back on hypocrisy to mask their real needs and feelings. When they do move to honest confrontation, however, these stress situations allow Helpers to establish their own positions and priorities. Their confrontation can be a gift to others through the Helper's truth telling.

Instead of provoking head-on collisions and confrontations, which Eric believed would be counterproductive, he preferred to be gentle with his sons, to reason with them, to give them a safe haven where *they* could vent and rage and know that he would not flinch: he would be there to support them. He felt (with a little puff of pride) that he understood their needs better than anyone, and what they needed was a safe place to sound off, to be as out-rageous as they could without judgment or censure.

Whenever he had time, he offered to drive back and forth with them to their various commitments; in that way he was able to spend time alone with each of them. They were both excellent soccer players, and Eric was a fan of the sport, so there was a nat-ural connection around practices and matches. Eric had a knack of getting people to open up to him, and his sons were no excep-tion. A gifted listener, he seemed to know what people were about to say before they said it. From their early childhood his sons had shared confidences with him about what was happening in their lives. Ultimately Eric knew that they were good boys, and he trusted them. Without their mother's knowledge, he'd condoned several of their more reckless adventures.

In essence, Eric's open relationship with his sons demon-strated what freedom meant to him: the ability to know the appropriate relationship between himself and others and the appropriate measures of *giving* and *taking*. He realized that his sons took for granted this gift, his ability to sense what they needed and wanted. That was okay in the context of Eric's recognition that as their father they expected him to give—all fathers gave to their children. A danger for Helpers lies in their inflation of relationships into something they're not, reading more into them than there is. As he grew older, Eric was grateful that he'd acquired an ability to sense what was his true relationship to others, his true contribution to them.

As adults, his sons questioned his judgment about many things, maybe because he'd been so permissive when they were adolescents. But he also knew that in other ways they trusted him, cared about him, and wanted him to be around them. He didn't know many other older men who were so loved by their grown sons.

Vicky—I'm Here to Help You

It was ten in the morning, and Vicky was still in her bathrobe and slippers. She sat in a comfortable armchair with two-week-old Carrie in her arms. Carrie's head rested heavily and warmly on Vicky's shoulder. They'd been anchored to that chair for ten days now, ever since Vicky brought Carrie home from the hospital.

At night it was a wrench for her to put Carrie into her pink-and-white bassinet, to be separated from her. Vicky was openly pleased when Carrie woke to feed, and she nursed her in the armchair, where they then fell asleep together. That's how her husband found them most mornings. He was understanding, but, as he said, "Life goes on." He needed attention, too; she knew that. A hot meal when he came home from work, conversation. She had to eat and shower and attend to chores around the house, which she did when Carrie was asleep. Yet for most of those first six weeks, Vicky and Carrie stayed bonded in that armchair.

Vicky was enthralled with her little girl. The wonder of her, the perfection of her skin, her tiny fingers and toes, her blue eyes so like her father's, the shape of her face so like her maternal grandmother's. The life force in her small body astonished Vicky. Carrie's face would pucker and redden in inexplicable rage, and she'd yell with vigor powered by all the air in her lungs.

Vicky recognized that she'd become one with her baby. Once or twice before in her life, she'd had this feeling of giving herself to someone naturally and openly, without any agenda. She can name the emotion as humility, the joy of giving to others without expecting anything back. Vicky was aware of the purity of this feeling. Of how different it was to give of herself from a sense of security, of self-identity, rather than from a sense of self-sacrifice and blurred boundaries. She didn't need anything back from Carrie; she experienced pure pleasure in giving herself to her baby.

Visitors came and went in those first weeks, close family and friends bringing gifts and meals. Anything outside herself and Carrie did not seem to exist for Vicky. Usually she was the most attentive of hostesses, well groomed, her home warm and welcoming. Her concern for others had always been a quality noted by them. She made people feel special, but for now it was obvious that she lived only for her baby girl. Visitors gave advice: You're spoiling her. She'll never want to be left alone. You'll be sorry later. Older women voiced amazement that Vicky never lost patience with the baby, never seemed put out or exhausted, never seemed to want time just for herself.

When Helpers feel as secure as Vicky did in the early months of motherhood, they experience their emotions more deeply. They're more in touch with themselves, and from this position they can claim their own selves, rather than give to others by giving themselves away. Secure Helpers allow their own emotional needs to surface, and they find ways to satisfy them. Vicky loved feeling at one with her baby. This was something her friends and relatives did not understand in the current situation; they were unaware of the subtle shift in Vicky's motivational behavior.

The dynamic of giving to others is a complicated inner puzzle for Helpers. They feel pride in meeting the needs of others and pride in avoiding their own needs. An inner dialogue can often sound like this: "I don't have needs. Me? *You* have needs. I want to take care of you—*that's* my need. But I don't have any needs for myself."

The sting in the tail for those connected to Helpers is that resentment can build if Helpers feel they've been taken for granted. The inner dialogue can continue: "Why haven't you attended to *my* needs? You're not paying any attention to my needs, and therefore I don't like you very much after all. I'm getting uncomfortable about this. Soon I'll drop you."

Why do Helpers weave a veil of forgetfulness around their own emotional needs or often deny even to themselves that they *have* needs? In order for Helpers to become more understanding parents, a step in the action program is to move from false pride in not having your own needs to acknowledging with humility that you are human like everyone else and *do* have needs. Helpers have matured when they can state their need: "I *need* you to listen to me." "I *need* you to tell me where you are going." "I *need* from you a sense that you value me without my having done anything for you." They know they've matured when awareness dawns that the pride they take in being able to meet others' needs is actually a trap that keeps them from developing a sense of self and robs them of their self-identity and the freedom to act spontaneously on behalf of themselves.

The gift of the Helper is true giving, true altruism, true allowing. Vicky knew instinctively that what she was doing was right for her and Carrie. Besides she felt herself to be in the flow of an inner life force: soft, feminine, passive, receptive, maternal. Real life was not this straightforward, she knew that, but she'd get back to real life later. This was her time to be at one with her daughter.

Vicky had waited a long time for Carrie. She was in her late thirties when Carrie was born. Originally she'd arranged to take maternity leave for six weeks from her job as a human-resource manager in a large public company. After a month she knew that six weeks would not be long enough, that she couldn't go back to work and put Carrie into day care, so she asked for six more weeks. During that time she requested a year's leave of absence, but this was not granted. She wasn't unduly concerned about that decision. Her whole life had taken on unforeseen priorities. After Carrie's birth everything shifted for her. She knew she could work from home as a consultant if she wanted to or if they needed the extra money.

When Carrie was older, Vicky would go back into the work-force, but not on the full-time basis of ten-hour days, traveling, the stress of meeting deadlines, the energetic exhaustion of working with high-functioning people—circumstances she thrived in before. Vicky felt guilty about abandoning her coworkers, especially the handpicked team she had cultivated and nurtured. She was proud of her team. Part of the Helper's gift is an ability to bring to fruition the potential in others. But this may be another trap for Helpers, a door through which a false sense of pride can enter.

Helpers single out those individuals with whom they want to forge a connection, usually people who will make them look good or through whom they can become the indispensable power behind the throne. Vicky had picked a few good people for her team. She felt deeply that she'd enabled her "selected" people to succeed. Vicky's subconscious response to their success could be along these lines: "*You* got the promotion in Marketing, but you wouldn't have had it without *me*." "You couldn't have done that without me," pride sings; "you couldn't have done this without me."

No, Vicky was not going to return to work full-time. Her daughter needed her. And maybe, if they were lucky, they would have another child soon. But for now she was not going to miss out on the early years of her little girl's life. She had too much love to give her. Besides, who could ever know how to meet Carrie's needs as well as her own mother could?

PERSONAL ACCOUNT

Katherine, a Helper mother of two daughters, gives this account

I loved the cuddles and closeness of my daughters' babyhood. Nursing was a particular delight, perhaps because in everyday life when I was a child I was brought up to be reserved and unemotional. There were no kisses and hugs in my family—no physical contact of any kind—but now, with a baby at my breast, I felt invulnerable. No, perhaps it would be more accurate to say "irreplaceable." I never gave my children a bottle, because it was so important for me to be the only one, the irreplaceable caregiver.

I take immense pride in my children's achievements: the possessive thrill from that first crooked smile, that first step, the first stumbling attempt to read. Then on all the way through school, college, and adulthood, their achievements still have the power to make me feel a little larger than my own self. I feel a rush of pride that is more intense than, and different from, any pride I allow myself in my own achievements.

My children are such a gift. I delighted in them so much that discipline was hard for me. Once decisions were called for, especially decisions about discipline, I was out of my depth. I'm thinking particularly of when they were adolescents and I found it almost impossible to set the necessary limits. I gave them far too much autonomy too soon. Looking back now, I can see I ran some appalling risks simply because I couldn't bear the idea of coming into conflict with them. Once there was a huge pop concert on Boston Common, and my daughter, then aged twelve or thirteen, wanted to go to it with a girlfriend her own age. It was madness to let them go, but because I couldn't stand to disappoint my daughter and without a thought of the danger, I gave permission.

Perhaps my main strength is my ability to merge with my children, to see things absolutely from their point of view and so share their emotions. Interestingly enough, I was two different people when I was interacting with either of my children, because they're so different. I became what each of them needed. I do see that this can also be a weakness. My other strength is really part of the same paradigm: I can and always have offered my children unconditional love. No behavior on their part alters that. When she was in her late twenties, it emerged that one of my daughters was gay. She did not "come out" in a definite way but allowed the fact to become apparent to us. I've helped her and her partner financially and supported them as a couple ever since. Perhaps this "blind" support can be a serious weakness when carried to extremes. Unconditional love sounds fine, but it can turn into unconditional permissiveness.

Another example involves my other daughter, who is athletic, well coordinated, and physically daring. Once, when she was about ten, she climbed the dizzying vertical wall of a slate quarry. It was certainly dangerous, and I haven't been more terrified in my life than I was during the twenty minutes it took her to get to safe ground. I still think I was right in allowing her to push her limits in that and several other similar adventures.

My avoidance of conflict leads me into absurd situations that often involve lying and deceit. On one occasion I was looking after my daughter's house while she was on vacation. I was appalled by the extraordinary mess and disorder of the house and decided to do a massive cleanup. I have good reason to believe now that all this was taken as implied criticism—which it certainly was. It's utterly characteristic of me and my relationships that the episode has never been discussed.

Trust your children. I think I went overboard and trusted them beyond what was reasonable or age-appropriate, but all the same I strongly believe that a parent's absolute trust in her child is one of the greatest gifts we can give. Where I've constantly gone wrong is in failing to articulate that trust, my love, and perhaps especially to set any limits. I made the great mistake of confusing clear discipline with lack of love. My advice to other parents is not to fall into that trap. You don't have to practice tough love, but you do have a very real responsibility to set limits. 💜

The Best Strategy and Action Program for Helpers

Build Boundaries

Inherent to the Helper strategy is an instinctive ability to charm others (including one's family) into loving the Helper. It does take a certain degree of self-awareness on the part of Helpers to acknowledge this behavior pattern. A Helper on a panel said, "If I was intent on figuring out what you needed, I would work every single angle to get you to be aware that you needed what I was giving you. Somebody once said to me, 'You made me love you,' and I said, 'Well, that song was written for people like me.'" Helpers can put themselves into the "skin" of others, take on their persona, play the role of another as if it were their own being. Helper parents instinctively know what their children need and help them get those needs met—often to the detriment of establishing and upholding behavioral boundaries. It's frightening to Helpers when they find themselves without a role to play in relation to others' needs.

A Helper mother recounts that her husband and children often ask her what she wants. She answers "I want what you want." They ask, "But if we weren't here, what would you want?" She can't answer that question, and it's scary for her. She wants to please them and doesn't know of anything she wants for herself that she's able to pinpoint.

ACTION: *Try to stand back, give yourself distance from your children.* Learn to be aware of when you've merged with them (or other people) and are making decisions from their point of view and not your own. Try to build boundaries so as to stay within yourself, and *do not give that self away.* Be reassured that setting limits for your children is advantageous to their development. This may give rise to conflicts, but remember that you're helping them mature into reasonable, responsible adults, not entitled ones.

State Your Own Needs

As we've seen, Helpers are experts at manipulating others (by helping them) into getting their own needs met. This is a subtle ploy. Yet Helpers experience intense discomfort if they have to ask directly for something. They don't often put themselves in that position.

Helpers report that calling on someone (even someone they know well and feel comfortable with) to ask for help can bring them to tears or give rise to a choking sensation. It's that difficult for them. Helpers can't tell why this is so (swallowing pride perhaps?), but they'd rather do just about anything themselves than ask for help.

ACTION: *Practice telling your family what you need.* Don't ask for help—simply outline your needs in the daily tasks of running the household: "I *need* you to put your clothes in the laundry basket." "I *need* time for myself." Ask for feedback on how they're reacting and responding to you and family situations that involve you. No one in your family is going to cut contact with you. In fact, you may be surprised at how pleased they are (once they get used to the idea) that there are limits, boundaries, and consequences. From experience gained with your family, it will be easier for you to practice this conduct in other relationships.

This may be a difficult step for you, because as a Helper you try to avoid the feeling that you have—and can state—your own needs. You feel that expressing a need for something to someone is one sure way to lose your connection to that person. This is a misperception. An important step on your growth path is to learn to state your own needs.

Build and Adhere to a Sense of Self-Identity

Many Helpers report that they alter themselves to match energetically with, and so connect to, the people they interact with. This can be achieved by flexing themselves to take on the outer physical characteristics of speech and mannerisms of the person, as well as to respond to more subtle inner cues of energy, needs, and desires. The Helper intelligence tells them that this is how to make their way in the world; Helpers find it difficult to believe that relationships can be forged in any other way.

A Helper told me that she was very conscious of altering. She had many friends, and they were from different walks of and stations in life. A number of years ago her family and a dear friend threw a surprise birthday party for her. They invited people from her work, as well as from the neighborhood and from the group where the two women had met. "What a stressful evening! It wasn't any fun, because I was aware that my family was there and watching me. They know that with some friends I'm livelier, or louder, or more talkative, and with others I'm a little more intellectual or serious. There they all were in the same room, and it was stressful. I felt my family could see me clothed in hypocrisy."

For Helper parents, the instinct to shape-shift can be seen as a plus, as an ability to meet the needs of all their children at the same time in distinct ways. There's a certain pride in being "all things to all people." They do interact with their children with a somewhat (maybe outwardly imperceptibly) changed persona. These shifts are more evident in a one-on-one encounter with individual children.

It's difficult, though, for Helpers to know themselves when their identity is so tied up with everyone else around them. A definition of identity is that individuals are separate entities. If you're a Helper parent, it's hard to know where you leave off and your children begin, where you stand, and what your issues and feelings are.

ACTION: *Be aware that you're a juggler, that there are several balls in the air and you have to be careful about keeping your attention on all of them equally, or risk the criticism of having favorites or playing favorites.* The outrageous enthusiasm you put out to your extrovert son in rooting for his favorite sports team might be overpowering for your shy, sensitive daughter. The soulful, artistic self you become when you watch ballet with her may leave your son scratching his head in bewilderment. Remember that *you* have set yourself up as being all things to all people—*and* that you're probably not as successful all the time as you think you are.

Try to build boundaries around your *self* in order to become a better parent. Children sense when you're like putty in their hands, when you change personas, and they'll take advantage of your lack of firmness. They learn how to play you to their advantage. Sometimes your personality and those of your children are so different they may not want what you're trying to give them. Then you have a real problem and no communication. Solicit their input on how they'd like your interactions to take place. Now that you know there are distinctly different personality styles, try to see the world from their viewpoint.

You may be troubled or distracted by your own inconstancy, by the fact that you do change with different people. Many Helpers state that it becomes easier as one grows older to find out what *you* want and who *you* are. Not easy, but easier, to build and adhere to a sense of self-identity.

Give Help Judiciously

Often there is a degree of manipulation alongside the Helper characteristic of shape-shifting. A Helper parent on a panel said, "I'm my husband's wife, my mother's daughter, my children's mother, my grandchildren's grandmother. Compliance is a two-edged sword for me. Underneath my compliance is the capability for real manipulation; so what you see is not always what you get."

ACTION: *Accept that you can, but you don't always, give from motives of pure altruism.* Realize that a clue that you're acting manipulatively is when you feel resentment toward another person. This may mean that you don't really want to meet that person's needs. Often it can be those closest to you—your partner and sometimes even your children. Examine why you're feeling resentful and you will begin to see how you've been manipulating the situation. Yet, unknown to you, many people in interactions with you can see that you're giving in order to get. They perceive your actions as false altruism.

It's obvious from the above remarks and the previous discussion that we're dealing with a subtle and complex matrix of motivations tied in to your abilities to make yourself an indispensable part of the lives of those you love. You need to be able to separate out for yourself the various strands that underlie why you give to others. Remember, *you do* have a gift of giving of yourself, but use it judiciously. Try to give only when your help is asked for.

Set Limits for Yourself

Helpers are among the most outer-directed of the personality types. Their attention and energy move out toward others. They are relational; their lives revolve around their relationships to others. *And* Helpers are capable of true altruism, pure giving. Most often they know what this feeling is like, for instance, when they shower love on and share themselves with their children. They impart themselves to others from a deeply held subconscious belief that giving is the way to ensure their progress in the world, to gain approval and love from others, and to secure protection against life's exigencies.

ACTION: *Be aware that you can smother the recipients of your giving with too much energy and attention.* As the Helper parent Katherine said, unconditional love can also lead to unconditional permissiveness. However hard it is to keep the boundaries or insist on limits for yourself in your giving, try to do so; this actually helps your children.

Recognize False Altruism

Helpers strike a subconscious bargain to ensure that they get their emotional needs met. It goes something like this: "If I give support and assistance to others and help them to succeed, then I will be identified with their success, buoyed by their appreciation, gratitude, and love."

Often it's difficult for Helpers to remember this rationale, to know why they want to expend themselves, because giving is so woven into the fabric of their being. Many Helpers are aware that their subtext is to be loved, to be approved, to be proficient. They don't see this as a bad motive, especially with their children. They feel that they're furnishing them with something of value that will last a lifetime. And this usually proves to be the case. While many Helpers experience feelings of pure joy in being able to give to others, to help them grow, the sense of self-fulfilment can be undermined quickly if they feel that their efforts are not appreciated. Resentment can build against the person who has failed to love or approve of them.

ACTION: *Learn the difference between true altruism, of giving without an agenda, and giving to get something back—false altruism.* In interactions with your children and partner, you have an excellent opportunity to bring a level of awareness and inquiry into the nature of your giving. Ask questions of yourself: "How can I keep my sense of self-identity intact? What does that feel like to me? Why do I lose my sense of self with my children?" Try not to be so dependent on the goodwill of others, especially your children. Learn to take action without the certainty that it will be approved. This may seem risky and stupid, but get used to the idea. It is empowering for you.

Find Self-Validation in Your Ability to Empower Others

Part of the highest intention of Helpers is the desire, almost the obligation, to assist others in reaching their potential. Helpers direct their energy, will, and creativity to this end. They become the facilitator, especially in intimate relationships, helping their family structure an agenda and attain goals. They can find alternative ways to interact, so each of their children may have quite a different experience of them as a parent. They derive great pleasure from figuring out what their children need.

ACTION: *Accept that in helping your children to reach their potential, you may be setting them on a path toward greater independence.* Don't hold back because you fear they will become so independent they won't need you anymore. See their independence as a gift you're giving them. Your success in doing something valuable is an excellent form of self-validation. You know you can make a difference in people's lives, and this is important to you. You're a role model for others, proof that one can make a difference. Helping others reach their potential is part of the prowess of your personality type.

Know Who You Are

Helpers have a sense of self-pride and importance in the belief that they intuitively know what others need. They believe that their empathy and their ability to give are a boon they provide to others. In the Helper's eyes those on whom they've chosen to lavish this benevolence are fortunate to receive it, while those from whom it's withheld are somehow diminished. By bestowing their gifts in such a measured way, Helpers can create an inner sense of their own worthiness.

This helps to offset their more general sense that being worthy is tied in with how others react to them. If approval or love is not forthcoming, or is present and then withdrawn, Helpers experience the loss as personally devastating. They're worthless. They have no meaning or significance. Their pride is wounded.

ACTION: *Part of your growth work is to build an identity so that you're not dependent on the responses of others for your self-worth. You can achieve this by spending time alone; in being solitary you come to know your true worth.* It's good to be alone. You'll find it a blessing to be alone, to feel what *you* need, simply to be as you are. By being alone, writing in a journal, reflecting on your relationships with deep inquiry as to your motivations and responses, you can come to know who you are. Once you begin to know yourself, you can try to take that self into your relationships.

"Is This for Them or for Me?"

From the reports of Helpers, we know that they lack a central belief in a sense of self. Helpers know they lack self-esteem and self-image, which is not surprising, since their self-esteem and self-image are tied up in the responses they receive from others. For instance, as parents they select the areas of daily life that offer the greatest opportunity for their child to succeed in, and they put forth their best effort to make this happen.

Hard as this idea may be to accept for a Helper parent, part of the selectivity process is that they know that by helping their child they're also going to help their own self-image. If their child becomes the star athlete on the team or the star performer in the play, Helper parents can bask in the reflected glory. They remember with a sense of self-satisfaction the hours they've spent in the car driving their kids back and forth to games, to practice or rehearsal, and so on. The following realization gives them real pleasure: "They couldn't have done this without me."

ACTION: *Don't stop giving to and helping your children, but be aware of your motivation. Try to keep your self-image separate from their achievements.* If you *are* a Helper, be aware of how much of your self-image is caught up in your giving. Next time you feel the energy come on to engage in your children's life in this way, ask yourself, "Is this for them or for me?"

Please Yourself

We've discussed how important approval is to Helpers. They report that approval is like oxygen, a necessity they must have in order to survive. Helper parents believe that approval is something that's gained from or withheld by others, including their children. This is one of the mechanisms through which they become dependent on other people and a reason they experience such panic when thrown onto a dependency of their own sense of self. Often their attention goes to where the approval *is not*. If Helpers want to be engaged with someone who they sense is disapproving or simply not affected by them, they will turn on tricks, such as flattery, to gain approval. Another ploy is to make others feel special.

A Helper said, "I went to Europe with a friend, and after about three weeks she said, 'I've finally figured out your trick of how you get people to like you.' I said, 'I have a trick? Please tell me.' She answered, 'You make the person you're talking to feel like she's the most important person in the world and your life wasn't complete until you met her.' I was flabbergasted. It never occurred to me that other people would see my actions as flattery and manipulation."

ACTION: *Be more relaxed about approval.* Parenting can became a great deal more fun when you don't have such a focus on everyone's having to like you and approve of you all the time. Helpers subconsciously make their children feel special: "You're wonderful children who complete my life." There's nothing wrong with saying this to your children, but be aware of your motivation. Maybe you want that reflected back to you—that *you* are special because you have special children. You gain a great deal from your children. But what happens when one of them doesn't want what you give? Naturally there are going to be certain times when they don't like or approve of you. Ultimately you have to decide to do and act and speak to please yourself.

Be Yourself; You Can't Please Everyone All the Time

Self-image is tied in with Helpers' preoccupations with pride, selectivity, and approval. Image—looking good to others—is in part fueled by Helpers' highest intentions to perform to the best of what others need. Thus Helper parenting can take on the outer trappings of a performance. There's a degree of stage management, for instance, in setting up a conversation, or a room, for a dynamic interchange.

You're aware of everyone's needs and try to accommodate them all. You don't want anyone in the family to be disappointed, so you go out of your way to make them comfortable and happy. You may think of your house as a stage set designed in the way you've conceived that the family dynamic will be played out most successfully. The ways you arrange the rooms are gifts to your family.

ACTION: *Whenever you're aware that someone in your family is disappointed, or feels left out, or is resistant to your efforts to create the family image, don't ignore their resistance by becoming more cheerful, more Pollyannaish.* Confront that person, even though it's hard for you. You know all the ways to engage someone, so you can defuse his anger. Seek out a conversation about his objections, inquire into his resistance. You will garner valuable information and give the other person (child or partner) the satisfaction of knowing that he's been taken seriously. You will draw him into the family circle again. Think how wonderful you'll feel about that.

Positive Confrontation Is Good for Your Children

Confrontation is usually not an option for Helper parents. They believe that if they confront their children, they run the risk of losing their love and approval. Even though they may not like themselves for doing so, because in certain situations it's hypocritical (internally they strongly disagree with what their children are doing or asking for), complying with the needs of their children seems a far safer tack. What is also frustrating is that Helpers can't even *act* tough. They know when their children are stringing them along, and they need to set some limits. Yet they find it practically impossible to do so.

Action: *Try not to be too lenient in setting limits and in making consequences stick.* Always giving your children leeway and the benefit of the doubt is not wise, because you're encouraging them to be manipulative.

Find an alternative if confrontation is a no-no for you; praise them, and work with good behavior, and use that as a counterpoint to put the lid on bad and unacceptable behavior. Being nonconfrontational is a weakness and a shortcoming in a parent. Even playing with the confrontation in a joking way is preferable to being nonconfrontational. You can rationalize that it's better to have your child's trust than risk frightening them away by being tough. But what if your child's personality demands confrontation as a way of testing who's honest and who's not? While you are doing your best to cultivate her trust, the net result is she trusts you less and less, because you shy away from every opportunity for confrontation she gives you. There is a middle ground between being too confrontational and being nonconfrontational. I encourage you to find it for yourself.

Parenting Steps for Helpers

- Build boundaries so as to stay within yourself, and *do not give that self away.* Continually refocus on your own needs and feelings.

- Practice telling your family what you need. Articulate your needs and desires. Say, "I need help with this."

- Build and adhere to a sense of self-identity. It becomes easier as you grow older to find out what *you* want and *who* you are. Get used to asking yourself, *"What do I want? What do I need? What is my moral truth here?"* Act on the answers.

- Use your gift of giving judiciously. Try to give only when your help is asked for. Find out from your family if your help is needed.

- Unconditional love may lead to unconditional permissiveness. Hold the line with your children with regard to limits, curfews, and consequences. Uphold family rules even though this may lead to confrontation that makes you uneasy.

- Inquire into the nature of your giving. Is it true or false altruism (giving to get)? Learn to accept that your family's love and approval is for your*self,* not for how you've helped them.

- Know that you make a positive difference in people's lives and that this is important to you. Potentiate them equally. Don't give more to those who'll make you look good.

- Grow into a sense of yourself; you can't please everyone all the time. Find time to be alone. Try to forge your own path instead of helping "the authority" in your family fulfill hers. Learn to recognize when you're using flattery and manipulation. Allow yourself to be more demonstrative with spontaneous warmth.

- Be aware that some members of your family may be put off by the emotionality and neediness of your behavior. Pay more attention to rationality and logic in dealing with your family. Remember you are biased toward the relational; their personalities probably have other biases.

SUMMARY: THE HELPER PARENT

Positives to Build On	Negatives to Overcome
Gives invaluable support	Proud of being needed
Supports authority figure	Constant need for approval
True altruist	Selective about whom to help
Caregiver	
Capable of real connection	Curries favor
	Plays it safe, not a risk taker
Emotional buoy	Assumes many selves, manipulative
Empathic	
Nurturer	Flatterer
Facilitates potential in others	Can become resentful and angry if feels freedom is curtailed

The Organizer
Loving through Doing

Jane—Doing Is Great, but Done Is Better

Jane was a great mom: active, energetic, engaged in all aspects of her kids' lives. The mother of four children who ranged in age from fifteen to six (two older boys, two younger girls) she juggled, seemingly without effort, carpooling, laundry, shopping, cooking, and other tasks. She was also a member of the PTA at both the local elementary and high schools her children attended. Jane worked hard for the PTA. It was a positive experience for her, the opportunity to achieve in a way that was beneficial for the world. She put in great effort, and felt good about it. She hoped that the school was a better place because of what she was doing.

During the first five years of marriage, before her eldest child was born, Jane was a rising star in an advertising agency specializing in products marketed to women. For years she has been a freelancer for the same company, working out of her home, in the mornings while the children were at school.

As an Organizer parent Jane played out her strengths in the arena of positive energy, enthusiasm, and achieving goals. She inspired (and pushed) all members of the family to achieve their potential. The key to Jane's success was her organizational ability. She marched through her day (and her week) to the drumbeat of a carefully designed schedule; large tasks were broken into smaller tasks and smaller tasks into easy-to-manage steps. Jane marshaled her family into a team held together by the glue of the schedule.

Weekends she planned with her husband, and they included shared household chores as well as organized outings for the whole family, usually something educational: a visit to the science museum, a hike in the woods, attending the theater or a musical performance. Lists of tasks generated by a computer scheduler were posted on the fridge every Sunday night, held up by funky, colorful magnets the children loved. Jane was defensive when friends told her that her household seemed regimented. She countered by showing them the schedule and pointed out that every day there was a slot for *FUN!*

Jane controlled fun time. She did not wield control for the sake of power like a Protector parent, or to feel safe like a Questioner parent, but in order to reach the goal. She thought along these lines: "If things spin out of my control, then everybody's going to be in so many different places that we're not going to get this job (fill in "vacation," "having fun," etc.) done. So I'll hold all the pieces together."

During fun time Jane expected the children to read, work on a hobby, listen to music, play together in the yard. She herself gardened or walked the dog together with her daughters. Often, during the days when Jane could not fit in a block of time to exercise, she felt this as a deficiency, a failure. She hoped that as the children grew older she would have more time to do things for herself.

Everything in life came back to completing tasks. Organizers expect others to work as hard as they do. Never mind if others in the Organizer family feel passed over, pressured, or alienated by the process. For Organizers, time wasted is time lost forever. This is another illusion of control, evidence of self-deceit, a belief that you can actually prioritize and schedule life into blocks of sequential time.

Jane got along well with her eldest son, who was involved in many activities and interests and organized his life into tasks (quite sensibly, she believed, relieved that at least one of her children had learned that knack from her). She often remarked to herself what similar personalities they had. Her second son, when he reached the age of thirteen, started to challenge Jane's way of organizing his life. She knew that their internal rhythms and ways of seeing the world were quite different.

"Fun for me is vegging out in front of the TV," he told her. "But to you, that and napping are among the seven deadly sins."

He was correct, that was the way Jane felt, but she stopped nagging him about the TV. She didn't want him to withdraw from her even more. His withdrawal constituted a failure for Jane. It's difficult for Organizers to admit failure. This is how Jane reacted to the challenge of her son: "Well, my way isn't working for him. But this is good, because now I know I need to be more careful with the girls. I won't make that mistake again. In fact, it's a great opportunity that he challenged me, because now I know to back off being critical of the TV watching. There must be other ways I can help him spend his free time successfully, rather than doing nothing." It was not on her radar screen that her son might have a valid need to veg out.

Organizers reframe what they think is failure into success, even partial success. This was what Jane was doing with her son. It's an intense experience for Organizers when they realize that most other people don't think of life in terms of failure and success; either something works or it doesn't. Success-or-failure is an Organizer construct on life.

Jane's hands-on involvement in her children's lives shows a person *doing* rather than *being*. Procedure and product are more important than time to process emotions. Organizers are often not emotionally available and are often unable to cope graciously when things do not go their way or start to fall apart. When they are stressed, part of their attention is split onto an internal taskmaster counting off all the tasks that have to get done, while they find themselves losing their ability to prioritize. There's a sense of not being able to move into action, of spinning wheels, of becoming more and more frustrated and frightened. For the family this manifests as a higher level of control mode and a greater expectation for them to do what they have to—*now.*

But at the right time Organizers can fully experience emotions and support and love their intimates unconditionally. Feelings of love allow them to encircle their loved ones in an embrace of warm emotion.

Her daughters were still too young to voice their opinions, but Jane could sense that neither of them was going to follow in her footsteps as a highly organized person. She sighed. They were going to make life much more difficult for themselves than it needed to be. This galvanized her to even greater effort to impart to them a sense of how satisfying it was when she felt her energy manifest itself around *doing* and *being busy,* and task after task was completed. Often at night, as Jane was falling asleep, she thought back over the day, of all she had done. Relaxed then, she drifted on that feeling of satisfaction.

When Organizers feel secure, they slow down, relax, stop driving themselves and everyone else. There's space for feelings to surface and time to think about themselves and others. This is when they can be demonstrative and loving and even commit some of the "deadly sins"—like napping.

But slowing down, letting emotions rise to the surface, can also be a discomfiting place for Organizers, because doubts emerge when they slow down. Faced with fears, questions, and doubts, Organizers find that emotions can be overwhelming. When the discomfort level is too high—especially about intimate, intense family issues—they quickly kick into action mode again.

Like other Organizers, Jane believed that she was the one

who was getting everything done for everybody else, so she projected an innate sense of self-importance around her. In whatever arena of life, this perception abets the Organizers' drive to accomplish. It's hard for them to accept and learn that in fact the world operates quite well without them.

Kevin—Picture Perfect

Kevin was a supersalesman for a large pharmaceuticals company, and he spent many weeks of the year crisscrossing the country on extensive business trips. He thrived on the feeling of being on the move, of being a cog in the machinery of the greatest economy on the planet. The sales-performance awards lining his office attested to his ability to close out the opposition. He liked having money for the material comforts he could give his family: the suburban house, the expensive watches, the cars, the vacations. His wardrobe was extensive—he had far more clothes than his wife did. Kevin knew exactly what to wear for each client and to each meeting to make that all-important first impression.

On his desk at the office, occupying pride of place, were several photographs of the family, shot every few years as the children grew and changed. Kevin was taken by surprise when someone at work looked at the photographs and commented on what a great family he had. He smiled with appreciation and made a suitable response. But he felt caught out. He realized that he was so focused on closing the next sale he hardly even noticed the photographs. Kevin played the part of the salesman so well that it was often hard for him to separate himself from his job. The photographs were props to build his image as a great father with a great family: picture perfect. Kevin needed to become aware of his self-deceit.

The father of the boy and girl emerged on the weekends. Relieved, Kevin put on his old jeans or sweats and tackled the odd jobs around the yard. He often talked his children into working alongside him, so he could catch up on their lives. "My family gets to see the other side of me," he said, "my more real side. Comfortable clothes, relaxed, the family man."

With the family (as elsewhere) Kevin played to the team. A subtle inner mechanism operated to draw others to him; he was a great persuader. Almost involuntary changes in voice, gesture, and manner made sure he had everyone's attention. These adjustments were quite automatic. Kevin could jolly his reluctant children (at least for now) into spending a few hours on Saturday doing yard work with him. This was part of the reason Kevin was a supersalesman: "Once I have you in front of me, my belief is that I can sell you anything, because I know how to package ideas." This is an essential Organizer illusion, but most Organizers hold to this belief and can come across as phony. Kevin's children were beginning to see the agenda behind his wanting their company in the yard. It was to salve his conscience for not spending more time with them. While Organizers think they're on a roll and everyone is on board their bandwagon, others see them working to sell their agenda.

Organizers *do* parenting. For Kevin, doing was tied in to image, and the right image was projected to ensure approval (especially self-approval). More self-aware Organizers become conscious of when they don personas and can separate out the pseudo from the essential self. While Kevin knew there was a difference between his work self and his at-home self, in either situation he was playing a role. To others these two types of Organizers may at first glance appear to be different personalities; however, the underlying psychological patterning is the same. For the Beaver Organizers—"What I do speaks about who I am"—doing is encompassed into who they are. Peacock Organizers are a more obvious form of the image type—"Image and how I look are of essential importance." Kevin was a Peacock at work but more of a Beaver at home.

On vacations Kevin was the model of the hands-on dad. He

spent all day with the children: playing frisbee, swimming, shrimping, taking sailing lessons together, organizing the shopping, the cookouts, the excursions. His energy and enthusiasm swept them along from one activity to the next. In his drive-forward style, he embodied the quality of hope. Organizers are adept at delivering hope, both in creating the expectation (vision) and in bringing it to fulfillment (getting it done).

Organizers report that when they're running on hope, they accomplish seemingly without effort. It's as if all they have to do is put themselves into a universal flow of energy and instinctively they know the right moves.

When Kevin was in the flow, everything fell into place: The parking space opened in front of the restaurant. The maître d' gave them a table with a view of the ocean. Everyone's favorite seafood was on the menu. The wonderful sunset they'd driven thirty miles to see took place as if on cue shortly after they were seated. Kevin smiled happily at his family. "We're a team. We're all doing this together."

Kevin loved to do things for his family. His hobby was carpentry, designing and building furniture. He built almost all the wooden furniture in the house. He chose expensive lumber like mahogany and oak, and he delighted in intricate touches and finishes. Working with wood was so elemental, so different from the high-powered environment at work (although he has all the high-tech equipment any carpenter could want and all the fancy gadgets from trade shows). He said that he liked his children to come in and chat while he worked, but he didn't encourage them to try the tools, didn't stop what he was doing to teach them. Basically he didn't like being interrupted when he worked. It slowed him down.

As he crafted the furniture, he imagined his children sitting at the desks he was building and doing their homework as they moved through school. He built his dreams for his children into his work and mused that maybe one day they'd pass those desks on to their children. When Kevin put the completed items in their rooms, he knew that the solid wood said, "I love you very much. Look what I've done for you." He was convinced that the more he *did* for them, the more they'd know what he felt for them, how much they meant to him.

Kevin occasionally attended his children's activities—baseball games, soccer games—but he often begged off, explaining to his wife that he was moving so fast during the week, on the weekend he didn't like to go anywhere. He always explained his absences to his children and believed they knew well enough that he was interested in all they did, that he supported them even though he wasn't watching them. Lately, though, he'd seen a knowing look in their eyes when he broached this subject. Kevin had an uneasy feeling that something was going awry between him and his children.

Although there are Organizers who are the exception and in whom self-awareness rises naturally, most Organizers only come face-to-face with their true feelings when illness or work-related or family-induced crises stop them in their tracks. Questions about self-esteem and worthiness, doubts around self-value, gnaw at Organizers when they're forced to take a good look at themselves. Over time they learn to become aware of the differences between what they are stating to be the truth and their honest feelings.

Kevin said, "Look, kids, you know I love to spend time with you, but if you're on the field, I'm not with you anyway, so let me get on with building the desk." He was protecting an image that he believed would bring him approval. The image said, "Look what a good father I am. How many other guys build their kids' furniture?" At first honesty and truth telling can feel risky for Organizers—"No one's going to like me for saying this"—but then honesty becomes liberating and self-verifying. What Kevin should say is "I'm sorry, I simply don't like to sit and do nothing. But I know you like me to watch you. So let me come for the first half, and then I can spend the rest of the morning in the workshop."

PERSONAL ACCOUNT

Heather, an Organizer mother of two sons, gives this account

I like the sense of building a team with my children, of being together for a common goal, being a family. Whether it's having fun, going on a trip, helping them with their homework—we do it together. We talk it over. Sometimes I have to lay down the law, establish boundaries, insist on certain standards, but mostly we can talk things over and come to decisions together. Also I like sharing their triumphs and disasters; it makes me feel part of them, so I do take a keen interest in their academics and activities. Now that they're older, I like being their friend, still being on the same team.

I don't like being buffeted against. I don't like it when my children take my words so literally that I then become the boundary they push up against. I don't like the feeling I often have that I'm the keystone that holds the family together. I want everyone to accept responsibility for that. I don't like it when they're sick. I feel so helpless. I'd rather be sick myself than have to stand by when they're ill, no matter how old they are.

My strengths as a parent revolve around energy and enthusiasm. I could keep up with both of my children from when they were little till they went to college. Also I don't get into a panic easily. I expect things to turn out right. When one of my kids was eight, he froze on a mountain path right where there was a precipitous drop of five hundred feet. He couldn't move. My heart was in my mouth, but I kept my voice calm and calmed him down. My older son, who was ten, was already over that traverse. He knew that it was a grave situation, and he listened to me, and together we helped the younger one across. It seemed to take forever, but it was perhaps ten minutes. A day or two later I took the boys back to the spot. I believe in the "get back on your horse when you fall off" theory. This time my younger son went over, back and forth without incident. I did this because I want them both to be independent and unafraid adults, and this was a useful lesson.

It's hard for me to see weaknesses in myself because I'm such a positive person. I don't dwell on the negative. I know I'm strong, and it's hard to think about weaknesses. Maybe that's a weakness in itself. My children watch me striving to succeed all the time, so they may not know it's all right to fail—as long as you pick yourself up and try again. Also I'm impatient, and I know I try to pack in more than I can handle. I juggle a lot of commitments, so I can't always give 100 percent of my attention at the moment they demand it. I give them full attention, but preferably on my schedule, or we find a compromise time.

A few summers ago, when both my kids were in college, we went to a favorite beach place for two weeks, the first time we'd all been together for years. We'd often gone to this place all through their childhood and adolescence. On the first night there they asked me what we were going to do the next day. I had nothing planned, because they were adults now and I thought they would want to go their own way. I was going to hang out on the beach. Their question made me think about how I used to plan activities for everyone every day, perhaps robbing them of a sense of initiative and adventure. With hindsight I see that my energy and enthusiasm had a downside, too.

My children are pretty clear-sighted about me. They say I taught them that there are many mountains to climb in life, to make full use of their opportunities, to fend for themselves financially and not expect a handout from the world, to contribute to society as a way of sharing their good fortune. But they also see another side—that I come on too strong sometimes and say things that are honest but also hurtful. They see me sometimes as too unemotional. They want me to tell them I love them, not to express my love through doing things with them and for them. One of them asked me if I practice "tough love," which took me aback, because I know how much I love them, and I can't believe that—even for a moment—they wouldn't know that, too.

I want to tell other parents not to overprotect their children. There's great freedom in being independent, learning self-sufficiency. Let your children take some knocks, but of course be there all the time to offer love and support. Let them know you love them unconditionally. Sometimes when we nag away, they may forget we do it from love. 🩵

The Best Strategy and Action Program for Organizers

Slow Down, Pay Attention

Organizer parents can take on many roles during the course of one day: the quartermaster getting the family up, fed, ready for school; the homework resource; the practical, concerned healer of minor wounds; the conscientious soccer mom or dad; the loving caretaker; the supportive spouse. Often Organizers change clothes several times a day as they subconsciously flex themselves into these roles.

Parenting is one role, work another. Children know quickly when they don't have their Organizer parent's attention. Dad or Mom has his or her mind on work while they're all doing something together.

ACTION: *Try to be aware of when your mind is in multitask mode.* Slow down. Take a deep breath. Push down on the impatience. Practice keeping your attention on where you are, who you're with, and who you are. You know how important your children are to you. What can be more precious than your single-minded attention on what your children (of any age) are telling you or what you're doing together? They will blossom in the sun of your attention.

Stay Present in One Conversation

Organizers don't listen very well. They filter out negative criticism as well as what they regard as extraneous information. Their children will tell them again and again, "You're not really listening to me." Or "I told you that before, but I knew you weren't listening." Or "You always change the subject, I know you're not interested in what I say."

ACTION: *Be aware that if you're not the one talking, then you're not particularly interested in what anyone else is saying.* That is, unless the conversation affects you or serves to further your (positive or negative) image, which is also tied in to the image of the family. Stay present in one conversation. Organizers report that even as they listen, their minds are spinning in several different grooves about the next task: what I'm going to do, how I'm going to do it, and what the alternative ways are for doing it.

Let Others Do It Their Way

Organizers want to be in control. They establish their authority through the image of being efficient achievers. With an almost limitless capacity for hard work, they organize their lives by breaking up goals into tasks. Efficiency—seeing a way to do things more quickly, more competently—is a trap for them. Not too many spouses or children take kindly to being shown, over and over, a *better* way to do a task. Organizers are probably correct that their way is the most efficient, but efficiency is not at the top of the agenda for other people. Take a five-year-old making a bed: it's going to be a while until the sheets are on straight. But if Organizers become impatient and do it for the child, they undermine the child's sense of self-esteem and accomplishment.

ACTION: *You are so efficient that it's hard for you to realize that others in your family will do the job their way, even though the way they go about it may look inefficient and time-wasting to you. Give them space and freedom to do it their way.* Rest assured that the world can and will operate without you.

Cultivate Self-Worthiness

This goal orientation and focus on tasks has many implications for Organizers. They gain approval by achieving their goals but run the danger of becoming human *doings,* not human *beings.* Organizers gain many rewards in American society, with its emphasis on energy, achievement, image, on being a winner. Organizers definitely want to be seen as winners, especially by their families.

When you get right down to the bedrock inner mechanisms of the Organizer, living life itself is a goal, and gaining approval has its place in the life-goal matrix. This can be hard on the Organizer's family. They are part of the Organizer's striving toward success. It's hard for an Organizer to stop moving forward, climbing upward, not unlike the Energizer Bunny. Children can feel inadequate and dwarfed by the Organizer's achievements, or feel pressure to achieve themselves, or emulate their parent, however hard or counterintuitive it may be for them.

ACTION: *Be aware that your sense of an inner self is often nonexistent. Work on finding* self-satisfaction *in what you do and accomplish.* Try not to share your latest triumph with your family—for at least a day. It's more important that you first hear and respond to what your children are feeling and doing, rather than the other way round. Cultivate a sense of your own worthiness, so you don't have to keep on looking for it outside yourself.

Practice Honesty: With Yourself and with Your Children

Organizers gravitate naturally to leadership positions. They enjoy being authority figures; they feel comfortable with responsibility, accountability, and the commensurate recognition and sense of importance these things bring. This makes for excellent parenting skills, especially when their children are preadolescent and still buy into the agenda. (With older children, a sensible Organizer parent will negotiate the agenda.)

Organizer parents are a positive force for good in the family. They have an innate sense of how to support others to help them achieve their goals. Their enthusiasm, high energy, and positive attitude inspire confidence. They are good self-promoters (and family promoters) and natural networkers, and they can ease the way for their children. When it's important for them to do so (such as saying when *they'll* do something for their family), they back up the hype with solid results; from earliest childhood they've gained approval for what they do. With an Organizer at the helm, there's a sense of unstoppable forward momentum.

ACTION: *Make sure, by talking it through with your chil-dren, that it is their goals you are both focusing on, not a version of what you want them to achieve. Help them to articulate their vision.* This is a gift you can share with them, your ability to help them actualize their vision.

Try not to tell your children to undertake something—and that they can count on your support—if you're doubtful you can deliver. To motivate others you have to walk the talk. Promote a sense of honesty and integrity about what you're doing. Other-wise your children will pick up quickly on anything that's fake and phony about your stance, and then they'll begin to doubt the veracity of whatever you say.

Operate (Sometimes) at Your Child's Pace

Organizers have an ability to do several tasks at the same time. They practice this behavior not only because to them it seems an efficient use of time but also because it gives them an adrena-line rush to do so. Others may look at the Organizer parent and see a hamster unable to get off a wheel, but the Organizer feels great.

Organizers report a definite sense of confluence when energy, effort, and multitask activity come together. If the main task is, say, cooking, it becomes almost a game for them to find ways to cook, but also to do the laundry, unpack the groceries, help both children with their homework—*all at the same time.* When the energy flows, it's a natural high.

ACTION: *Try to slow down and pay selective attention. You might even enjoy operating at your children's pace, seeing the world anew through their eyes.*

Children know when it's more about you than about them. You can't fool them. They will tell you, if you stop to ask them, that they often feel like stations on the production line of your life. You may achieve all you wanted to do (as in the above example) and look around for applause, but you'll find that your audience has disappeared. You may feel that you're on a roll and having a great time, but to others you seem a little frantic and maybe even foolish, running around in so many different directions.

Beware of the Inner Taskmaster

For Organizers, reaching the goal, achieving the vision, and manifesting the end product are of major importance, the source of their approval. They throw everything at the given job, flexing into the appropriate image so they become identified with what they do, clamping down on feelings, bringing the full bore of their multitask abilities into play, but no attribute is as powerful for them as their ability to perform through organization and task orientation. Their focus is on tasks. Many other personalities keep lists, but the motivation for the Organizer is that the list becomes a map to navigate what is otherwise the chaos of life. Prioritized lists are an Organizer specialty. If it is on the list, it will get *done.*

ACTION: *Try going a week without making a list (not even a mental one). Catch yourself when you find your mind going to a list.*

Lists are generally a good organizing tool, but sometimes they can backfire. When your child reads her name on your list, followed by a string of tasks related to her, it's not a great leap for her to see herself simply as another job for you to do. Explain to her that she is unique and special and *that you love her,* and her name on the list is a way to help you run *your* life. Tell her you know that other people, other parents, are different. Let her help you find ways to take her name off the list, without your having a panic attack over thinking that she's going to disappear into the general confusion of life.

You Are Not What You Do

Identification means aligning oneself with a person or group with a resultant feeling of close emotional association. For other personalities, identification may go no further than a feeling that one would like to emulate a mentor or identify with a place, or an ideal, or a religious concept. If you're an Organizer, identification takes on another level of meaning: merging with the role of being a parent so that you see yourself as the quintessential role model for the parenting job. Organizer parents may actually pity other parents. They're convinced that they are the type of parent every child would want. In situations like PTA meetings, they try to persuade other parents to think and act more as they do!

One of the life tasks for Organizers is to be on the lookout for moments when the illusion of who they are fuses with what they do. Children can be helpful in this, as often their perceptive observations can cut through the persona. Jane's son's remark that naps were one of the "deadly sins" according to her is an example. Kevin's children's knowing look when he explains why he won't be at their games is another.

ACTION: *Try to be aware of when identification with your role is blinding you to reality. Ask your children or your spouse for a reality check.* Try an approach that encourages cooperation. Say, "This is the way I see myself in this situation. Is this how *you* see me?" Let them see that you are heeding their responses and trying to build them into your worldview. The simple action of asking for a reality check can help to remove the identification blinkers.

Love Your Children Unconditionally

Organizers put enormous store on success and achievement, and this is usually a major sticking point for children of Organizer parents who are not like them. They ask, "Why do you want me to always be first? The first to ask a question in class? The first to be picked for a team? The first to be invited to a party?" Many children of Organizers, especially when younger, wonder if the Organizer loves them, especially if they can't perform to the Organizer's (often unspoken) expectations.

ACTION: *Ask your children more frequently, "How do you feel about school today?" and less often, "What did you do in school today?"* Create an atmosphere of sympathetic listening and acceptance of their feelings and activities. Love them unconditionally, *and* let them know it by both your actions and words. Often you believe that *doing* so much for your children conveys to them how much you love them. Practice telling them "I love you" until that expression is a natural and spontaneous part of your interactions. Encourage them to open up to you by setting aside time to *really* listen to them.

Accept That We All Live Our Own Lives

Organizers avoid failure. It is well nigh impossible for Organizers to take Rudyard Kipling's advice from his poem "If": "If you can meet with Triumph and Disaster / And treat those two impostors just the same." Triumph and disaster are not impostors to Organizers; they form a solid reality in the Organizer world. Organizer parents don't take easily to living in the flat, even plateau between the peaks of triumph and the valleys of disaster. They constantly seek the high of forward movement and the energy of being upbeat.

Organizers gain approval by doing well, by achieving, by believing that they are loved for what they accomplish rather than for who they are. This belief leads to a lifelong dance with image issues; winners are loved, approved of—there are no prizes for second place. The family is taken from one successful peak to another. There is fun, excitement, movement. Organizers are very present in the family dynamic: when the energy lags, they provide it; when silence falls, they rev up the conversation. Failure involves not being able to operate at that upbeat level.

ACTION: *Some of the most powerful motivational forces in your life are the fears of boredom and failure. Accept that there are times when you have no control over events,* and if something goes wrong for your family, don't judge yourself as a failure. Be aware (and be thankful) that you don't operate the universe. Live in the hope and trust that others (even your children) are responsible for their own lives and for the consequences of their actions.

Image Is All-Important

Organizers project an image they can believe in and sell to others, so they become caught in a self-fulfilling loop of projection, image, approval. A panelist reported that her Organizer mother used to insist that the downstairs rooms of the house always be perfectly tidy, in case unexpected guests dropped by. The upstairs was a mess—her mother never took visitors upstairs. But her image was wrapped up in visitors' seeing how well organized and beautifully she kept her home: picture perfect. This woman and her siblings saw their Organizer mother as living by a double standard, and it undermined their belief in her. She became suspect, phony at times.

There is something of a Machiavellian sense that the ends justify the means in the ability of Organizers to instantly switch roles and images (one moment the harassed, impatient mother, the next the charming, gracious hostess). And in most instances the end is for the greater glory of the Organizer (and by extension her family).

ACTION: *You set great store on being a winner, on the image of success. This drive translates to your children, who may feel they are letting you down if they're not winners, too. Make sure you let them know you love them just as they are,* whatever they do or don't do. I know I'm repeating this, but it is fundamentally important in Organizer parenting.

Being Loved for Who You Are; Stop Seeking Approval

Like the Helper parent (but for different reasons), Organizers have an unslakable thirst for approval. It's as if they look in a mirror and are not alive unless they see someone else smiling back. Because approval is so important, they set up a comparative yardstick of how well they are doing. Organizer parents compare themselves to others, for instance, in how not to become mired in the emotional problems (it seems to them) other parents encounter with their children. They tune out criticism with what in extreme cases can be an almost narcissistic belief in their superior abilities. (Moralizer parents also compare themselves with others, but they do so on an internal scale of judgment.)

Organizers certainly seek approval from both their children and their spouse, and they'll keep on telling them about what they've achieved until the acknowledgment is forthcoming. As they grow older, children can learn to deflect this drive, with comments such as "We know you're great, you know you're great. Why do you have to keep telling us?" Or "We believe in you. Don't you believe in yourself?"

Organizer parents bask in the approval of others; they're elated when people stop and say, "Oh, I've heard such good things about you and your children." One reaction can be "More, more." Another, more complex reaction is to be filled with gratitude internally but deflect the approval externally: "Oh, it's nothing really, and anyway Jimmy should get all the credit. His MVP award has little to do with me."

Organizers assume that they can and should *make* good things happen for their family. Taking the vacation they can't really afford, ensuring that everyone's together for Thanksgiving when college-age children are scattered far and wide, putting effort into keeping everyone in touch by phone or e-mail; they take it upon themselves to make it all happen. They seldom stop *doing,* rarely backing off to see if the family will remain intact without their efforts. (Usually their children are independently in excellent communication with one another. This often comes as a surprise to Organizer parents.) And why is all this effort necessary? One Organizer reports that putting a process in place and seeing it through to the end product in and of itself constitutes her approval. Organizers get their approval when they know they've done the job well, but an added fillip is other people's acknowledgment.

ACTION: *Practice living with the idea that you're loved for who you are, not for what you do.* Practice it until it becomes a constant habit of mind and replaces the notion that you are *not* loved unless you're achieving, unless you're a winner. Be passive in your interactions for a day, a week. It may seem annihilating to you to wait, but practice this as a step on your growth path. Wait a few days to call your child at summer school or college; don't send any e-mail for a week. See what comes to you.

If you are honest, sometimes (to your dismay) you may find yourself competing with your children (particularly the older they are) for attention and approval. For instance, if your daughter holds the limelight for too long at a dinner party, you ask yourself, "What about me? When can I talk?" Acknowledge the feeling, and try to see where it is coming from. This is a complicated issue, for you know, too, that you revel in the attention your child is receiving. Thinking this through may be the beginning of freeing yourself from the bind of always having to be the center of attention, of needing approval.

Stay Present in Your Feelings

Organizer parents seem to be forever optimistic and upbeat. They don't often pause between an idea and moving into action for long enough to be ambushed by emotional responses. In an intrinsic way Organizers have put their interior life on hold in the name of performance and activity. Habitual conditioning with regard to how to win approval is in part what creates the need for constant activity and for the Organizer to suspend feelings to complete tasks.

Family dynamics are often charged with emotions, and because Organizers fear that feelings will hold them back, drag them down, and then they will not be able to *do* for their family, they can come across as unfeeling and distant. This is often exactly how they *do not* want to be perceived, because in fact they are roiling with emotions.

One Organizer parent reports that her fifteen-year-old son was involved in a cycling accident. As a strange car pulled into the driveway and she saw him emerge looking dazed, his crumpled bike sticking out of the trunk, she felt panic sweep over her, followed by a strange calm. She thanked the people who picked him up off the road, and then she took him to the bathroom to clean the cuts, helped him change, called the doctor, left a note for her husband, drove him to the emergency room, went in the ambulance with him to another hospital for a CAT scan. Later that night, when she was finally home, she felt herself grow cold with horror at what might have been, and she broke down and sobbed. But until that moment she was focused on task after task after task.

ACTION: *You are being somewhat dishonest, deceiving yourself and your loved ones to suspend your feelings while you get the job done. They may feel that you're still emotionally with them, but in fact you're not present.* Learn to *stay* present. Organizers are energetically passionate, they have deep feelings and can express them verbally and physically, but the time must be right. It's an important gift to yourself and your family if you can learn to express your feelings spontaneously, as they arise.

Your Life of Feelings Is Waiting for You

As long as attention is outer-directed, on tasks and on others, getting caught up in emotions can be put on hold. Why is it so important to Organizers to suspend feelings?

The subconscious mind is a powerful register, and they've conditioned themselves to believe that their value and worth are tied up in what they do, rather than in knowing their inner world. Because the emotional world is relatively unfamiliar, and because Organizers don't believe that they can handle their feelings, they find emotional intensity overwhelming. Once feelings take over, Organizers don't know if they can survive the power of those feelings. The mother of the injured son *believes* she's incapable of coping if her feelings are present; she will let him down. Organizers have little practice at being in constant connection with their feelings. They haven't sacrificed an inner life; they simply aren't familiar with the idea that there is one available to them. Organizers keep the schedule filled: if there's no free time, there's no time for feelings to interfere.

ACTION: *Your children can be your teachers in helping you to access your feelings.* At their birth, in their earliest years, you feel their innocence and dependence, you open to their trust, you can release yourself emotionally in loving them. Reach back to those feelings and try and recapture them. Try to bring that affect into your dealings with everyone in your world, but especially with your children. Not only are you shortchanging them when you're so busy *doing* for them that you're not consciously loving them, but, just as important, you are shortchanging yourself.

Parenting Steps for Organizers

- Practice keeping your attention on where you are, who you're with, and who you are. Be aware that you suspend your emotions to get the job done. Children pick up quickly when this happens that you're not emotionally available for them. Your focus on tasks rather than feelings can lead to hurt and misunderstanding.

- Stop and consider the consequences of your forward momentum. The world can and will operate without you. Accommodate to others. Alternate ways of doing something are as valid as your own.

- Work on finding *self-satisfaction* in what you do and accomplish. *Hear* your family when they say "We love you," irrespective of the success you do or do not garner in the world.

- Promote a sense of honesty and integrity about what you're doing. Guard against being the instant expert when your children ask you questions. Be aware that you exaggerate positives and neglect negatives. This can lead other people (especially your children and partner) not to trust you, not to have confidence in your judgment.

- Forgo the image. Operate at your children's pace. Slow down and interact with the family wholeheartedly, reminding yourself, "I'm at home now." Stop pretending you have it all together. Let your children see your exhaustion, fears, tension, doubts. This allows them to feel it's okay to be a human *being,* not a human *doing.*

- Stop seeking approval. Practice living with the idea that you're loved for who you are, not for what you do. Be passive in your interactions for a while. See what comes to you if you wait.

- Beware of the inner taskmaster. Take note of when you're compulsively doing for your children (instead of sharing feelings with them). They may feel that you regard them as a product, an extension of yourself, especially when their triumphs (or setbacks) are experienced as your own.

- Focus fully on your feelings. Tell your family members you love them. Share your emotions verbally and physically. Don't live by the adage that what you do for them speaks louder than words.

- Acknowledge your partner's contribution to parenting your children; don't take all the credit for a dual effort. Help your partner keep his or her boundaries intact; don't insist that your partner always jump on whatever is *your* current bandwagon.

SUMMARY: THE ORGANIZER PARENT

Positives to Build On	*Negatives to Overcome*
Self-confidence	Image of the perfect parent
Reliability	Values results, impatient for progress
Keeps focus on tasks	Pushes down on feelings
Natural authority figure	Believes own propaganda
Goal orientation	Assumes is loved for actions rather than self
Multitask thinker/doer	Difficulty in opening to feelings
Competitive	Avoids failure
Drives self and family to succeed	Wants to be a winner or the family to be a winning team—at all costs
Efficiency	Views family as a project, brushes aside feelings

CHAPTER 4

The Dreamer
Connection Is Everything

Jack—a Rich and Passionate Life . . . but Something's Missing

Jack was a good father—at least that's what his children told him. Sometimes he could accept their judgment with equanimity, but most of the time his memories were redolent with regret: "I had many good times when they were growing up, but if only I spent more time with them in the summers when I had the opportunity to do so. We did accomplish a lot together, but why didn't I take the long weekends off when they wanted me to go camping and fishing with them? We've had memorable and nostalgic moments of connection and sharing, but why did so many of our conversations involve mundane matters like money, tuition bills, or their part in paying back loans? Why do I never take what they give but always want something else? Take this past Father's Day, for instance. For years I've told them that Father's Day was every day of the year, not the day decreed by commercial opportunists. But why did I feel diminished when they didn't acknowledge me on Father's Day this year?"

Jack felt he came up short as a parent in not being able to forge the unique connection he believed each of his children deserved. There was only so much time for family, and he chose his primary connection to be with their mother; she came first. Jack found that relating to four children and their mother had its pitfalls as well as its privileges: "I admit that I found their childhood and early adolescent years stressful and uncomfortable. There were too many people making too many demands on me."

Jack shares with us what many other Dreamer parents report as well. Stress arises for Dreamers when they feel an emotional pull in too many directions. In this situation they lose their sense of personal boundaries, their sense of inner balance. Jack concentrates so hard on making connections to *all* his children, to give them what they want, that he feels the connection is no longer forming inside himself. A large part of Jack's stress is that he feels phony when he loses his boundaries: "I'm connecting, and it doesn't feel as if it's from a deep place. They see me as on a roll, but I'm simply going through the steps of being a good father."

There were many family stories of the times when they all set out on an expedition and then one of the children expressed a need that was not part of the day's plan. This request would sway Jack off his agenda. When their mother wasn't present to keep the outing on course, Jack would abandon the original plan in order to address that child's needs, to give her what she wanted at that moment. He felt he was being dependable, reliable. The other children were seldom as sympathetic to their sibling's pleas. Jack's availability could be seen as selfless devotion, but it also speaks of a lack of boundaries. Jack admitted, "I lose myself, I lose my equanimity, I lose my plan. This used to happen in business, too. In latter years I've become aware of this tendency. I catch myself in the moment and ask, 'Why have I left the plan?'"

Dreamer parents experience life with a melancholic flavor—witness Jack's what-ifs at the start of this description. Yet, when asked, several of Jack's children said that their father was not only melancholic but prone to bouts of depression. To those on the outside, a more overt form of melancholia can look like depression. Melancholia has a bittersweet nuance for Dreamers, and many say that they enjoy the edge it brings to their lives. Depression for Dreamers (as for any personality) can be filled with pain and suffering, but Dreamers feel that spending time in the depths (as well as the heights) of experience allows them to know life fully, and because of this they are more authentic than many other people. For many Dreamers, depression does not carry the negative charge placed on the term by society at large.

Again Jack is a case in point. One of his daughters was mildly autistic, and Jack explained his deep connection with her this way: "There's a sense that I can stay there with her in the dark places of her mind when no one else can. I've been there. No one else I know can feel as intensely as I do. I can stay there for a long time resonating with the emotional pain of others."

There is a profound interiority to Dreamers. Many Dreamers in the counseling professions do excellent work with the most troubled teens and adults, because at a deep level they can empathize with others' anguish.

Jack lived a rich and passionate life, yet he was constantly aware that the special quality, the drama of his life, was contained in the fact that the glass was half empty. For instance, when he looked at the lives of other fathers, most often he felt diminished: "Why do they have more time to spend with their children? How come they can afford to go to Florida every winter? Why do their children win all the prizes at school? How come *he* gets tickets to every baseball game?"

Envy often manifests itself as competitiveness. Competition can be compelling. At one time Jack wanted a position on the PTA, and he formed an emotional attachment to the idea. The position went to someone else. Jack was strongly enough attached to being elected that he wanted (internally and momentarily) to annihilate the person who won. He made it known how hurt and put upon he felt. Even in matters of envy and competition, Dreamers are ruled by emotions involving connection.

As in his exterior life, which was ruled by highs and lows and moved in fits and starts, Jack's interior world did not follow a sequential pattern, either. All the mythic moments of life involved some meaningful connection. If you ask Jack—or other Dreamers—to tell a story, he will never begin at A and end at Z. The events are related in order of importance from the dramatic highs to the lows. Dreamers operate from an inner terrain that feels like a roller coaster. This can create difficulties in parenting when children are looking to their parent to provide a stable environment and what they get is a roller-coaster ride.

Angela—on Being That Special Parent

Angela loved her children. She knew that other parents love their children, too, but her love was something special. She wrapped them in a warm cocoon of love. Her dreams for them were that they fulfill their unique gifts: her son played the cello, her daughter trained long hours for gymnastic competitions. Angela's joy in her children could never be fully realized; something would always be missing. This she knew as a fact of life, and it filled her with melancholic sadness. Sometimes she was overwhelmed with regret that her life had to be unfulfilled this way. She was astonished that neither her husband nor her children were aware of the fragility of special moments, the effervescent impermanence of reality.

A moment was perfect, and even as she realized its perfection, it was gone. For instance, she was often enraptured by her son's cello playing; the lingering purity of the deep notes registered pangs of longing in her. Then he stopped bowing, and the music ended. She yearned to keep those moments alive, those moments when she felt a deeper sense of herself and her connection to her son and their lives.

This focus on something missing was not a new realization for Angela. She'd felt this kind of sadness from childhood. The great moments, anticipated or spontaneous, when she felt life at its fullest, were inevitably marred by her realization of a flow the other way, to emptiness. The fullness/emptiness phenomenon that Dreamers experience in a broad sense characterizes their inclination toward tasting life as bittersweet, melancholic. At a subconscious level Dreamers are all too familiar with the paradox that the seeds of growth and fulfillment are also the seeds of decay and disappointment. Dreamers have a sense of the highs (rising to moments of perfect connection) and lows (abandonment to emptiness, or to losing that connection) and little of life lived in the middle. Part of the action program for Dreamer parents, described later in the chapter, is to try to even out and balance a life that is either high (elation) or low (depression) or both and to find in the mundane tasks of everyday life an equanimity that will help them stay on an even keel.

Growth for Dreamers occurs when they can experience equanimity. Equanimity can be defined as balance or calmness or tranquillity. For Dreamers, balance arises when the extraordinary and the mundane are present together; they realize a richness in that.

Angela knew she had a hard time setting boundaries with her children. She felt such a connection to them, she was so engaged in their lives, that when they said they needed her, she tended to drop whatever she was doing so she could accommodate them. She believed that every interaction deepened their connection. Angela could see the downside of her overwhelming responsiveness. Her instant availability might inculcate a feeling of entitlement in them. She sensed that her children depended on her more than was good for them—or her.

One fall she had a call from the director of the camp her twelve-year-old daughter had attended the summer before. The director told her that one of her daughter's cabin counselors had received a hate letter from Angela's daughter. Angela listened carefully to what the director had to say and asked her to mail a copy of the letter. One look at the handwriting and she knew her daughter *had* written the letter. But the date revealed that it had been mailed during the time when a friend from camp had been visiting their home.

When Angela spoke to her daughter, she did not confront her but adopted an attitude of curiosity. The story spilled forth easily. The two girls had really grown to dislike this counselor while they were together, and the friend had come up with the idea and the content of the letter. Angela's daughter was swept up in the friend's enthusiasm and never gave a thought to the effect on the counselor. Like her daughter with her friend, Angela was all too often swept up by her children, when perhaps she could serve them better by keeping her feet on the ground, keeping her boundaries intact.

However, in the letter incident Angela felt secure in the line she took with her daughter. She knew the correct action to take. Together they came up with a plan to set the record straight with the counselor. Angela liked the feeling of knowing she was right and could see the direction ahead. This was so different from the times when she was at the mercy of intense emotions, each one overwhelming. The pressure she experienced in extreme emotions stemmed largely from not knowing how to process them *and* from knowing that other people process their emotions differently.

At those times she was grateful that eventually the intensity faded. Then she could think reasonably and order her life to bring some structure and sequential logic to what she was thinking and experiencing. The times she liked herself least were when she became self-critical and her anger took an internal, indirect form, expressing itself as judgment and criticism at her husband and children over little things like an unpaid bill or a spill on the kitchen floor.

When Angela was a child, her mother helped her father develop their small business. Angela experienced her mother's absence as abandonment. As an adult she discussed this feeling with her siblings, and they were amazed at her response. They pointed out to her, "But Mom made sure we were taken care of. She was around enough so we didn't get into mischief. She was always there when we were sick or in trouble."

What Angela remembered was her shame that her mother was different from her friends' mothers. And on an intimate level she never felt the connection with her mother she hoped she had forged with *her* children. Angela's mother took care of her physical needs, but there was a disconnection, a gulf of missing emotion. *A real fear was that if Angela didn't do what her children asked of her, they would abandon her, too.* She was aware that she'd carried a dull ache in her heart since they were born, pain arising from the knowledge that inevitably life would take them from her—even as she helped them grow into independent people.

One of the reasons that Angela was so grateful to be a mother was that she could remother herself while she mothered her children. In an essential way, though, through her children, she felt a spiritual connection to the universe. She had borne life inside her; that miracle connected her to the universal: conceiving life, bearing life, nurturing life is the ultimate interconnection with life processes themselves.

For Angela and other Dreamer parents, parenthood in many ways eases their yearning for a sense of belonging. They feel authentic in belonging to their children in this intimate way—as their primary caregiver. Angela felt she had found the place where she was meant to be, where she could be present. For this she was profoundly grateful.

PERSONAL ACCOUNT

Bob, a Dreamer father of two daughters, gives this account

The feeling of family is wonderful and delicious, but often elusive. Most of all I like the feeling of parenting: helping to guide, nurture, and enjoy my daughters. I love being there for them, whether it's sharing their joys and troubles or being able to help them with advice or other types of support. Helping guide my children is a delight even when the interactions are sticky and uncomfortable.

I don't like being ignored or forgotten by my children. Sometimes, especially during their adolescence, I've felt taken advantage of with little response or caring and almost no appreciation from them. I also feel awful when they seemingly choose not to want to spend time with me. Being divorced has meant much physical and emotional separation, and this has been excruciatingly painful for me. Another way of saying this would be that I like being able to be a good father, and when I don't have access to them, I don't see myself as being *able* to be the good father.

My strengths are definitely stability and dependability. With much chaos in both of my daughters' lives, I've been the only person to always be supportive in every way. When my younger daughter was little, I loved carting her to gymnastics classes, piano lessons, or dentist appointments. In fact it gives me pleasure to be of service to them. I also think that my being a role model serves them well. I'm reliable: I've had the same job for twenty-nine years, lived in the same house for seventeen. I'm a loyal person to my friends and family.

My older daughter had a drug problem when she was in her early twenties. Her husband took their baby and went out of state to live with his family. Her mother (my ex) flipped out and would not deal with the situation. My son-in-law arranged a residential rehab treatment for my daughter a few hours' drive away, but someone had to convince her to go there for several months and get her there.

Even though she's my adopted daughter, I took charge of the situation and convinced her that entering the program was the best thing she could do. I also drove her to the program. My daughter needed help, and I wasn't going to let her down.

My weaknesses are my tendencies to be overly emotional

and to take personally their responses to me. I'm deeply saddened that after the divorce I missed out on having them grow up under the same roof with me. I think that because I was hurting from this, I tended to make too-subjective judgments on their not wanting to spend more time with me. It's as if I were being cheated of the life experience I most desired. I was envious of the attention they gave to their mother and the experiences she had from their living together.

When my younger daughter was around ten years old, she went to overnight camp for two week-long sessions. She had a one-night break at her mother's house between sessions. My work schedule had me out of town for a few additional weeks after her camp experience, which meant I might not see her for six weeks. I felt so guilty that I really pressured her to find one hour to spend with me on that single-night break. She did carve out an hour but had a negative attitude while she was with me, and I lost my temper. After our meal, at which she was obstinately unresponsive, I pulled the car over and screamed at her.

I think this scene had more to do with my not feeling like I'm a good father than with her attitude. I wanted to spend quality time with her—I missed her a great deal. But there was a part of this that was about me, not her. My putting pressure on her to satisfy my self-image needs is not one of my proudest moments.

For many years this daughter has had great difficulty appreciating me, and it was painful. On the other hand, her older sister is grateful to me for being there for her over the years, and values my steadiness, reliability, and vision. After her recovery from drug abuse, she phoned me one time and said she finally understood what I tried to do for her during those traumatic times, and she thanked me. That felt wonderful.

My younger daughter once said she was afraid of me, even while acknowledging I've always been there for her. She's also told me she hates my sense of humor. Many times I take her aloofness or disconnection as an uncomplimentary statement on my being her dad. I guess she feels I'm overbearing at times.

Happily, our relationship has now blossomed into one of openheartedness, trust, and mutual respect. I don't see or speak with her any more frequently than I used to, but a wonderful spirit of sharing and appreciation has evolved between us.

My advice is to love your children unconditionally but also be able to detach, so you can set limits to help guide, nurture, and teach them. This is tough when you love your children deeply and see them making mistakes that will be painful to them. Experience is the ultimate teacher, and a truly loving parent will allow his children to learn from their own actions. 🪷

The Best Strategy and Action Program for Dreamers

Develop Inner Equanimity

Dreamer parents (like all others) want life to be perfect for their children. For Dreamers, though, there are so many fantastic journeys and experiences they can have with their children. In the fantasy stage what the dreams have in common is that they're perfect. One Dreamer parent told me, "I want my children always to be happy. Envy for the unattainable arises with the realization that life doesn't map that perfectly, doesn't measure up to fantasy or how it is in a perfect realm. Still, one can dream. . . ."

Dreamer parents may be able to imagine that in every situation they can do something better or differently. Then they watch other parents and children and observe their dynamic and think, "Oh, God, we should be doing that." Their attention is constantly going to what they *could be* doing or what they *wish* they were doing, rather than staying with what they *are* doing. Or they wish they had on the outfit one of the other parents was wearing. It's almost as if they want to be somebody else. What happens is that they lose themselves, their boundaries, and that reinforces the fact that they're lost anyway. They have to struggle to gain themselves back.

ACTION: *Take a large step on your growth path: try to move from envy to equanimity.* Equanimity is balance or calmness or tranquillity. Having equanimity is being able to operate in the ordinary with a sense of inner balance. Learn to find the miraculous in the everyday. Shop at Wal-Mart occasionally, not always Bloomingdale's. Take your children to Burger King sometimes, not always to the place that serves gourmet burgers. Find as much pleasure with your children in washing the dishes together as in designing a creative poster for school.

Your Achilles' Heel: Avoiding the Ordinary

For Dreamers, feelings of unworthiness and inadequacy can be defended against, paradoxically—but quite logically—by adopting a stance of feeling "above," "better than," or "special." Dreamers want to rescue their children from an ordinary, boring life; it's important to make them feel special. If a child indulges in some casual doodling, the Dreamer parent will immediately arrange art lessons.

Dreamer parents can exhaust themselves by constantly giving their all to make each interaction with their children an extraordinary and meaningful experience. They want their children to acknowledge that *they* are different from other parents. They yearn for this sort of comment: "My mother (father) knows who I am and helps me see who I am. We have an unbelievably strong bond." Of course, acknowledgment like this is rarely forthcoming.

ACTION: *Try to understand what your children need from you, not what you need from them. Try to keep yourself focused on that and not always be pulled away when things feel ordinary.* Seeking to avoid being ordinary can be a real Achilles' heel. The effort and work it can create for you is enormous, because you want life to be so deep and meaningful, so special. Learn the boundaries of your parenting. For example, when you hover too closely, your child may say, "Please get out of my personal space." You may be affronted and feel, "What an ordinary response." Obviously, what feels like connection to you may be the wrong thing for this child; it feels like smothering. It's important for you not to try to remove yourself from the ordinary, not to try to bring something to others that you think *they* need because *you* need it.

Believe Your Children When They Offer Appreciation for You

As we know, the focus of attention for Dreamers goes to what is missing. The following Dreamer gives a clear report of how this perceptual lens focuses many of the other classic Dreamer preoccupations: "There's no defense against feeling that something is missing, that I'm worthless, unauthentic, vulnerable, and I get depressed. One of the joys of learning about other people's worldviews is that you can realize that people are trying to connect with you by the way attention comes to them. We're all different, not better or worse. This is so helpful with your family, especially your children. You learn to accept what they give to you and how they do it."

Dreamer parents often report that no matter what positive feedback they receive from their children, there's always something missing. The more they know that their children approve of them, the less comfortable they feel. They dance around wanting to be heeded, respected, and appreciated, but they're unable to assimilate that approval. A Dreamer mother said, "I have a yearning for acknowledgment, because I give of myself endlessly and oftentimes what I experience is common disregard."

ACTION: *Try to become superaware of where your attention is, especially when it goes into the default mode of focusing on what's missing.* You are the victim of a faulty belief system built around your feelings of worthlessness, of being less than others, believing that deep relationships aren't possible for you. Basically you have to teach yourself that's not true. You *do* connect often, in a profound and deep way. You need to learn that in fact we are all interconnected, just in different ways. Believe your children when they offer appreciation for you, whatever form that offering takes. And show and tell your children how much you love them, not as half of the deal of waiting for them to love you back. Give your love unconditionally.

Use Your Connection with Your Children to Help Support Their Feelings

Dreamers have a finely tuned conceptual vocabulary to describe the nuances of connection, and they can precisely describe these nuances. For Dreamers, life *is* connection. They ask, "Do I have it? Is it missing?" These are the parameters of life's possibilities; everything else is secondary. One Dreamer said, "I try to connect by engaging energetically with each person so that I can match him or her. The key connection is down and in myself, to a centered place. If I'm up and out, it can feel like I'm frantic. I have to shift and come back down, reconnect with myself. Now I can experience people out there and see where their energy is."

Dreamer parents know how their children feel; they're intuitively connected. Their children don't have to tell them anything about how they feel; if they do choose to tell their Dreamer parents, they've already understood. But Dreamers can be off base in areas where *they* hold strong feelings and may project those feelings onto their children. The projection may be off.

Dreamers yearn for connection because they're acutely aware from childhood that they feel a sense of something missing. This perception is tied to feelings of loss or abandonment, an inability to fit in (shame), of not belonging. It's easy to see how this blind spot can be overcome by developing an acute intelligence about connection, to scan for it internally, to come to know what authentic connection feels like and what it means, to have an ability to name different kinds of connection. Unlike Helpers, who are outer-directed, other-referenced, and who anticipate others' needs in order to form a sense of self from the responses they receive, for Dreamers, connection arises internally.

ACTION: *Work on clarifying your feelings, literally separating yourself from other people, so that you can see and value others and hold on to yourself.* Know where you're coming from. With your children in a one-on-one situation, you have an inherent connection that creates a bond between you. But that is not enough; it's important to be able to communicate with them (especially with adolescent children) in ways that encourage them to understand some truth about themselves.

You need to help them support their feelings about themselves. Recently I heard of a seventh-grade girl, probably the best soccer player at her junior high school. She was elected team captain, a position usually filled by ninth-graders, yet she chose not to take the position, because she didn't think that at her level of maturity she understood what leadership entailed. After listening to all her reasons, her Dreamer father said, "Many kids your age aren't thinking these things or aren't able to speak about their feelings like this. Yet you seem to care about them a lot. You're probably different from your friends." His daughter acknowledged that might be so. It was a meaningful moment of connection for them.

Respect Personal Boundaries

With such an imperative drive toward connection, it's not surprising that many Dreamers have issues involving personal boundaries, their own and others'. Dreamer parents are aware that their children often don't know where the appropriate line of behavior is drawn. Children don't know where the line is because Dreamer parents haven't drawn it clearly or shown them at what point in life the line changes. For instance, parents are allowed to have private time with their spouse or partner, and children should respect that boundary.

ACTION: *Learn how to set boundaries for yourself.* The other side of the mirror is that through your intense desire for interaction with your children, you may violate *their* boundaries. You care so much about your children that you interact with them in ways that may be uncomfortable or inappropriate for them. Experiment with holding back before you jump in to praise, help, or go after them. You'll begin to get a better sense of what defines the parameters within which they're comfortable interacting with you. This does *not* mean you should hold back from your unique way of loving your children. As a Dreamer this is one of your gifts to them: unique creativity in parenting.

Try Not to Take Interactions Personally

Dreamers belong to the Attacher triad of personalities, with a matrix of characteristics that have to do with feelings. Dreamers perceive that they experience life more deeply than many other people do; it's one of the ways they feel special. Certainly they have emotionality and feelings close to the surface. Dreamers find it difficult to be distanced and objective about the behavior of others, especially their family. They take interactions personally. For example, remember how Bob, the Dreamer father we met earlier in this section, described his subjective reaction to his younger daughter's unresponsiveness when they were together.

Another Dreamer parent verified this perception: "People at work or people I don't know well think I'm exceptionally patient. But parenting is a situation where I'm so emotionally involved, my patience doesn't last long. I know I take parenting too personally."

ACTION: *Try to build boundaries for yourself in your interactions, especially with those closest to you.* If you can learn to work positively with your attention and redirect it from what's missing to what's present, you can begin to be less emotionally reactive.

Rather than reacting personally to negative interactions with your children, first start an internal inquiry. Ask yourself what's going on in your life that may be making you more reactive than normal. Then ask your children what's going on with them that they're behaving the way they are. If they're not forthcoming, use your intuitive gift of connection to help them figure it out for both of you.

Live with a Less Intense Desire to Open Yourself to Others

For Dreamers, being vulnerable is being open about the need to connect with others and to let down their guard when it comes to yearning for that. One Dreamer said, "Connection is extremely important in my life, to the point that it may put me at a disadvantage sometimes; it makes me vulnerable. As a parent I yearn to achieve this connection, too—I can't help myself. I drop little hints: 'I feel happy when such and such a thing happens' or 'I feel sad.' I hope my children will pick up those hints and respond to me on an emotional level. But if I say that and they start talking about a fishing trip, I know the connectivity isn't there. I know that maybe I'm coming on too strong for them, making them uncomfortable."

ACTION: *Learn to live with a less intense desire to open yourself to others.* You probably have a hundred watts of connective energy, while your family operates at twenty. Learn to operate at their level; that way, when you do open yourself, you'll be met with the response you want.

Make Positive Use of Your Unique, Creative Gifts

Dreamers have a sense that they're somehow special, different, and indeed many Dreamers *are* uniquely gifted in the realm of creativity. It's difficult to define creativity precisely, because it has so much to do with intuition and intuitive energies. Dreamer parents believe that they give their children a gift in that they're unique, unlike many other parents. They trust their intuition with their children to know if something will or won't work. Creativity, change, improvisation—these are among the tricks they carry in their parenting bag.

ACTION: *Trust that you're skillful with intuition, that you know a lot of different ways to connect with your children.* Inevitably at times you're going to feel as if you missed something: "Maybe I should have handled this another way?" Know that you can't do everything differently all the time.

Find Your Authentic Self

The authentic self is a complex issue for Dreamers to understand and for others to understand *about* Dreamers. But it is a key component of the Dreamer motivational pattern. Many Dreamers are aware that they present themselves as an image of what someone else expects them to be, mainly as a cover-up for their own sense of deficiency, rather than the authentic inner self they would like to present. Dreamers experience this pull between authenticity and the creation of a pseudo image as an inner struggle.

How does this relate to parenting? There is pain and yearning for Dreamer parents in not being perceived as authentic. Subconsciously they're constantly checking: "How did I come across to them? Did I come on too strong? If they start not to like me, eventually they may abandon me. I don't think I can sign up for a yoga class in the afternoon—what happens if they want me to do something for or with them? I'll miss that moment. Once gone, it's gone forever."

After an interaction with their children, Dreamers may feel they've screwed up or didn't do something well. They experience pain (and shame) when they hear that the image other people (especially those closest to them) have of them is not what they think they are. It's painful because they spend so much time trying to imagine how they're perceived by others.

ACTION: *Learn to move beyond the pain, yearning, and melancholia.* You know that at times you've experienced a sense of bedrock reality, *the authentic you,* when everything comes together in a moment of truth. This can be described as a verifiable feeling in your body; the *you* that's experiencing this *is* authentic. You don't have to do anything with it. Simply allow it. You don't have to create anything. You can just say to yourself, "This is what's true for me."

Hold on to those moments. Inquire into them, find out how they come about for you. See if you can't replicate them when you're feeling at your most vulnerable, or experiencing shame, or feeling pain. Try to explain this dynamic to your parenting partner, to your older children, even to friends you trust; they can help you return to these moments to find your authentic self.

You Are a Good Enough Parent

Feelings of low self-esteem for Dreamers, as with so much else for this personality type, are tied in with the attentional focus on what's missing. If it's the truth (and Dreamers believe it is) that something is always missing, how can the Dreamer ever be good enough?

As a Dreamer parent said, "That's the story of my life, I guess—not being good enough. The way it plays out for me is anything I do or accomplish, I minimize, I don't value the good things I've done, although others do. I still have a low sense of self. For instance, a strength of mine is relating to others. Recently my teenage son wanted me to help him join another soccer club. I said he hadn't completed his goals at his current club. I knew intuitively he *had to stay* with his commitments. And, to be truthful, I wanted to stay to fulfill *my* commitments; I'd played a role there, too. Coaches, parents, and players were doing better because I had communication going between them that wasn't there before he joined the club. That was one of the first times I started to realize that I was of value. I could see that my being there made a difference. I held that boundary for him regarding staying at the club. Although it was tough for me to do so, it was also enlightening for me."

ACTION: *Continually get a reality check from those who love you that you* **are** *good enough.* Listen when they say you've made a difference in their lives. Trust the feelings you have that you know what you're doing as a parent. *Let it take hold deep inside you that you are that good parent.* And that you don't only fulfill the *image* you carry of being a good parent.

Even Out Mood and Energy Swings

Dreamer parents need to be aware of how their mood and energy can affect their interactions with their children. As this Dreamer parent said, "I've had to learn that my own ability to give off energy can be strong. Before I enter into an interaction with my children, I do a check on my feelings and make sure I'm in balance, because if I enter out of kilter from my last experience, I immediately see our interchange disintegrate, or my children will directly reflect my feelings. In our interactions any intense feelings that I'm experiencing will press the buttons of (especially) my adolescent children every time. But if I clear and settle my emotions, my children will also settle."

Dreamer parents often live on an emotional Ferris wheel— now high, now low—so their moods shift between these extremes. They have little experience of staying in the middle, of flat ordinariness. Their children may find it difficult to track their behavior, and at times their swings of emotion can be hard for children to handle. On one extreme they can try to outdo their parent's dramatics, while on the other extreme they can shut down, simply not be available emotionally. Either extreme is hard for Dreamers to interact with. The more they can keep themselves on an even keel, the more they can stay in ordinary moments, the easier it is for their children to reach out to them. And not always the other way around. Dreamers may be surprised to see that if they remain passive, good things will come their way.

ACTION: *Let your children feed you emotionally and you them—it's a mutual process.* It's exciting when you know that this level of connection is real. Though some children tend to be quite passive, if your moods and energy can reach them, if you see you can get through, then a dynamic is established. Sometimes with passive children you feel you have to work harder and harder to get a response. You have to escalate your own dramatics or your passion for whatever you're dealing with, or elevate your mood.

But remember that these children may interact mainly by listening to you. The more you go after them, the more they'll draw away from you. Respect their boundaries.

Other children tend to be overly engaging. Even if you try to be balanced and calm, their emotions trigger your own; you can't hide your feelings from them. This need not necessarily be a negative experience for either of you, but rather a point of contact and connection. You can discuss with them the impact of moods and emotions and boundaries, on yourself specifically and on others in general.

Parenting Steps for Dreamers

- Develop equanimity. Anticipate mood swings, structure ways to check and balance your energy. See that you are centered before you enter an interaction with your children. Learn to find the miraculous in the mundane.

- Reinforce your sense of worthiness. Believe your family when they offer appreciation for you, whatever form that offering takes. Know that nothing is missing; it's okay just as it is. Give your love to them unconditionally.

- Help your children support their feelings about themselves. Find ways to notice when your emotions and feelings are inflated. Be aware of when you're romanticizing another person's—or your own—feelings. Balance out mood swings.

- Be aware that you may violate others' boundaries. Don't lose yourself in the need to be special; that's when you most need to be centered. Remember, you feel unworthy and deficient to begin with, so don't take criticism or negative interactions personally.

- Learn to live with a less intense desire to open yourself to others. Connect with people at an appropriate level of intensity *for them.* Your emotional energy can be overwhelming.

- Focus on facts as well as feelings. Structure situations in terms of facts and logic, not always emotions.

- Avoid depression. When feelings of melancholy, sadness, and loss become overwhelming, get a reality check or ask your family and friends to help pull you back. Listen to the feedback that praises your worthiness. When your attention goes to what's missing, count the positives in your life.

- Know that you can't do everything differently all the time. Remember that the rest of the world runs on an ordinary and orderly schedule set by the clock and the daily calendar.

- Use your creative gifts in a positive way. Don't procrastinate when you view tasks as mundane; help structure a creative solution when you seem to be bogged down in feelings and experiences of ordinariness. Encourage yourself to undertake mundane tasks.

SUMMARY: THE DREAMER PARENT

Positives to Build On	*Negatives to Overcome*
Connectivity	Feeling special to disguise shame
Creativity	Melancholia, heightened emotions
Empathy in pain	Envy that others have what's missing
Passion	Wants the unattainable, egocentricity
Compassion	Needs to be different, special
Intensity	Inflating emotions
Understanding	Feeling unworthy, courts abandonment
Authenticity	Avoids the ordinary, mundane, mediocre
Intuitive ability	Romanticizes emotions, overdramatizes connections

CHAPTER 5

The Observer
Let's Step Back and See

Marie—Loving beyond Words

Parenting did not come naturally to Marie, but then neither did anything else out there in the world of interactions, people, and emotions. She felt that spontaneously following one's emotions was scary behavior, often even dangerous, and besides, she had difficulty even feeling her emotions. Far easier to keep a distance between herself and others, to act and move more slowly than the situation demanded, to measure her words. Words once spoken were difficult to take back; they had weight and heft and could cause far-reaching consequences that took her by surprise. Spoken words could also be unruly, messy, not neat and clear-cut, like ideas in her head. Often people didn't hear the rational sense of what she was saying anyway—they heard what they wanted to hear. So Marie said the minimum necessary to get by; that way she kept her life the way she wanted it to be.

She remembered that time in high school when she'd blurted out what she was feeling to a teacher about how he was conducting the class. Disaster. She knew it even as the unformed ideas and unthought-through words left her lips. She so seldom spoke in class that the whole group riveted its attention on her. Of course the teacher wanted to engage her in an elaboration of her outburst—he even seemed pleased she'd spoken up. But she pulled right back. She still remembers the feeling: her energy retracting, like a wave on the beach receding into the ocean. Oh, the force was still there, the energy and emotion that had propelled the outburst. But now it was safe, contained, in her head. She wouldn't utter another word in his class all year. He couldn't make her. But her mind roiled: she spoke ceaselessly to him, he answered her, their debates raged. No one watching her impassive face knew anything of the passionate interchange taking place in her head.

Marie liked life to be predictable. She divided her life metaphorically into a large chest of drawers, which gradually became a subconscious feature of her mind. Just as Organizers can multitask as a natural ability, Observers can move among the compartments of their lives, although to others the outer appearance may appear seamless.

Marie's large drawers contained smaller drawers, and within those were even smaller nooks and crannies. One large drawer was Home, another Work. There were several others. In Home nested Children, Husband, Pets, House, Garden, Activities, and so on. In Children were Love, Responsibility, Security, Homework, Vacations. The drawers had a way of interconnecting among themselves, so that, for instance, Vacations also appeared in a different context in Husband, Work, and other drawers. With this mental mechanism Marie was able to hold a big-picture view of her life, the pieces interlocking to make a satisfying whole.

As a life strategy for the Observer personality, the safest place to be is in the head. As long as Marie felt she *could* detach safely into her head, she could operate on two levels, and she functioned well in relationships *she chose,* both personal and professional. Minimalists by inclination, Observers are shaped by an intelligence that directs them to put out the least, especially of their energy and time; for then that is all people will expect of them. Marie knew she had to manage her energy resources, control time. An essential part of her life was private time and space to recharge her batteries.

Nonverbal language is also fundamental to Observers, a positive means of communication that translates into expressions of affection. Marie loved baking the cupcakes her children adored or laundering and ironing their clothes, anticipating what they needed and when. One way she expressed her love for her husband was to bring him breakfast in bed on weekend mornings, each tray embellished with a thoughtful object, like theater tickets or the newspaper clippings she'd collected during the week.

Intrinsic to this personality strategy is an ability to detach, to move into the head, especially if something is frightening or makes an emotional demand. A stereotype of Observers is that because they detach from feelings (akin to Organizers suspending emotions), they don't have feelings. This is not true. Neither personality is unemotional; both have the capacity for experiencing emotions. For the Observer, emotions are contained in a rich interior world, along with feelings, ideas, nonlinear thinking, and creative new solutions to problems. Extensive time spent on the preview and review of events is part of the Observer psychology. Observers like the idea of themselves as objective, detached from an emotional bias that may cloud reason. Often they seem to live a long way from their bodies.

It was for these reasons that when Marie first experienced an orgasm with her husband-to-be, she could scarcely comprehend what was happening to her. All previous physical sensations she'd been able to catalog and process, but during orgasm her body had a will of its own. The intense muscular movements had nothing to do with anything she'd ever known before. She learned at these times to give herself over to the powerful sensations, to enjoy the energy and force of them; for if she tried to make sense of them while they were happening to her, sex became a dispassionate, isolating event.

Inadvertently, by unbridling her sexuality, Marie embarked on one of the growth paths for her personality type. During sex she could relinquish (for a while) her inclination to be conscious of conserving her energy, her time, containing herself. Growth for Observers comes from not being so attached to these habits of mind, from letting go, allowing, letting spontaneity arise. For the same reasons she rated childbirth as among the peak experiences of her life; simply put, she gave herself over to the process.

Marie learned to be a good mother by observing other parents. If she could observe, read about, overhear, or otherwise gather information on the different ways other parents interacted with their children, she'd find a path to satisfy herself. "What does this child want from me now?" she would ask herself, repeating it like a mantra. She found it hard to act spontaneously on the answers that arose naturally within her. Often she would buy time for herself. She was creative in her interactions with her children, designing holding patterns while she sought rational responses that sat well with her. "Act in haste, repent at leisure"—meaningfully she repeated this aphorism to her husband when the deliberate pace and tenor of her life frustrated him.

Ben—Why Don't the Pieces of This Puzzle Fit Together?

By the time he was fifty, Ben had it all. There was the long-term marriage to the woman who'd been his high-school sweetheart, whom he still loved and had stood by through good times and bad. There were his three bright, well-adjusted children, planned to be born five years apart, so each could have the benefit of their parents' constant attention when they were babies. There was the large house with a swimming pool in the suburban neighborhood where his wife had always desired to live. Ben had moved them to a slightly bigger home with the arrival of each new baby. This current home featured the garden of his dreams, toward which he'd been moving steadily for twenty years, a garden he designed and redesigned in his head for all those years, which he now worked on with pride and joy. There was the job, his steady rise to a top executive position in a large public company. There was the respect of those he worked with and those who worked for him (now over a hundred people in his department). There were the perks: cars, use of the company lakeside cottage, annual bonuses. Most important, there was his time to be alone on weekends, when he rode his bicycle for long hours in the surrounding countryside. He valued this time to think about the past week and the week to come.

Ben couldn't remember a time when he didn't engage in this review/preview process; it was part of him. And while doing it he got to experience life three times: the preview (anticipation) of the upcoming event, the event itself (when often he could feel quite detached from what was happening around him and observe himself in the moment), and the review (reliving the event, the richest experience). Like other Observers, Ben's attention in any context went to gaining knowledge, the review/preview process a large part of this drive. Knowledge was the key to the universe. Without knowledge Ben was aware of an inner sense of emptiness, somehow a disconnection with life itself. While most of the time his rich inner world filled this internal space, he longed for knowledge that would connect him to something bigger than himself.

Ben believed that knowledge could provide safety for himself and his family. Safety was achieved through formulating a sane, rational grid to lay over an insane world. Belief that this grid existed was Ben's illusion and primary blind spot. He built the grid from the knowledge he acquired, information he sought, questions he asked.

So (the big question he asked himself as he pedaled down a tree-lined road one Saturday) why had the grid crumbled around his eighteen-year-old son? On Wednesday, after procrastinating for a while, he had agreed to meet his son at his son's counselor's office. That was Ben's first surprise; he hadn't known his son was seeing someone and, it transpired, he had been doing so for many months now. Ben didn't believe much in counseling. If you put your mind to it, you could rationally think through any problem for yourself. But his son obviously felt that counseling was important, so eventually Ben went along. It had been a disquieting experience on a number of levels.

Under the counselor's gentle prodding, his son had articulated his deeply held and (to Ben) completely irrational belief that his father was not capable of truly loving him and his siblings, because he was always so detached, so cool, so controlled. His son articulated, in tones of great anguish, that he'd never seen his father lose his temper, become impatient, speak with tears choking him. Ben did all his family asked of him, but it was as if he were operating on automatic pilot.

That last part was an exaggeration, thought Ben, but the rest was true. For the first time in many years, Ben remembered that when his father died, when Ben was eighteen, he had come in despair to his mother and sister, both exhausted from crying, and stated that he couldn't cry. He had tried, because he felt sad, but he couldn't cry. He felt that same emotional impotence now: not love his son and his other children? That was preposterous—he adored them. There were many ways of loving; how come his son didn't know that? He'd gnaw on that question.

Ben turned his mind to the week ahead. He was to be honored by the company at an awards luncheon on Tuesday. He felt good about that; the award was well deserved. He'd always been secure at work, competent. He knew what he was doing. He read columns of figures the way other people read novels. They made sense to him, conveyed whole worlds of knowledge, information he could turn into powerful concepts for the company. For many years he'd worked alone with a small team, crunching numbers. Leadership of many people had come as a fairly recent and somewhat unexpected development in his career.

The turning point had come gradually. About ten years ago, with conscious intent and clarity, whenever he was bored in meetings, Ben would minutely observe his inner reactions. He discerned that when he was about to speak, he was aware of a definite rush of nervous energy, one of the few times he could feel a sensation in his belly. He was used to backing away from that feeling, because it made him uncomfortable. He interpreted it as nerves, and it caused him to retreat even more from spontaneously speaking out. But on one occasion Ben took that chance and spoke up. He received such positive feedback that he realized he was not perceiving nerves at all; rather, this was gut instinct. He still found it strange: "When I get this kind of feeling, I immediately say and do what I'm thinking." Acting on gut instinct was the key to his leadership success.

On Sunday he worked in the garden. His midweek meeting with his son still preyed on his mind, but he tried to keep it in perspective. He felt that his son's responses to him had more to do with *his*—the boy's—emotional development than Ben's own shortcomings as a father. Yes, he was independent, self-disciplined, and self-contained. Yes, he did keep different parts of his life separate. But he amply recompensed his family with other gifts of his personality: rationality, coolness, a calm and balance that allowed him to see the big picture, enabled him to help them with decisions and the like. He also did whatever his family asked of him and more. And look what a life he'd provided for them! He didn't like feeling vulnerable. That meeting with the counselor surprised him and made him feel vulnerable.

Ben worked in the garden with his shoes off, up to his ankles in dirt. He looked at the trees around him and suddenly thought, "They're carbon atoms, the grass is carbon atoms, the dirt is carbon atoms, Mars is carbon atoms, and I, my children, all of us—we're all carbon atoms."

He had his perspective, the realization that he was part of something bigger than himself. The universe, the cosmos—he was a part of all that. He, who had not felt part of anything for so long, was part of all that, or it was part of him. Ben realized that no matter where he went or what he knew or did not know, intrinsically he was connected to all of it. When he died, he would still be connected to it; carbon atoms don't cease to exist.

Ben had glimpsed omniscience, knowledge of universal connection. It is the kind of knowing akin to the Dreamer concept of universal belonging. Both speak to a fullness of being in the moment, of being present, of the still point where being comes together.

PERSONAL ACCOUNT

Dave, an Observer father of a son and a daughter, gives this account

I like interacting with my children: teaching them, showing them how things work, telling them stories. And especially doing physical activities with them, such as wrestling and backpacking, teaching them how to do mildly dangerous exploits like rock climbing, snorkeling, and white-water canoeing. I treasure reexperiencing the world with them as they grow up. I like being there for them when they're in crisis. I'm a pretty good, nonjudgmental listener for my children, particularly one on one.

I don't like being a "parent." I'm not comfortable being part of a family. I mean, I can interact one-on-one with any of my family, but I'm not comfortable with family activities. My children have experimented with sex and drugs, and I refuse to get uptight about it. This kind of attitude has put me at odds with my spouse, other parents, and school systems.

My most important strength is that I have a good sense of humor. I'm also loyal, truthful, and strong. I don't play games with my children. If I take them to the doctor and the procedure is going to hurt, I tell them so and help them through the experience. I don't panic easily. I'm the one who usually takes them to the emergency room. Growing up, I've done most of the things they've done and will do. I've survived all this, and I

assume they will, too. I don't panic when they call with a problem. In addition to good listening skills, I have good counseling
skills. I can deliver simple, direct messages and then shut up.

An example that illustrates these strengths occurred when
I was separated and living a few miles away from the ex and
the children, who were in their early teens. I got a call from my
daughter, saying, "I don't usually meddle in my brother's business, but he's snorting speed. I think that's really dangerous."
I agreed that it was dangerous and said I'd deal with it.

I called my son and left a message. When he called back, I
said, "I have a message that I want to deliver to you. Among
my rich and varied acquaintanceship, there are no old speed
freaks. The reason is simple: speed freaks die young. That's the
message." I paused, then continued, "So what's happening in
your life? Are you reading anything interesting?" I had deliv-
ered a simple, clear message, no fear, no anger, no yelling and
shouting. A week or so later my daughter called again and
reported that her brother was no longer using speed.

My main weakness as a parent is that I don't like conflict.
I can deal with conflict, but it takes a lot of energy, and I find it
draining. In conflict situations I can move inside myself and
become an observer. I am not a good role model for being a
standard dad. I'm not much of a joiner. I detest most of what is
on television, and I can't stand to be in the room when the TV
is on, so I'm absent during that activity. I like to read and I like
alone time. So I can be seen as distant and an infrequent par-
ticipant in family activities. I don't like being pushed against. I
find the whole issue of testing limits boring and energy-
consuming, and I don't handle it well. I don't always manage
anger well. Sometimes when I get angry it comes as a surprise
both to me and everyone else involved. This can make me
appear unpredictable.

As I continued my study of intra- and interpersonal
dynamics, I began to notice that we had a lot of games in our
family. For example, I noticed that whenever all four of us were

riding somewhere, the children would invariably fight. It would start out as simple horseplay and continue until someone was in tears. This only happened when all four of us were in the van or the car. I found this uproar very distracting while I was driving. I also found it impossible to ignore. I felt like I was trapped in a small space with noxious stimuli I couldn't escape. I tried everything from "I" statements to physical violence to break this pattern. Nothing worked. Finally, on the way back from a camping trip, I said, "This is the last time I will ever ride in a vehicle with all three of you again. Any two, yes; all three, no." They thought I was just venting, but I meant it. I never rode in the same vehicle with all of them again. When we went somewhere, we took two vehicles.

My children have said of me, "If we expressed an interest in something—geodesic domes, kites, breadmaking, books— you would find out about it yourself and encourage us in our interests. You made a point of spending time with both of us individually." Or "You allowed me a lot of freedom, you encouraged me to take risks." Or "There was never any doubt in my mind that you loved me. You both told me and showed me that you did."

On the flip side my children share the following responses: "While you were usually very good with us on an individual basis, you didn't do so well with the family as a group. Whenever things were going really well, I always felt that there was a time limit on it, as if eventually one of us would screw up and set you off." Or this: "For me it was the distant times, when for one reason or another I felt that you were not sharing or even participating so much as observing."

Don't bonsai your child. Each child comes into this world with a unique set of gifts. Let these gifts unfold; nurture and support them. Be patient. The child may flit from interest to interest before beginning to focus. Don't try to mold and shape your child, but rather be a coach and a mentor. This isn't easy.

It means letting go of your ego and fears. The payoff is that the child grows up to be his or her person, and not your person. The risk is that the child may not succeed in the way that *you* define success.

The Best Strategy and Action Program for Observers

Show Your Emotions—It's Not Enough to Think Them

Interaction is not spontaneous behavior for Observers; they have to think it through first. They become adept and superfast at doing this, so interactions *seem* spontaneous. This Observer shares with us how she came to know how to interact with her husband: "I had to observe his family, watch how they were in relationship to him in order to figure out what he needed from me, how I was supposed to be with him. I would mimic their phraseology, their expressions. Often the feedback that I've gotten in my life is that I have a blank face and people find me distant; yet I'm not feeling that way on the inside." Like Marie and Ben, many Observers *observe* others in order to learn how to put their emotional affect out in the world.

Some Observers can come across to their children differently from the way they intend. Especially when they're trying not to be discriminatory or make judgments between their children, they can be blank-faced and perceived as unresponsive.

ACTION: *It's not enough to think that you have your happy or sad face on. For instance, when your children come home from school or activities, you have to be conscious that you're smiling, saying words like "Hi, honey, I'm glad to see you."* Your welcoming energy and emotions have to be there, too. It's important for you to know that most people want to be able to access what you're feeling: in the expression on your face, in your eyes, the sound of your voice, your body language. You have to train yourself consciously to display these outer manifestations of emotions, until they become a natural way of expressing yourself. Don't assume that because you're happy to see your children, they will somehow know of your response; know what you are feeling. You actually have to carry through with your emotions, put them out there. It's not enough to *think* your emotions; you have to learn to *embody* them energetically.

Role-Model Spontaneity for Your Children

How do your children know what their Observer parent thinks of them in a particular situation? Does the parent approve or disapprove? Minimalists in many areas of their lives, Observers can be minimalistic, too, in articulating praise or recrimination. Their preference is to think through and write out a carefully worded message of appreciation or disapproval, leave a note, or send an e-mail. If they have to be face-to-face, they would rather read to the other person what is in a note than spontaneously make a remark in the moment.

ACTION: *Your children need you to role-model spontaneity for them.* Even if the words don't come out the way you want them to, learn to trust yourself and let go. Speak to them naturally and freely. Try not only to praise them for their academic work or their good ideas or creative solutions to problems. Praise them, too, for expressing their feelings, for reaching out to others. With all your best intentions not to be subjective, your bias is to try to teach them that if they can interpret the world rationally through acquiring knowledge, nothing unexpected can happen to them, they can be safe. Remember, there is also safety in sound relationships and emotional interconnection.

Trust Yourself That You're Going to Do What Is Right

One Observer mother shared with us the story of the occasion when she had to rush her child to the emergency room. She felt as if she were in the middle of battle—she couldn't let *her* emotions get in the way. "I had to go on, because if I stopped, I'd become needy of attention, too. And *I* was not the focus of the emergency; it was my poor son who had fallen off his skateboard onto the back of his head. He was in shock and concussed. So I put aside what I was dealing with emotionally till later. I began to understand the arbitrariness of death while I stood looking at my son being readied for the CAT scan. I felt sad for him and helpless. But if I allowed my emotions to take hold at that point, I would probably have fainted." Observers do have a full range of emotions and use them on a regular basis. There is often enjoyment and appreciation, as well as frustration and pain.

This was verified by another Observer, a father: "The feelings are always there, but when you detach from them, you're detaching from an overwhelming sense that you don't know what they are. You need time to sit back, review the situation, figure out what you *knew* at the time you were feeling. I'm thinking about three or four crisis situations. When my youngest son injured his back by falling out of a tree, I was right there. Other people were freaking out and panicking. I was cool and clear. I made the right decisions. I focused fully on the needs of my son. At that time I detached from my emotions. Later I reviewed them. I can't tell you about my emotions until I sit back and think about them. At other times, especially when I'm relaxed, emotions will overwhelm me instantly." Both speakers demonstrate that Observers do have feelings, but they can detach from them.

ACTION: *Be aware that you are in the Detacher triad, one of three of the fear-based personality types.* The way you deal with fear is to keep it at bay by acquiring more and more knowledge. You do your best to have foreknowledge of situations that may beset you and your family. I'm sure you realize that you can never acquire *all* the knowledge necessary to deal with every situation, that at some point you have to trust your instincts.

You may spend way too much time in your head trying to make the details fit a big picture, not only with abstract parts of your life but also in relating to others. Trust that when situations arise, you're going to do what's right. *The way to feel personally secure is to know more and more that you can rely on your instincts.*

Ask for Time in Order to Handle Conflict

Although Observers are often stereotyped as being unemotional, this is not correct. As the above stories show, they are fully aware of their emotions. This Observer told us of his specific response to an emotional event: "When the feelings come in, sometimes it can be overpowering. Sometimes I can react, go over the situation as I suppose anyone else would. Though even while I'm still in the situation, I find I can separate and start thinking about it as it goes on. Afterward I'll spend three times as much time thinking about it. I almost feel it's a richer experience when I'm thinking about what happened than when I'm actually experiencing it."

In their inner world Observers can detach from experiences, and they may have no spontaneous connection with their emotions. Often, when feelings arise, the initial response is a knee-jerk reaction to separate, detach, go off somewhere alone and figure out what's going on. Once detached, Observers can put the emotions into a context and devise a plan for what they're going to do the next time something similar happens to them, so they'll be prepared.

When conflict arises, Observers will think about it; they don't have a ready response on tap. If they find themselves sad, rather than letting themselves feel sad, they'll think about everything going on around them, trying to figure out from where the sadness is emanating. Sometimes they simply recognize the feeling: "Oh, I'm feeling sad," and they can leave it at that. But most often they have to put their feelings into some sort of context or theoretical framework, flesh out why they're feeling what they're feeling. The following story describes this mental process in an everyday situation.

An Observer father comes home after a hard day at the office. As he walks in the door, he's aware of an outburst between his children, who both come running to him, both with their own side of the story. He finds it upsetting to deal with conflict, especially conflict between his children. His emotions come up unexpectedly. It's almost as if his ship gets overturned—he capsizes. The emotions take over and throw everything else out of his mind, to such a degree that he can't deal with them. The only way he can respond to something so emotional is to sit back, and after several hours he'll know how he feels. He says, "Can we talk about this later? I need to be able to give myself some time and space in order to help you with this problem." If his children come to him in tears, looking for him to solve their dispute when he's already emotionally drained, basically he's going to run (even if he doesn't actually leave the room).

ACTION: *Don't back out of conflictual (or any) interaction with your children without an explanation of your behavior.* They will feel misunderstood and abandoned. Learn to ask for time, as the father did in the above story. *And reassure them that you love them.* You're not backing away from them, but you want to give them your best when you've regrouped. This way you get ready to handle something that might be small in and of itself but big for you because of the emotions it's bringing up in you. Learn little phrases to get you the distance you need. If asked graciously to do so, your family will support you. The cooling-off period benefits everyone.

Make an Effort to Share Yourself with Your Intimates

Observers are aware that they can retract, be present physically but have no true presence. This way they can retain their privacy even when among other people, and so keep the drawbridge to their inner citadel firmly drawn up. An Observer said, "In middle school I learned how to become completely invisible. So invisible, in fact, that Mademoiselle used to mark me absent in her French class even though I was sitting in the third row. That's how it is when I retract—you can't even see me. But going that far away from yourself may not be good."

ACTION: *Work at being less secretive, especially with children.* Not being fully present in your interactions with them is disconcerting, even disturbing to them. Children pick up on whether or not you're present, with all your attention. After a while, if you are continually absent, they may not trust you or believe that you love them (remember Ben and his son). Bit by bit learn to share parts of yourself with others. As we have seen with instincts, privacy and holding yourself back have to do with issues of trust: when to trust others. A good way of thinking about privacy is that there are different "yous" interacting with different situations, different groups, different people with whom you have no impetus to share anything. You can have an intense experience with your partner or with a child, but to someone else who is also important to you, like another child or the children's grandparents, you won't even mention the previous experience, because it's *yours.* This behavior obviously involves a type of hoarding of yourself, a desire to be private. Try to align the different yous into one entity.

Be Aware of Your Need for Energy Management

Outside intrusions are interpreted by Observers as a drain on their essential energy. They are aware of the need to withdraw, to be private, to recharge after a period of interaction. Being a parent can be energy-intensive or energy-draining. For example, like most other Observers, Dave mentioned earlier in this section that he liked "alone time."

Privacy ties in with the Observer ability to mentally compartmentalize different parts of their lives in order to protect their privacy. By compartmentalizing they can ensure that their defenses are intact against having separate parts of their lives flow into one another and hence out of their control.

Compartmentalizing is also a way of conserving energy. Attention and thoughts stay focused on one compartment and don't spill over to others. If you're focused on a task with one child, or on having fun with another, or interacting with a certain group of people, you don't think about anything else. Especially feelings—they're not going to intrude.

Another Observer parent said, " I can go through with whatever it is we do, no problem. But I have to know that I'm going to have that hour afterward to recover. So I can give of my energy, but only with the intention of having time to recharge. There have been occasions when I don't get that time, when the situation keeps going and going and going. I find then that I *can* just go with the flow. But it's difficult to put myself spontaneously into that mentality of flow, as opposed to being forced into it by situations."

ACTION: *Time and energy management are not merely psychological needs for you; emotionally, they're a must. If you are open and frank about it, your family will understand that you need time and space to be alone. Build this into the household routine from the outset.* Everyone then knows that you're no good to anybody when you feel drained and frazzled. Family members will accept that you have to be alone if you've done too much. If you're scraping the bottom of the barrel to put your energy and your interactive self out, they'll know that, and they'll want more of you. At that point close the door and switch off all the gadgets that connect you to the world. Do whatever you have to do to give yourself some downtime.

Manage Your Big-Picture Thinking

Gaining knowledge is the Observer's focus of attention. Yet Observers are equally sure of the elusive nature of ultimate knowledge, the final pieces that will unlock the universal puzzle of their lives. There is irony and frustration in being so driven to pursue the possibility of knowledge that is totally certain, while at the same time knowing that it may not exist at all. This Observer parent, a first-time girls' club soccer coach, said, "For me, when I'm preparing the team for a game, I never quite get the feeling that we're finally ready. I never think I have enough knowledge of the drills, of game plays, for us to compete in the league. This is for reasons that I don't want to seem stupid, or because surely there are other schemes I haven't thought of, other details I missed or forgot about. Something may have happened yesterday I don't know about yet. I'm continually questioning myself. But I find on the other hand that if the team takes the field on game day and starts off well, I get into my action mode: this is on track, I'm ready to go with this."

Having, or striving for, a big picture allows Observers to feel safe. Unlike Moralizers, who down-chunk processes into details to keep control, Observers amass details so they can see the interconnections and build a big picture. With the big picture they feel they can take off in any direction and respond to any situation. Most Observers know that the big picture is a mental illusion, but it helps their self-confidence, even boosts them to action. If Observers don't feel they have the big picture, they feel uncomfortable, because they see only fragments and don't know where the pieces go—and therefore where they themselves fit. The Observer mind works as if it were solving a puzzle, seeking the pieces that create the whole, where everything falls into place and a big picture forms.

Observer parents talk about how they try to get their children to think about the ways that things connect, how each element leads to a bigger picture. Observers report that achieving a big picture is probably the most exciting intellectual process there is. It's what they're always thinking about.

ACTION: *You need to be constantly aware that not all personalities think this way; building big pictures may be quite alien to other people.* Your children probably don't think this way. When you're on them about forming interconnections and big pictures, remember that these may be totally foreign concepts. Be aware of how you feel when people ask you to articulate your thoughts on the spot, to react in the moment.

Remember that you revel in a complex mental world. Knowledge is all-important to you. That, and using it to find other ways to look at problems. This approach has worked so well for you that you want to encourage your children to take the same approach to problem solving. Some children are highly resistant to this; they like predictable, literal thinking, not mental gymnastics. Many others prefer to be told what to do, not to have to think about it much, and so on. Don't persist with pushing this level of complex mental effort if it is falling on deaf ears. Try to figure out where your children are coming from and how *you* can adapt to their mental world rather than the other way around.

The same goes for silence. You value silence as a signal that the child (or others you are interacting with) has to *think* about a response. But silence has a charge for many personalities. Some are comfortable in silence; it allows them time to think. For others, silence is uncomfortable, because in it they are thrown back on their inner resources, unable to concentrate on outer actions or reference themselves through other people. When you're a parent, ultimately it's not important what you think about the big-picture syndrome or what silences convey to you; what is important is what your children know, feel, or believe inside themselves.

Practice Social Skills

We've discussed the difficulties Observers have in connecting to others. But what does it feel like to *them* to be in interactions with others?

For one Observer parent, in order to feel valued, she has to know that she's been seen and noticed for the specifics of the way she manages things: "When I take a more visible role in a relationship, whether at home or at work, it's because someone went out of his or her way to have a special connection with me, to recognize me, to reach out to me one-on-one. Someone noticed that I was making an effort, putting out energy. Then I would feel more confident to go forward with the activity, feel safer in that situation. After I had children, I wanted them to know I was like other moms, so I observed different parenting behaviors in others. Now I've interacted as a parent for so long, and with other parents and children, that it's second nature to me. The energy comes out. I operate naturally. Throughout my life, though, initiating conversation, speaking up, is neither natural nor spontaneous for me."

The following Observer pinpoints another dilemma: having the desire to be included in the group, but not having the social skills to approach others. This Observer father tells us, "If you're at a social function, look around: the person who's standing and watching you (and the other guests) is probably an Observer. I'm not antisocial; I want to belong in a quiet way. It's just that I can't do small talk with lots of people. I wait till the conversation shifts to something I'm interested in, something intellectual or from the sports world. Then I'll talk to that person if the opportunity arises and we're alone. I'm not going to compete for anyone's attention.

"If you're the host or hostess, it's up to you to draw Observers out, if you want to. It's almost a relief if I'm standing there apart from the group and someone comes over and pulls me in. I want to be included, but many times I don't have the skills to approach the group. It's good to be drawn in. If Observers respond positively to your prodding, it's an indication that they want to join. But it can definitely become an intrusion if they don't want to and some-one's always pulling on them." From a third Observer: "I have few friends, few relationships, but a rich interior life. I had one good friend in grade school, another in high school. My roommates became my friends in college. My wife is also my best friend. My children are my friends, too. That's sufficient."

ACTION: *Learn to cultivate social skills.* Your children need *you* in many instances to initiate social contact for *them* (not the other way around). This is hard for you and may seem of little value, but—especially when your children are younger—your behavior models social interactions for them. It is part of your growth path to learn to connect with others on many levels. Try speaking spontaneously, adding something to the conversation when a response arises within you rather than waiting for an appropriate moment that may never materialize. Initiate some of the conversation; don't always wait to respond. Work with your tendency to say something only when it's ready to be said or when *you* deem it important.

Try to ask those around you (begin with those closest to you, who will understand and want to help you) to help you structure initial conversations. One good method is to practice *talking* about what you've observed in a given situation and what you think about it. This is an excellent way to begin a conversation.

This practice will work well for your quiet Observer child, too. Encouraging him to share what he's observed and what he's thinking about it allows him to contribute to the family conversa-tion by displaying what he does best: thinking. Generally, Observers are not articulate or coherent in the moment, but after a while they can respond by telling you exactly what they've expe-rienced, if it was appropriate, who had an interesting point of view, where the conversation flowed. You'll be astonished at the depth of their observations and perceptivity, because at the time it may have looked as if the Observer were simply sitting, not being particularly present.

Parenting Steps for Observers

- Do not merely *think* your emotions—learn to *embody* them. Be aware that you tend to share little of yourself; successful relationships are a two-way street. Push yourself toward personal engagement. Interact beyond your comfort level. Learn how to express emotions—for instance, join a theater group.

- Be aware that you can come across as noncommunicative and secretive. Practice spontaneity, take risks, experience what it is to be fully alive in the moment. Truly connect with your family. Be present for them (not only in your head) to share and enjoy interactive experiences.

- Trust yourself more and more to rely on your instincts. Learn to access your instinctual energy, and trust what it is telling you.

- Ask for a time-out when you enter situations of conflict. Learn little phrases to get you the distance you need. Establish a comfort zone for yourself. Manage your energy by building in downtime to be private and recharge.

- Remember that you revel in a complex mental world. Others in your family may not value (or rely on) the world of the mind as you do. But do share the rich ideas and insights you have. Utilize your gifts of synthesis and creativity with big-picture formations.

- Develop social skills. Your children need you to interact on their behalf. Tell your intimates that they should not assume that little show of enthusiasm from you equals boredom. Often you interact by simply being present and listening. Realize, though, that you are often oblivious of how retracted you appear.

- Share your gift of rational thinking, of keeping a cool head in charged situations. You are invaluable in a crisis.

- Thinking can replace doing for you. You prefer not to move into action until you have all the information and knowledge about a situation. Set reasonable deadlines (ask your family for help on this) to circumvent the procrastination that comes from gathering too many ideas.

- You can withdraw from situations without knowing you've done so. You are physically present, but you've detached from your emotions and are inside the citadel of your mind. Learn to read the distress this is causing those closest to you. Constantly check that the drawbridge to your*self* is down and that you are accessible.

SUMMARY: THE OBSERVER PARENT

Positives to Build On	*Negatives to Overcome*
Rationality	Requires privacy, guards time and energy
Calmness and balance	Draws back from personal interactions
Objectivity	Secrecy, overvalues independence
Creative synthesizing of ideas	Prefers nonengagement in emotions
Big-picture thinking	Tendency to be minimalistic in the physical world
Predictability	Lacks spontaneity, emphasizes controlling emotions
Independence	Overvalues the self, takes a detached, observing stance
Nonjudging	Compartmentalizes, keeps family, work, other areas of life separate
Restraint	Noncommunicative, interactions can be problematic

CHAPTER 6

The Questioner
"Be Prepared"—That's My Motto

John—Never Let Down Your Guard

Finally they were in Belize on a long-anticipated family vacation. It was March. They'd left behind the snow and ice of the East Coast for two weeks in the tropics. They were all excited, perhaps overwrought. The flight was without incident, but John couldn't put aside his doubts about how unwise it was for everyone to fly together. Maybe his wife should fly back with the two younger boys and he with their eldest? He'd broach the subject of separate planes with her in a few days, once they were settled in the condo. She'd found it on the Internet, on a cay that was also a marine nature reserve.

Quite safe, their regular travel agent had assured them. Belize is one of the safest Central American countries to visit. "How does *he* know?" thought John. "He's never been there." Local conditions changed all the time. One coup or another, one dictator or another. The U.S. Marines were always going into these places to save the day for this or that fledgling democratic movement. And no one knew about it. You put on the TV on some Sunday morning, and the fresh-faced announcer would be saying that the marines had landed in Belize overnight, a full-scale amphibious operation, destroyers at sea, and so on. They'd secured the embassy, were airlifting personnel to safety. U.S. citizens were advised not to travel to Belize till further notice. All Americans in the country were being held at the embassy compound.

Questioners, like Observers, are among those who detach, withdraw into the mind. For Questioners, the retreat into the head, like the whole momentum of this personality type, is to find safety. But safety is a projection, an illusion, because nobody is more or less safe in objective reality. Yet the sense of seeking certainty and finding it seems real to Questioners. For Observers, there is a great opening up, a relief, a sense that one can cope with the world because one is in one's head. The concepts of questioning, seeing the worst-case scenarios, being doubtful, are positive means whereby Questioners can test the hypothesis that the world is not safe. It seems to make absolute sense to Questioners that the only way they're going to find security is through questioning. If you don't question, how can you ever be sure? Maybe the only surety you can have in your life is that you are not sure. And that's okay. For John that's a good place to be.

"Who knows?" John mused, reclining as far as the airplane seat let him, his eyes closed, his mind in the grip of his old friend, the worst-case scenario. Right now someone back in New Jersey could be turning on the TV to be greeted with the news of this operation. While here he was, about to land in the place, deliberately putting his family in danger and, what's more, paying handsomely for the privilege.

The airport was directly on the ocean, which was as blue as the brochures had shown it to be. John had been skeptical. But, right on time, the resort driver was waiting for them with open-air transport. There were no other passengers. This resort was away from the tourist places, remote, pristine, as his wife preferred.

She was obviously delighted, and the children's eyes were alert with excitement and anticipation.

John was in a sweat, and it wasn't only from the heat. It was not a good sign when everything went this well. Usually it meant that something was going to go wrong; sooner or later the other shoe would drop. The driver handed John the keys to the vehicle, and a simple photocopied map. There was a lengthy explanation in Spanish and English. The driver was staying on in town. This was it, then, the unanticipated glitch; he had not prepared himself to drive his family through jungles and over unfamiliar mountain roads. John offered the man money, but the driver laughed and shook his head.

John's sons were looking at him strangely. The younger one moved toward his mother. The mood of elation and happy antic-ipation of moments before was beginning to shift, dissipate. John could sense the change. With a tight smile his wife held out her hand for the keys. "I'll drive. You know I like to drive." John shook himself mentally; he was hung up by his thoughts, the old mental trap. But he would never let his family down; his boys would not grow up with the doubts and questions that accompanied him. As he often did, John found courage on behalf of his sons to over-come his fear. The situation was stressful, but he kicked into action mode. Despite his qualms, he found the van as easy to operate as his automatic sedan back in their New Jersey garage.

Relaxing now, he could feel the knots leave his stomach, the dryness ease from his throat after he swallowed a few times. They made their way through the town without incident. Now that they were on the rain-forest road, the boys' spirits rose. The scenery was spectacular. John realized that he was excited, too; they'd never left the United States together before. He'd always wanted to go to a tropical locale but he was afraid to—so much could go wrong with three babies. But now they were no longer babies: thirteen, eleven, and nine. John had wanted to supplement his high-school Spanish, to learn the language a little better before the vacation, but of course there'd been no time.

Suddenly, around a bend, there was a roadblock in front of them. Armed soldiers were lounging about, one of them with his hand raised. John's fears flooded back, almost overwhelming him. He understood enough Spanish, even this patois, to know they were joking with one another and deciding whether or not to take everything out of the van. But they didn't, and John drove on. A fine mist covered this stretch of the coast, making it cooler, less sunny. John's internal radar was on high alert. He said little; encounters with any authority made him extremely edgy.

It was Sunday, and people were drinking. He watched them lolling at the side of the jungle road, while paying careful attention to every car for signs of dangerous driving. He noticed that there were five men in the truck ahead drinking beer. The truck stopped; they all jumped out to pee, so he knew they were drunk. He couldn't drive around them on a rise, on a curve, on a single-lane road. John felt trapped. His panic rose, but he beat it down. He turned to his boys in the back. Despite his tension, he couldn't help smiling at their amazement at the men peeing on the road. They would never know of his panic. He would hold things together for them.

By the time they made it to the resort, the afternoon haze had turned the sky and sea gray. The condo was right on the beach—perfect. He tried to put all thoughts of tidal waves out of his head. Everyone was exhausted, so they retired early. Before turning in, John went out on the deck to look at the ocean. Almost inevitably he heard a small plane overhead, and then another. At sea he saw large, dark shapes: could they be troopships waiting to stage a landing? There was a stutter of shots in the distance, then, shortly after, another long round. John was resigned. His worst fears had come back to haunt him: "Great, I've brought my family to a revolution."

He moved slowly to the bedroom, thinking, "What now?" His wife asked if he'd heard the fireworks. He looked puzzled. She said, "It's a national holiday. I thought you knew. That's why the driver wanted to stay in town. For the festivities."

The next morning he heard small planes again and realized that the resort had an airstrip. Those dark shapes out in the ocean turned out to be large rocks. John breathed deeply, felt his body relax. It had all worked out as they'd planned. But he stayed on low alert, subconsciously scanning for hidden dangers. Not to do so would be plain dumb.

Lucy—There's Nothing Good or Bad, but Thinking Makes It So

Lucy found parenting something she had to work at. She coped when the children were ill, or when she had financial worries, or when she was presented with some other challenge. She preferred to hunker down for the siege or be on the ramparts on behalf of her children. As long as she perceived herself and them as underdogs, she could be relied on 100 percent. But the doubts arose when everything seemed to be going well; she knew she couldn't put faith in good times.

Lucy was a single mom. She'd been married twice, but both her daughters had the same father, her second husband. The first marriage lasted six months; it was a disaster, the divorce uncontested. Her second marriage lasted for ten years before her husband died. His death confirmed every fear she'd ever had about the uncertainty of life.

She loved her children fiercely, more like a tigress than a gentler creature like a doe, but there was often an uneasy tension between them and her. Lucy acknowledged her role in the dynamic; basically the tension arose because of her ambivalence regarding authority and authority issues. On any given day, as her children came home from school, if she'd received two more bills in the mail that she didn't know how she was going to pay, she would be off the charts on her internal fear scale. Usually she loved the moment when they came home, but if she was worried about something like money, their whole connection was soured that day. She questioned them too sharply about school; there was a suspicious tone to her comments, an edginess to all their interactions. By the next day the domestic situation was more resolved and certain. When the girls came home, Lucy was their best buddy: she wanted them to kick back and have fun. As an authority figure, Lucy oscillated between being too lax and too authoritarian. This was disconcerting for her children.

Lucy, like many other Questioners, also charted an erratic course at work. She liked her job, she didn't like her job. She trusted her bosses, she didn't trust her bosses. When the organization was doing well, she was bored. But when it appeared to be in trouble, her sense of responsibility and loyalty rose to the fore and she went far beyond the terms of her job description to help it right itself. Her girls became inured to the trail of jobs Lucy left behind her. Through all those years somehow she paid the rent, clothed them, and put food on the table.

Then she got a job at an environmental agency and stayed there for the rest of her working life. In many ways she felt she *became* the cause of saving the environment in her state. A fearless lobbyist, organizer, and protester, she was a well-known figure at the state capital as well as at rallies. Until they were old enough to decide whether they wanted to be involved or not, she always took her girls with her to protests. They admired their mother's energy and commitment. No one watching her would know how counterintuitive her behavior was for Lucy. Questioners have a fear of putting themselves in the public eye, of being noticed. But Lucy found the *fear* so paralyzing in and of itself that before she even knew she was doing so, she plunged into whatever it was that was making her afraid.

She practiced her hobbies with great intensity, too. Country music fans, she and her second husband used to attend concerts often. He played the guitar a little, and Lucy loved to sing. The girls remembered happy times when their parents put on shows for them. Lucy was an intense, ardent person in general, not only about country music. Her "on the edge" exploits proved it. She was seen as a different kind of mom. Calling attention to herself with her activism in the environmental movement was unusual enough, but in her forties she developed a passion for racing powerful motorbikes; you couldn't help but notice her. It was the danger she craved. Continually she wanted to push the envelope against her ever-present fear of what she was doing. She lost herself in the power of the machine to carry her far beyond where she would normally dare to go in life. Racing became a natural drug for her, a high. When she realized she was becoming addicted to the sport, she gave it up.

This was the pattern of her life: oscillation, swinging back and forth. It depended upon where she was in her internal debate regarding authority issues. Questioners have a sense of internal misalignment toward authority. The world is seen in terms of *me* and the *authority*. It's easy to see how this is part of a fear-based strategy: "Time is the authority. My job is the authority. My cause is the authority. Bike racing is the authority. My responsibility to my children is the authority. Life is the authority." Questioners give away their power to the authority, far more power than the authority has over them. Then they get resentful and the oscillation picks up, back and forth, back and forth.

Lucy's parents were coming to stay for a few days, a rare occurrence. For weeks and weeks, she'd been preparing the girls for the visit. In her head she had ordered and tidied the house, set up one of her daughters' rooms as a bedroom for her parents, thought through their meals, even bought the groceries. Three days before the visit her eldest daughter asked, "When are we going to get the house ready for Gram and Grampy's visit?"

With that query Lucy stepped out of her head and moved into action. She clicked into high gear, tackled all the tasks, got the preparations out of the way. Like other Questioners she was aware that she could get caught in a pattern of procrastination. Usually an energizing moment arose that freed her, when she said internally, "Okay, let's go." Then she could charge into dealing with whatever it was she was procrastinating over. But if she had to structure something, she did it in her head first, and she often got stuck there. Yet at work, for instance, if the routines were set up for her, doing the tasks was a piece of cake.

The visit was a success. Surrounded by the people closest to her, those she knew for sure loved her unconditionally, Lucy was able to relax, let down her defenses, open her heart, and find universal, unconditional love and peace of her own. Sitting before the fireplace one night, listening to her father telling her daughters a story about her childhood, Lucy could feel love and peace throughout her body. She was open and trusting, letting go—an almost counterintuitive state for the ever-vigilant Questioner.

PERSONAL ACCOUNT

Jody, a Questioner mother of a son and a daughter, gives this account

The best part of being a parent was the wellspring of love I discovered in me; a feeling of joy and wonder at the beauty of this creature that I helped bring into the world. And then I wondered if I could ever love so much again. I had another child, and the wellspring was even deeper. I found that there was a strength in me I didn't know I had. I learned that nothing stops me from doing my best to keep my children out of harm's way. Being a parent gave me newfound courage to stick up for myself as well. I enjoy the challenge of being able to cope when different situations arise, and I can help my children find their own way with love and support and without making them dependent. I also like getting my husband's perspective and working as a team to foster our kids' growth on every level.

What I like least is the worry. I hate it when I don't know if my children are safe. I don't like it when I'm unsure of what is the best thing to do: have I been too controlling or given them more freedom than they're ready to handle? I don't like it when I'm so unsure of the balance.

I devote a lot of time and energy to parenting. I feel it's my most important job. I give them room to make mistakes. I share explanations for why I do things, and I work at keeping the lines of communication as open as possible. My children know I care and that I work hard at honoring who they are and supporting them in their goals and dreams. I'm sometimes stricter than other parents, and at other times I'm more liberal. I try to gauge it by what I think is truly best for my kids, not by what others think.

For instance, recently I let my kids go to an annual four-day concert out of town. Usually a friend and I go with them and let them bring their friends; we all stay in a hotel. This year I did let my son camp, but my daughter stayed with me. They sat far away at the concert. I gave them their space, but I was there if they needed me, even if it was only for the ride to the hotel.

The other kids talk with me and don't feel too weird around me. I'm not their friend, but I work at not judging them, and they feel accepted. I don't condone their getting out of hand, but I try to let them test the boundaries in as safe a way as possible. I'm ready to let my son have freedom, if only because I know there's no choice—he's eighteen. I trust that he's been given a strong foundation, and I also know he'll make mistakes. Even though it isn't my dream weekend, I feel good knowing they can enjoy something I wouldn't feel comfortable simply sending them off to.

On the other hand, I do know I worry too much. Sometimes I get into worst-case-scenario thinking, and even though I don't even tell them half of what *could* happen, it hampers all of us. My worry can throw a wet blanket on something they're excited about, and I feel overly anxious when I *could* be sharing their excitement. I also worry that I'll create unnecessary fear in them.

Sometimes I lose it with them because I let my feelings build up, and then I'm mad at myself for not dealing with the feelings as they arise. Or I'm not even sure what those feelings are. I'm worried, so I either yell at them or lecture on and on and on. When I'm not grounded, they know it.

A couple of years ago we went camping with friends who also have teenagers. I found out that the boys had gotten into the beer cooler while we'd been out on the lake. I was so furious—mad at myself for leaving them alone, feeling that they'd betrayed my trust. I went right into deciding that my son would now become an alcoholic. I came up with all the reasons that he probably already was one, knew I could never trust him again, knew that life as we knew it was now changed forever.

Recently my children have said, "You and Dad are the best. You know when to yell and when to hug. We both have talked about it, and our friends say they wish they had parents like you. When we get maddest and yell back, it's usually because we know you're right." They also say, "You worry too much and don't get excited when cool things happen." or "You care too much."

My advice to other parents is to stay balanced, take time for yourself so you can keep the faith in times of stress and worry. Enjoy each stage your children go through. When you are frustrated or your priorities are confused, take the time to reset them. If you're out of sorts, everything can become distorted. I think of parenting as a fishing line: I let it out as far as I can, and when it seems too far, I reel it back in a bit. It's okay to keep adjusting that line. Try to give them the security and faith they need in themselves, so that they can swim free. They need to know on their own what it feels like, when they need to swim hard or go with the flow, when to rest in the water—and especially to realize that something much greater than themselves (or their parents) will keep them buoyed, if they keep the faith.

The Best Strategy and Action Program for Questioners

Not All Questioners Are Alike

Questioners are among the most difficult personality types to understand, because they fall on a spectrum ranging from highly fearful, phobic (e.g., John who's always on the verge of caving in to his fear) to counterphobic (e.g., Lucy, always moving into action against her fear). Most Questioners embody to some degree elements of both ends of the spectrum. John is aware he's fearful. As a phobic Questioner, he has motivations that are easier to understand. This personality *knows* (the blind spot) that the world is a frightening place and that one way to cope with fear is to figure out what's the worst that can happen; there's a degree of safety in knowing. Inherent in this strategy are practices to mitigate one's fear, such as going toward people in a warm way, being friendly to head off dislike and potential harm from others.

Counterphobic Questioners go against their fear, and in the most overt manifestations they can often look like confrontational Protectors. Lucy would be surprised to learn that fear is among her primary motivational drivers; she thinks she's fearless. The intense discomfort of being trapped in fear is so disturbing that these personalities go into whatever is frightening them in order to alleviate the discomfort. If you're a counterphobic Questioner and scared of heights, you'll take up bungee jumping. When you're *in* the fear, you can overcome it. If you're scared of water, you go sailing across the Atlantic solo. These are extreme but real-life examples. Like Lucy, if you're scared of finding life speeding out of your control, you take up motorbike racing. If there's been a family argument, before the repercussions can even begin to settle, the counterphobic Questioner is challenging you for your response. Questioners need to know what's certain and safe; they can't leave an argument unresolved.

No one on this fear spectrum is pathological or paranoid. Questioners are as normal and high-functioning as anyone else, but their personality strategy tells them to keep up their guard; it makes sense to do so. Paranoia plays out in gentle and subtle ways in most cases: the parent who's always asking, "Yes, but . . . ?" because of fear of the family's landing itself in a problematic situation, unaware of all the possibile things that can go wrong. Keeping the family safe is territory Questioners view as their responsibility.

Although most Questioners report that they are both phobic and counterphobic, one style usually predominates and is the fallback mode.

Afraid for Your Children: Of Everything and Anything

The world is a frightening place, and most Questioners are amazed that other personality types don't know this or heed the dangers if they're told about them. The habitual practices of their strategy—scanning, doubting, worst-case-scenario imagining, questioning—are sensible tactics in a lifelong battle to keep disaster at bay. One Questioner parent was amazed when he realized the counterphobic element in his parenting behavior. He relied on going toward his fear to help him discipline his children. "When I began to understand my parenting style, I became aware that I *attack* my children's interaction with my authority. I *go after* them for dissenting from me and *pound away* at them about how important it is to pay respect to others. I don't care to admit it, but I like the feeling of confrontation. I'm afraid of it, so I get pushed toward it. Mental or emotional fear I experience as challenges and go right toward them."

Another Questioner reinforces this observation: "It's been something that I constantly, constantly see in myself, how I push out the fear that I feel inside and don't recognize as fear."

Questioners are often frightened of other people's anger, because they know how powerful their own is.

ACTION: *Become aware of what creates fear in you.* It could be the unknown, even if you've done something similar before. Fear is a key motivational factor in your parenting. You are not afraid of your children, you are afraid *for* your children—of anything and everything. Fear can take many physical forms that you can learn to recognize: a clutch in the stomach, a dry throat, a faster heartbeat, a wave of nausea, a tightening in the chest, a shaky voice, sweaty hands, trembling knees. You need to know in what ways your body signals fear to you, because most often you don't know you're afraid. When you become aware that you are afraid, metaphorically take a good look around your life and see if you can pinpoint the cause of your uneasiness. *It's always easier for you to deal with what's known.* If there's no reason inside yourself to explain your unease, then look around to see if your child or someone else you're with is anxious. You may be picking up on another person's anxiety and projecting it onto yourself. In either case the best way to cope with your fear is to get a reality check: ask people you trust if what you're feeling and perceiving is valid, if it has reality.

Ambivalence Involving Authority and Trust

Many Questioners feel powerless in the face of life's uncertainty and capriciousness. Questioner parents can't overestimate this basic motivation. How can they be authority figures to their children if they have no authority over their own lives? This feeling expands into a general sense of being life's underdog. From this point of view life itself becomes the authority, a rubric that can include many phenomena. From here, Questioners are always up against the wall, underprotected, watching their backs, scanning for safety. Questioners give away their power to authority, view it as more powerful than they are. It's most often a case of "us against them," when Questioners align themselves with underdogs or underdog causes. They and their family become the underdogs. If Questioners feel safe with an authority, they will be less wary. But as soon as the authority shows any signs of disarray, the Questioner becomes uneasy, filled with questions and doubts. Some Questioners are deliberately rebellious about wanting to test the authority (life), not as in a power struggle but to see if they can be safe and secure with the authority. (They're unlikely to experience either state for long. Life changes.)

One Questioner describes this motivational behavior: "Everything is an authority. I'm in the car with the kids, we're late for school—the clock is the authority. I'm going too fast. A police officer stops me. The fear rush comes up, but by the time he gets to the window, I'm all warmth and affection."

Blindly obeying authority can inculcate feelings of inchoate anger. Another Questioner tells us, "I always obey authority. An interesting thing is that I thought I was the most trusting person in the whole world. I trusted everybody. I didn't realize that all those questions had to do with *not* trusting. I thought I was just trying to get clarity, especially where my children are concerned. I know I get resentful when my time is taken up, or my energy, or someone has authority over me. I think that's when rage comes into me, when everybody is demanding something from me, including the clock."

Trust is fundamentally counterintuitive to Questioners. The idea of trust is just *so* stupid. They don't trust themselves, so how are they going to trust anyone else? For Questioners, take the word "trust" out of the dictionary—it doesn't exist. Many Questioners are bewildered when others ask them questions about trust. As they have never trusted, they are unaware that they don't have trust.

Questioners favor a nonauthoritarian family ethic. You're comfortable with not being in charge of everything that happens, not having to be part of every decision your children make. You try to develop a nonauthoritarian relationship with your children. But children need you to be an authority figure. Unfortunately for you, simply by being a parent you are perceived as an authority figure by your children. If you question them, sometimes they'll see that as confrontational. The very parent-child roles you have will at times set you up in a "them against me" situation. Your oscillation around authority—now the one in charge, now one of the gang—is disconcerting to them.

There is another motivation at work here that you are well aware of, and it has to do with trust. Authority issues are shot through with trust issues for Questioners. The ideas of trust and trusting don't feel safe at all; you feel this opens you to certain victimization. *Nonetheless learn to trust yourself with your children. You are trustworthy.* Like the Dreamer parent who may not feel good enough, some Questioner parents may not feel trustworthy enough.

ACTION: *Try to be consistent.* Set up discipline processes as the need arises if that will help you heed your antiauthoritarian concerns; then keep your end of the deal. Enforce consequences. You're actually helping your children develop into responsible adults. Trust their love, their joy in you. And when, inevitably, there are clashes or they let you down, it is most important that you still trust their love. Learn to separate what they do as normal children growing up, rebelling and challenging, from how they feel about you. Try never to let them see for even one moment that you doubt their love for you. Never let on that by their actions they may have corrupted some of your feelings for them. You know you love them deeply, steadfastly, but sometimes your behavior may convey a different message. Constantly tell them you love them. Make sure they know this is so.

Trust Your Child's Loyalty

For Questioners, the concept of faith is tied up in the idea of loyalty. They know that loyalty is a major motivation for them, so they look for it in others. If those people are loyal, then

Questioners know they are faithful and can be relied on, because that's the way it works for them. Questioners' loyalty is often directed to intimates and family, but especially to the underdog (which in many cases is how they see their children, especially when they are young and helpless, unprotected, dependent on the Questioner). Questioners are loyal; it goes with the territory of being responsible. Once they're committed, they're responsible to see parenting and marriage through all the ups and downs.

ACTION: *Be aware that your loyalty can come across as overbearing concern for your children.* They may feel smothered and confined within the ambit of your loyalty. Be aware that subconsciously you may be seeking from them a commensurate sense of loyalty. If this is not forthcoming, it doesn't mean they love you less or are less concerned about you. What it means is that they love you differently. Often your loyalty can be fairly idealistic, and others can't—or don't want to—keep the same standard.

Sometimes you can mistake your instinct to discipline your children as being disloyal to them. Loyalty in personal relationships is such a key motivation for you that your inclination to discipline them may then remain hidden. Trust yourself in these instances to do the right thing; don't confuse needed disciplinary action with disloyalty.

Try not to be reactive when you think your children are being disloyal to you or the family. It *is* hurtful when you feel that despite having parented them over such a long period, they are disloyal. It can feel like a betrayal, and your worst-case-scenario habit may kick in. Try not to go down that route. Question them about their motives for their behavior. Most of the time you'll find that they're testing their wings, brushing up against your authority, behaving as normal, growing children do. Disloyalty doesn't figure on their radar screen. However hard trusting is for you, remember to learn to trust your children.

Aim for More Objectivity in Protecting the Underdog

Questioners often view *themselves* as life's underdogs. After all, they give away their power to authority, and what is an underdog if not powerless? From this position it's easier to explain the fear, the doubts, the negativity, all the other mental constructs that arise with a constant necessity to question the world. This Questioner parent is acutely aware of her inner motivations and how they manifest themselves: "In my home maybe you'd expect me to relax and take on mental pursuits because I operate so much from my head, but interestingly enough, my focus is on relationships, because relationships are where I can reach security. A set of intimate relationships can establish my safety zones. I feel protected by them, and I will protect those relationships with my life. I do everything I can for my family. My primary concern in parenting is not the values and beliefs I convey, although those are important, but that my children grow up in a safe environment. My anger is directed at those parents who don't value that safety, who put their children down, or who are bullies."

ACTION: *Try not to be overzealous in protecting the underdog, whether it is your child in some trouble with another child or in fights between your children.* Children need to make their own mistakes, fight some of their own battles. That's how they develop a belief in themselves, gain their self-confidence. Don't intervene unless necessary or called on to do so.

This is hard for you, since your inclination is toward protecting the underdog. It's difficult for you not to attack anyone who seems to be overbearing, or, as one Questioner parent put it, "I become the bully to the stereotypical bully types."

In arguments between your children, if you intervene, pick sides, and root for the underdog, this strips away your objectivity and makes you less effective as a parent. Your children won't value your judgment in the long run.

Beware of Constant Vigilance

The focus of attention of Questioners goes to scanning the environment for hidden dangers: the unexpressed intentions of others toward them, the host of unexpected occurrences that can ambush and assault them. A Questioner parent reports the concept of scanning accurately: "When I walk into a room, if I feel uneasy, then I have to look around, and if there's no reason inside me, intellectually or physically, that I should feel uneasy, then I'll start looking around to find somebody else's anxiety."

The attentional focus of the Questioner goes to scanning to seek certainty, as if there's an internal radar system always running. This type of scanning is quite different from, for instance, a Helper's, whose scanning is relational. It's a ceaseless scanning for danger that obviously becomes a part of the Questioner's motivational conditioning. However, there is a gift present in the continual scanning. If others give the Questioner room to speak up, particularly in family discussions, Questioners love to voice their doubts and troubleshoot. They will define the problem so everyone can reach clear and logical conclusions.

ACTION: *For your children's sake, try to rein in your constant vigilance, your constant uneasiness.* Otherwise they may grow up unnecessarily lacking in confidence and fearful themselves. When they're adolescents, they may rebel against your perpetual wariness. Certainly they will begin to question your judgment.

Be aware that you may project your fear onto someone or something, and that it has no reality. You may be like the sentry in the sentry box who often raises the alarm when it's only the wind moving shadows. This can also occur in relationships: you tell your children what they are thinking when *they* haven't been thinking that at all.

Again, an important antidote to scanning and projection is to seek reality checks from those around you whose judgment you value.

Be Wary of the Role of Devil's Advocate

Questioner parents put great store in clear, logical thinking, and they communicate from this perspective. And naturally they would like their child to develop these habits of mind. They try hard to encourage their child to think along several paths that incorporate these patterns. They ask, "What's your main idea here?" or "How and why did you come to your decision?" or "How do you use this theory?" They are trying to teach their child a skill, to draw conclusions from the available information. Essentially they want to teach their child how to work logically with theory and concepts.

Questioners are skeptics and may display skepticism as to whether their child's ability to apply logical thinking is adequately developed at school. They seek certainty and are never sure that their child has got the point of what they're talking about, until the child demonstrates that she's got the point. Many children may find this type of probing onerous.

More than likely when Questioner parents were students, they never took things at face value. They were probably strong devil's advocates, always challenging and questioning, not to bring down authority or the facts, but to make sure that what they were hearing was truthful and accurate. As parents they find they are still the devil's advocate for the ideas they support.

ACTION: *Remember, your children may not understand your devil's-advocate passion for logical thinking.* When you question them about their comprehension of what you're saying, when you push them to think things through, to think logically, they may not realize that you're questioning *their thinking and not their selves.* They may take your intellectual, mental rigor personally and back off from engaging with you. This would be a pity, for you have much to offer your children in the realm of thinking skills. Remember that we are all different and that we think and communicate differently. You are programmed to think (for instance) in terms of pros and cons; your children may *never* think that way.

Set Short-Term Goals, and Stay Focused

Questioners procrastinate for several reasons, all of them having to do with being unable to let go of mental prohibitions involved with taking action: thinking replaces doing. When ideas are still in the Questioner's head, they can be submitted again and again to a process of argument and counterargument, but once actions are taken, they have consequences. Once words are spoken, they've been made public and cannot be retracted. Questioner parents are fearful that if they have not thought through all the scenarios, their words and deeds will be misinterpreted, misrepresented. The fear is partly of becoming a target, of being public, partly that they may not fulfill their responsibility and duty to their children. One Questioner father said, "The task I'm supposed to complete is like a dead body in my car. I'll be driving along all happy until I start to sniff it. Then I remember and get in a panic, and I'm totally energized, and I get it done."

ACTION: *Try harder to overcome procrastination.* Recondition your thinking to suggest to yourself that actually you *may not* be a dutiful and responsible parent *because* you're procrastinating, and not the other way around. Be assured that you can easily take action, manage tasks, reach short-term objectives if a structure is present. Setting clear objectives and goals is a way to overcome procrastination. If you keep tasks short and focused, the energy stays high. Longer-term tasks are harder for you. Some Questioners do the last-minute things first to create that energy, to push themselves to action.

Safety: Let Everyone Have an Opportunity to Speak

Sometimes the only way for Questioners to feel safe is to be in charge. They don't want the limelight and are not on a power trip; in fact, they recoil from taking on the responsibility of being a leader. But if *they* do it, they know it'll be safe for everyone, and that's important to them as parents. There are a number of other ways Questioners can create safety: Looking someone in the eye is one strategy. Or asking questions so others can voice their fears and concerns. Or trying to draw people out, using humor a lot, and making fun of themselves. Questioners often share their own experiences as a way of making others open to them. If others don't respond with equal openness, Questioners' scanning mechanisms go into high alert.

It makes sense that *as* Questioners are afraid of being victimized, they are constantly vigilant. If in any environment in which they operate they are not given the opportunity to express their questions and doubts, then they keep up their guard and wait for their worst expectations to materialize. But if they feel safe—which to a large degree means being able to express their opinions, doubts, fears, and questions—they can let down their guard, be spontaneous and creative. This freedom of expression is obviously of fundamental importance to Questioners. It's interesting how many Questioner parents state the precept of soliciting and listening to everyone's thinking as a golden rule of their parenting.

ACTION: *Rein in your preference to create an open format so that there's room for expression, for hearing everyone's opinions.* In your family, everyone's having the safety to speak out is important to you. You hold a different awareness for each of your children. You're protective and supportive. You encourage your children to say outrageous, funny things, to express themselves. You use humor, often offbeat humor, and humor is a connective bond in your interactions.

While this atmosphere of fun and cooperation is to be encouraged, once again I caution you against going too far in creating this environment. By all means enjoy your children and have as much fun as you can with them. But realize it is harder then to pull back and hold the line when you need to do so for your children's sake, once they're so used to your letting them say and do whatever they want to.

Parenting Steps for Questioners

- Fear is a key motivational factor in your parenting. You're not afraid *of* your children, you're afraid *for* your children—of anything and everything. Be aware that you may be projecting your fears and emotions onto them; get reality checks. Ask your family for help in sorting out real dangers from imagined threats.

- Being a parent, you are perceived as an authority figure by your children. Find a consistent way to model this role. If you tend to come across as confrontational when all you're doing is voicing doubts, modify the way you interact with your children. Be aware that you give undue authority to others and feel weakened as a result.

- You are a trustworthy enough parent. Learn to trust your children, too. They'll make their own way in the world regardless. Be aware that loyalty, trust, and faith are two-way streets. Trust the reassurances of love, regard, and esteem you receive from your family. Give freely of your love, and don't be scared that emotion will sweep you away.

- Build boundaries around your inclination to jump in and protect the underdog. As far as it's reasonable to do so, let your children sort our their own battles. Don't intervene unless necessary or unless you're called on to do so.

- You may be like the sentry in the box who often raises the alarm when it's only the wind moving shadows. You tell your children what *they* are thinking when they haven't been thinking that at all. Ask them for feedback and reality checks when your projection comes their way.

- Be aware of overplaying the devil's-advocate role. You feel safe with your family to express your doubts and questions. But in asking questions too sharply, while *you* may know that you're after logical clarification, your family may feel personally attacked. Your doubting attitude may come across as negative and carping.

- Find a process to overcome procrastination. Ask your family for help in structuring short-term tasks and goals as a way to short-circuit procrastination. Be aware of times when thinking paralyzes your ability to move into action. Don't shoulder too much responsibility and overcommit.

- Try to get in touch with your body and emotions; an exercise program and interpersonal interests are important to balance your mental world. Try to be more spontaneous with your emotions. Show others your love, appreciation, and gratitude.

- Parenting is for life. You can't bail out on your children when the going gets tough. When your children act out (as inevitably they will) and challenge you, hold your ground and don't let doubts sweep you away. It's more important that they know that *you* love *them* and are there for them than for you to know that *they* love *you.*

SUMMARY: THE QUESTIONER PARENT

Positives to Build On	*Negatives to Overcome*
Loyal, sticks with the agenda	Fearful, scans for danger
Responsible, endures	Fear can be paralyzing, undermining
Protects the underdog	Struggles with authority issues
Questions incisively	Doubtful of self and others: "Yes, but . . . "
Logical	
Rational	Self-sabotaging, fears that success brings hostility
Clear-thinking	Defensive, afraid of own and others' anger
Troubleshooter	
Skeptical	Suspicious, devil's advocate, seeks safety
	Procrastinates, track record of incompletes
	Cynicism, little faith in others and the world

CHAPTER 7

The Entertainer
Let's Have Fun! Let's Play!

Connie—a Magic Circle of Imagination

Connie loved life. She felt that hers was a particularly fortunate one. From when she was a little girl, she knew that the world was hers to enjoy and explore. When she was five, she was given a glass ball with a fairy castle inside. All she had to do was shake the ball and snow fell, a princess appeared in the castle. Throughout her life she believed that the world was that magical glass ball she held in her hand. One shake and new possibilities and options opened for her. Connie hated limitations of any kind. As a toddler, when she was left outside to play, she would wander into neighbors' houses. Her parents put a harness on her with a long line and tied it to a tree. She'd find ways of getting free and wander off again. She thought it was a splendid game.

Bright-eyed and bushy-tailed, outgoing, with a sharp wit and sense of humor, she took everything in her stride; life's path was even and smooth. In many ways she felt entitled to this fortunate life. When she looked at other people's lives and relationships and saw how messy they could become, she threw herself into life even more avidly, put even more energy into being upbeat, positive, engaging. She knew that this was the way to ward off pain, suffering. Even if life did hit a few bumps in the road, from previous experience Connie knew that youthful zest and enthusiasm, always looking on the bright side, would see her through. She embraced a jaunty positivism, enjoyed being a living icon of eternal youth. She didn't see any value in dealing with negativity. Life was too short.

Entertainers like Connie are rewarded by American culture. They embody many popular American characteristics: upbeat energy, wisecracking wittiness. They are charming partners in relationships, take-charge leaders, models of infectious youthfulness and optimism, upholders of egalitarian and democratic attitudes and responses; they're engaging, articulate entertainers who tell great stories.

Connie did well at school, had many friends, took the opportunities that life presented to her and turned them into great adventures. There were so many options open to her: the world was a banquet, and she wanted to taste everything, was excited about everything, wanted to do everything. Connie *believed* she could do everything, and that was exciting in and of itself. When she was first married, she loved riding horses, and she made herself into such an expert horsewoman that her husband believed she would reach her dream of owning and running a riding stable. Then she decided she liked horticulture and landscaping, so she became a horticulturist and started working at a large public botanical garden. When she became a mother, she loved entertaining her babies so much that she wanted to teach kindergarten. It was then she *knew* she'd found what she loved to do. She was committed to children, so she didn't change direction as much anymore.

As many Entertainers mature and grow, they experience a shift from the expectation that the experiences life offers are a cornucopia of delights created expressly for their tasting to a sense of finding some fulfillment in the routine, the mundane, in knuckling down to do committed work. By dedicating herself to children, Connie let go of an almost addictive need to stoke her inner excitement by keeping too many options open for herself, feeling entitled to taste everything. She settled down into a type of sobriety. "I can say no to those options. I can commit myself and follow through on this." This doesn't mean she'd lost her zest and youthful enthusiasm for life—far from it—but her energy was redirected.

Among Connie's gifts as a parent were optimism and an ability to enliven the lives of others through storytelling. She was inventive about activities. Not only did she make up mysterious and fantastic stories or turn bedtime reading into interactive performances, but her children developed skits with her. These became legendary family and neighborhood projects. The children helped design and make costumes, and had great fun in rehearsing and then producing the story. Many neighborhood children were drawn to the magic circle of Connie's imagination and fantasies. Some danced, others played instruments. Connie was delighted at the whimsy and flights of fantasy the children displayed; she became fascinated by the way children thought and wanted to find out as much as she could about child development. She went back to college to do graduate work in this field.

The Entertainer strategy directs these personalities to live in the head, to spend as much time as they can there, fantasizing, imagining, planning. Both Observers and Entertainers are in the Detacher (mental) triad, but while Observers are inclined to make connections in order to put a big picture together, Entertainers like to see the interconnections in associative patterns of ideas. Connie loved to plan her children's activities; they sat for hours sifting through all the possible ways to make an idea for a skit or a short performance work. In the interactive arena, parenting is a natural for Entertainers. Their passion for options, plans, and escape into the world of the imagination plays out in games with their children. Connie brought gifts of tremendous enthusiasm, firing of the imagination, opening of the mind. Any idea that the children came up with was discussed and seriously considered.

When her children were older and went away to summer camp, Connie anticipated the time she'd have for herself and planned many activities she'd put on hold since they were born. But in fact she was content to stay put; to her surprise she found she'd arrived at a stage of her life where she relished her privacy. Once she was alone, her mind did not slow down. Rather, it sped up. A monkey-mind ballet ensued, with her imagination leaping and cavorting through the tree canopy (freeform ideas) interconnected by vines on which they swung to and fro in a dizzying display of mental gymnastics. Often she had no idea what she'd been thinking about for hours on end.

She allowed herself the time and space to do things she'd thought she'd never do again, like reading and writing for herself. She realized she liked to be alone some of the time, liked to run her thoughts without any constraints, wherever they led her. There were no limits in her mind.

Dan—Don't Fence Me In

Ever since he was a boy, people were drawn to Dan. He had a charming way of disarming one's reserve, caution, or shyness, and, drawn to his enthusiasm for life, people become his friends. By the time he was in his mid-twenties, he knew hundreds of people in many parts of the country and the world, all of whom he referred to as "my friend." He *was* a good friend: interested in people's lives, supportive, asking questions to draw people out, suggesting alternative approaches to problems. Friends felt the full surge of his ebullient energy.

His only child, a son, the apple of Dan's eye, fell under his father's spell, too. He was Dan's great buddy until he was about twelve and entered a stage of adolescent judgment over what he considered to be his father's immaturity. For instance, Dan, a great practical joker, never missed an opportunity to replace the spoon in the sugar bowl with a cake fork. His son thought this was childish behavior, and in fact he was perceptive: many Entertainers carry the sobriquet of "the eternal youth."

As a consultant Dan traveled constantly. Far-flung clients were party to the boy's growth and development from his baby days forward. There was always a new pack of photographs in Dan's wallet. Strangers knew of the boy's exploits on the baseball and soccer fields, of the first fish he caught, of the time when he first "dated" a girl at the local town social. Somehow Dan managed to make the routine seem remarkable, wry, and nostalgic. What didn't please his son was when strangers, Dan's clients on business trips, came to stay overnight and greeted the boy with unusual warmth while reminding him of childhood anecdotes he'd rather forget and certainly resented their knowing. As his mother said, with Dan's outgoing bounciness there was little that was close to the vest about him.

When Dan was home, father and young son were inseparable. Dan loved to take long drives on weekends. There was something freeing about driving with the windows rolled down, the air rushing in, the radio blaring forth, the open road in front of him. Dan's favorite golden oldie was "Don't Fence Me In." He had the song recorded on all his personal tapes and CDs. As soon as it came on, he would sing along with the old cowboy who asked for space on the range to roam in. When his son was five or six, Dan would place him on his lap behind the wheel and let him experience the thrill of "driving" the car at high speed.

They also spent a good deal of time in museums of natural history, science, and technology. Dan entered into his son's interests and hobbies with gusto. Each summer they took two trips together, Dan choosing one, his son the other. For instance, when his son was eleven years old, Dan took him to the Baseball Hall of Fame, and his son took him to the Smithsonian Institution. Entertainers are egalitarian in their approach to life; they equalize authority with others. Of course Dan was cognizant of his responsibilities as a father, but in many ways he treated his son as an equal. Similarly, when Dan was a student, he had treated his teachers as equals. Dan never respected someone because of his or her position; to gain his respect, one had to earn it.

Dan was often late to fetch his son from school or sports practice, or to deliver him to the dentist and to other appointments. In fact, Dan was often late for his *own* appointments, but his clients treated his tardiness as a quirk: "That's Dan for you." His whirlwind arrival, full of jokes, stories, and high energy were a welcome diversion from the daily routine.

The habitual pattern of lateness of many Entertainers is part of this personality strategy that directs them to being somewhat elusive, not easy to pin down. Of course, this ties in with the Entertainer motivation to keep options open. Dan formulated a rationale for this behavior: "I will say that I will be at the meeting at eleven A.M. and in that moment I mean that I will be there. But if at ten-fifteen A.M. someone calls and something else comes up, life becomes exciting. I have to be at a meeting at eleven, but maybe if I get there at eleven-fifteen, it will be okay. Then I can still fit in this other option *and* do the meeting."

Dan's son became inured to waiting for his father; he knew he'd show up eventually. Sometimes, though, when Entertainers miss a commitment, the picture can become a bit broader, reframed as part of a cover-up. "Did I say eleven A.M. *today?* It was next Wednesday, right?"

Entertainers believe that being a little slippery around the edges of their actions is a well-disguised ploy, but it can be noticeable to others. They reframe the facts in their heads. They think they're being creative and original, justified in reframing, because that way they're avoiding the consequences of causing pain to anyone.

When a client, friend, or family member, for instance, pointed out that Dan was late, and his excuse paper thin and transparent, he did not react with equanimity. His backup style was to become sarcastic and use his verbal facility to defend himself, sometimes with cruel intent. Entertainers do not take kindly to criticism. Criticism is stressful for them, not because they're in the wrong, but because they've been caught out. Entertainers are fully aware that with many balls in the air, resisting limits, keeping their options open, there's always a danger that they won't be able to keep the juggling act going. They're addicted to this danger; it's exhilarating to always walk the thin line. Another personality type, the Moralizer, also reacts strongly to criticism. But Moralizers find criticism devastating on two counts: first that they've erred and second that they now have to take on responsibility for righting the wrong.

Dan's wife (a Moralizer, as it happens) called him on his evasiveness whenever she was aware of it, but his son learned to let Dan be; ultimately he came through with most of his commitments.

PERSONAL ACCOUNT

Larry, an Entertainer father of two daughters, gives this account

I enjoy so much about being a parent, especially emotions such as mutual, unconditional love and the joy I get hearing my children laugh. Also simple things, like going to swim together or walking hand in hand. Then there's the more profound side: helping them deal with life's youthful crises, like fights with friends or uncertainty at school. I see and learn so much anew with them. We walk in the woods often, and they always notice little things in nature that escape my attention. Not just a tree or a leaf or even a bug on the leaf, but the fact that the bug has a broken wing or a caterpillar is beginning to spin its cocoon. Every fallen tree represents a loss of oxygen, and they worry about the well-being of the planet.

I love watching my kids develop in all aspects: first struggling to hang from the monkey bars for just a few seconds, then climbing like monkeys, fear replaced by a spirit of daring and pride (but fortunately hanging on to some caution). Swimming, reading, the glee of realizing they can add numbers. They're fast becoming my best friends, but it's a unique kind of friendship. I'm obviously the parent, the adult, and in the friendship I have control or the dominant position. But there's a trust and a positive kind of taking-for-granted that doesn't exist in other friendships.

There are a few things I don't like about being a parent: one is that there's not much downtime or personal time. This is similar to the pleasure of sharing in a new relationship with a partner, but missing the freedom of being alone and making all your own decisions. Another is the fact that I now worry about the future. I worry about so many things, like bad drivers damaging their bodies, bad teachers messing up their minds, boyfriends hurting their hearts. It doesn't matter if the fear is realistic or not, or imminent or not. I worry just the same.

I feel stronger as a person by having produced and raised two such wonderful human beings; who would have thought it? I also feel weaker, more flawed. Often I don't seem to be able to provide clear, consistent direction that will dictate their appropriate behavior for life and entrench those values that we consider important. I'm constantly reminded that I can't answer all my children's questions. I've yelled when I shouldn't have. I've been at a loss when trying to handle parenting situations that are new to me, like what does one look for in a school for one's children? In a teacher? How much to let them learn from their own experience? It's easy making decisions that affect only me, or even my wife and myself, but for kids it's hard. They don't come with instruction manuals.

I fear that I am too tough. I say no to something they want to do or insist they do something they don't want to, like cleaning up or going to bed early. Or else I'm too lenient by not insisting they eat five pieces of fruit a day or be sure that their hair is neatly brushed before leaving the house. Mostly, though, I'm available, tolerant, loving, and I *enjoy* spending time with my kids, which translates into a decent job of setting values and limits. Our spending time together is really important to me. I chose a job that compromised on challenge and responsibility but increased my ability to spend time with my kids, attend recitals, and such. My older daughter points to the following situation involving swimming as an indicator of good parenting: she was frightened to go under, and I kept encouraging her, but I was also patient when she explained her fear. I let her get there in her own time.

On the other hand, I'm aware that I'm overprotective in everything from preventing even small opportunities for them to hurt themselves to avidly guarding what they watch on TV. Also I'm not as consistent as I would like to be. For example, I set a specific bedtime but then find reasons not to stick to it, and I give in to their reasons/excuses to let it slip. My younger daughter says I break my own rules, like the rule for no TV during the week, yet I get to watch. This may have an "I'm the adult" justification, but it does confuse the kids. I do it, anyway!

Nonetheless they've acknowledged that they know I love and care for them. They tell me I'm patient in important things, such as the swimming situation I mentioned, that I like to have fun. I'm one of the dads who'll run in the playground with the kids rather than always stand on the sidelines watching. I like playing card games and doing projects. As a family we enjoy doing yard work together. We'd love to find more time for this kind of fun. I'm always there for them.

Listen to everyone's advice, and then ignore it (if you don't listen, they won't stop giving it!). Read books that reinforce your values and approach. Figure out what works for you and your children relative to schedules, routines, and so on. And play, play, play! ❧

The Best Strategy and Action Plan for Entertainers

Be Alert to Others' Response to Your Perpetual Optimism

Entertainers believe that if they make their worldview upbeat, positive, and energetic; if they throw ideas, fantasies, and plans at it; if they keep their options open, that becomes the way of the world. That is, until perhaps life presents the Entertainer with a painful reality check, the opportunity to see through this blind spot.

Entertainers are almost unrelenting in their determination to see the bright side, to put a positive spin on events. Their optimism is often rooted in the desire to escape from mental pain. While Questioners employ a strategy of worst-case-scenario thinking to contain their fear, Entertainers employ a strategy of *best*-case-scenario thinking. They can't bear to be negative, not while the lifelong defense mechanism of escaping into a mental world filled with limitless options works so well for them. An Entertainer parent remarked on how she has a need to make everything less somber: "It's a whole lot easier for me to be able to have others see the better side of the worst side they're looking at."

ACTION: *Remember, your children may become sad or down on themselves, or they may go through painful crises with their friends.* Unlike you, they let the process happen; they don't avoid pain. Some people *need* to process their pain, and it can take days or weeks. There's usually a point when you want to say, "Okay, enough. You've been doing this for days. We've gone over those problems. I feel sorry for you, but can we move on? You need to snap out of this." Your children may find your perpetually upbeat energy jarring, out of sync with their needs. Learn to go at their pace; don't try to move them at your own. Let your children be themselves. Honor and respect their differences from you.

Are You an Entitled Egalitarian?

Entertainers don't easily recognize that they carry a sense of entitlement. They find this characteristic of theirs difficult to put into words. Oddly enough, in many ways entitlement is tied in to their desire to be egalitarian. Feeling entitled to assume an equal footing with anyone else is a way of lessening any authority's power over them, including those that set limits. Entertainers feel entitled to ignore rules, disregard limitations, take risks.

Entertainers are part of the fear triad; their strategy directs them to lessen their fear by equalizing authority. If everyone is on the same level, Entertainers can use a charm-and-disarm approach to move the authority to their side. Entertainers can become markedly antiauthoritarian if the authority seems to want to limit or restrict their options in any way. Feeling entitled and superior are two strands of this overarching strategy they use to justify their behavior. They bring authority inside themselves, claim it as their own. *They* choose to commit themselves, *they* decide on this option or that one, *they* keep the deadline or not—authority is internal.

ACTION: *Remember that it's your preference to equalize authority.* You'll tend to want to practice this egalitarianism among your children and yourself; in fact, your family relationships are often about leveling and equalizing the group so that everyone belongs. If this is your agenda, stick with it. All too often your future-looking energy doesn't allow you to manifest this (or other) dynamics in ways you'd like. Your concern for everyone is definitely there, but while you move on to the next project, you may leave your children confused and ambivalent about your intentions and authority.

Remember, too, that many other personality types desire a sense of hierarchy and don't experience a feeling of safety or fairness when everyone is regarded as equal. They may *want* you to assume a hierarchical authority role. Ask your children about this. You may be surprised by what they tell you.

Know That Parenting Is a Lifelong Commitment

It's not that Entertainers are unable to commit to their families; it's that they see potential in other options. But once they say they'll be there, once they commit to something, they will see it through, *because it is their choice.* Commitment lasts for as long as the Entertainer decides it should. In a powerful mental construct, Entertainers can feel that they've fulfilled their commitment by completing *in their heads* what they've undertaken; they don't have to actualize it in the world. Parenting is of a different order: it's a lifelong commitment, and because it's interactive, *it is* in the world. One can leave a marriage but not stop being a parent.

Most Entertainer parents are just as dedicated as other parents. They flex their psychological paradigm about options and limits to fit their parenting role. In other words, they try to open up the options for themselves and their children within the boundaries of the parenting dynamic. The Entertainers we've already met—Larry, Connie, and Dan—are all examples of this.

ACTION: *Instead of resenting the loss of personal time and downtime, especially in your children's early years, allow yourself a feeling of unlimited time to interact with and enjoy them.* You'll find you have a knack for inventing games, seeing the world anew through their eyes, sharing the spontaneous fun and exhilaration of their world. You'll have permission to revisit the inner child you've never quite left behind.

Learn to Identify and Stay with (Even Painful) Feelings

While some other personality types might see Entertainers as glib, superficial, slippery, with too many quick answers and fast-changing schemes, this clearly is not the whole picture. For example, Larry shared with us that he has fun, is inventive and interactive, enjoys his children, yet he's aware of his flaws and foibles and is almost overly conscious of the pain that life may bring his daughters.

160

At base many of the positive characteristics of the Entertainer mask a flight from fear. Emotional and psychic pain arouse the greatest fear—they're avoided whenever possible. By being upbeat, talkative and bright, intellectual and rational, Entertainers avoid what is painful. There's a fear that if they go too deeply into one area, they will be found lacking, which is painful, so they become fascinated by many ideas and interests. The same dynamic is at work with commitment: they fear commitment and the pain it may bring so they seek options and no limits. Ironically, many Entertainers don't know they're limiting themselves in not being open to emotional commitment that is both joyful and *painful.* There's strong motivation for emotions to be filtered and processed intellectually.

This Entertainer cites a poignant circumstance when she knew she was keeping pain at bay through an intense effort to intellectualize death: "When my son's best friend died in an accident, I was at sea about how to approach his mother, his family. My son was crying and grieving, and I went to this devastated mother and spoke on an intellectual level about death rituals. To me the event was experienced on an intellectual plane as an interesting conversation about rites. I want to alleviate the pain for everyone else instead of feeling it for myself. I don't have the words to talk about my emotions that other people do. It's one of the reasons I get into the interesting, intellectual aspects of whatever sad thing is happening."

ACTION: *Try to identify your feelings, learn to name them.* See if you can pinpoint times when you feel a disconnection from your family, from your children, from the losses life brings, from the longing in your life for the nonmaterial things you don't have and that you want, but feel that it's too painful even to think about them. Think about them. Try to feel the emotion associated with them. Work particularly with anything to do with the feeling of loss or of what's lost. Try to enter the emotions surrounding the things you regret doing or saying in your life. This is the pain you avoid. Getting acquainted with your pain will make you a more rounded, more understanding parent. Like other Entertainers who are so good at pushing down on pain, you may find that your personal growth might not begin until you start experiencing what pain feels like. Become aware of the degree of difficulty you have finding your way into the world of emotional experience.

Notice When You're Putting a Positive Spin on Reality

Entertainers' worldview is not simply a question of saying this is true and that isn't or yes, the world is a terrible place, yes, the world is a wonderful place. They pay attention to a certain aspect of that reality, but in their heads they imbue it with the possibility that at a future time they or someone else will conceive a brilliant plan to interconnect truth and untruth, terror and wonder. In the meantime it makes sense to reframe reality to reflect the possibilities of this perfect future. Reframing can be denial, rationalization, or thinking things out in a way that isn't an honest or reliable reflection of reality—not to be deliberately deceitful but to hold on to the glorious possibilities that are inherently present. For instance, Entertainer parents won't say an interaction or an altercation is painful, they'll say it's interesting. They'll instinctively put on a positive spin; even if it was an awful experience, they'll reframe the negative to give it a more positive view.

ACTION: *Notice when you're putting a positive spin on reality.* If you're reframing more than usual, you may want to ask yourself if something painful is going on with you or your children. It's your escape hatch to deal with pain. Be aware that the way you reframe may look to others as simple denial: "Oh, well, that didn't happen like that." Or "It was a learning experience. Now I can move on."

Be aware that passing through painful situations honestly can be a positive experience. Maybe you couldn't have become the good parent you are today unless you experienced that pain. Often experiences may not take place the way you would prefer, but when you're through them, you have reserves of experience to draw on for the future. Think of it as a positive option to incorporate past experience.

Get Out of Your Head and Ground Your Vision

In many ways the Entertainer energy feeds on itself, so there is a constant need to replenish a high level of excitement: intellectual and emotional interests, other stimuli. This state of mind can be described as overindulgence, a desire to sample the positive opportunities life offers without any limits. As this Entertainer mother reports, she can be uncomfortable in situations where she feels limited: "I think sometimes I can probably be overwhelming to my kids, because I'll abandon one plan and try another one before we've exhausted the possibilities of the first or understood what I was trying to get at with that plan. If I don't like something, I'll try something else. I don't linger too long on any one thing. If I'm arguing with my daughter and the suggestions that I give her don't work, I'll find some other approach. That's such a natural place for me to be. I'm never wedded to one thing so much that I can't abandon it and do something else if the first doesn't happen to be working. Even if it's working well, I might do something else that doesn't work quite as well, because it seems more interesting to me."

ACTION: *You need to be far more concrete with your children.* As a parent you spend a lot of your life planning, thinking through unrealized ideas. You need to knuckle down to a committed practice of bringing projects to a conclusion for your family. You'll feel enormous satisfaction in the visible, concrete public manifestation of your vision. Let your children be a grounding force to get you out of your head and into action. Otherwise your free-floating mind-set, like a helium balloon without a string, may lead to negative consequences.

Try Not to Make Your Family Plan the Rule

We have seen why the Entertainer strategy directs this personality to having many options, but there is an equal drive toward planning. Many Entertainers use the words "fluid" or "fluidity" to describe the way their minds work. The planning patterns are like individual drops of water in a stream: there is fluidity of movement; the drops are picked up by other drops and become larger and larger units of themselves. The drops fuse into the greater whole. Those smaller elements may be fascinating daydreams, intricate thoughts, futuristic ideas—all parts of planning. What may look to others as evidence of scattered thinking are, to the Entertainer, coherent elements of a mental stream out of which plans cohere. Listen to this Entertainer parent: "My parenting is fluid. When I sit down to plan a family event, I see it as flexible, pliable as plastic wrap constructed around an idea. I usually remain true to the central idea. But we can drop other things into it. I consider suggestions from my children to take us in some other direction. I try to help them make connections and see patterns—that's the way my mind works. I love to make connections; I think my kids do, too."

Entertainers pay attention through planning. They have a fascination with ideas: "I always have a handful of interesting ideas that change the way I see my children, the way I'm trying to get through to them, the way I frame a problem."

Eventually a few ideas will settle, and a pattern forms. Entertainers love interconnections, creating patterns with ideas: "I think that information doesn't have meaning except when you make a pattern of it."

ACTION: *Try not to make your patterns of and plans the rule for your children. Different personalities have different ways of thinking about and processing the world.* Be aware that you may experience frustration with those of your children who think in a concrete, detailed way—the children who prefer facts to ideas, reality to fantasy. They don't easily see the patterns you value so highly. Try to enter their world, the way they think, try to see things their way. You may find this fascinating. Remember, some children are fearful of change. They want to do the same things over and over because it's safer to do so. Learn to curb your impatience with them. Try not to entice them to take risks—they may judge *you* as flaky, unreliable. Remember to be physically demonstrative with your children and *show* them your love. They cannot read your mind, be in your head, to realize your love is present. Demonstrate love and emotions.

Slow Your Racing Mind in Family Interactions

The Entertainer mind works so fast that it can trip over itself. There are many circuits running at the same time. One Entertainer described how, in a workshop, she followed a guided visualization: "Everyone had to close their eyes and imagine an empty house. We were to decorate and furnish, walk through the house and visualize each room, the color, the shape. After I'd been sitting for thirty minutes, I'd finished, fitted, furnished, lived in three houses in different parts of the country while the group leader and everyone else were still working on that same house."

This feature of racing mind is generally regarded by Entertainers as a huge plus. They gain great pleasure from their ability to think fast along different tracks. But they're aware also of a downside. An Entertainer parent: "My mind moves rapidly. I'm comfortable with that, but I know I'm too fast for lots of people, including my children at times. I assume they can follow, or that it's as interesting to them as it is to me to go off on tangents. I've had to teach them how to give me feedback. I can have at least three different tracks in my mind at once, literally have mental conversations with people while I'm thinking of something else.

So I've taught my husband and children to verify appointments with me and such. If it's something important they must ask, 'Mom are you there? Now, repeat it back: you're picking me up at three from soccer today.' It's pathetic, but they've learned they can be left high and dry, so they must not to assume I heard them."

ACTION: *Remember that often you fail to share with others the associative leaps between ideas that your mind takes.* This sometimes puts your family at a loss to understand your elliptical thinking. You get so caught up in your own mental energy that you tend to leave your children and others behind. Ask them to tell you when this is happening. Some children feel insecure when you jettison one plan, seemingly without a moment's thought, for another. It doesn't feel safe for them. On the other hand, there can be no parent as exhilarating to children as an Entertainer, because nothing will ever be the same way twice.

Try to Stay in the Present

Although it's difficult for them, Entertainer parents *can* quiet their minds, focus, be present in the moment, pay undivided attention to their children. This relative sobriety (contrasted to their default mental mode of the headiness, of being among future plans and options) is perhaps the most valuable gift they can give their children.

ACTION: *Try not to become resentful or impatient.* Much activity related to parenting is repetitive and mundane. If you shift your mind-set, parenting can provide you with many opportunities for fun. Above all, try to stay present and in the moment, to appreciate what you're experiencing. What can be more important than honoring your child with fully focused attention while he tells you something or shares his dreams or fears? Fun for you is in new interests, new mental challenges, living in the future, not being dragged down in mundane matters of the present. Let your children motivate new challenges for you as they develop and mature. Find fun in turning an area of inexperience (dealing with a teenager when your eldest child turns thirteen) into a challenge. You know that if you're not challenged, you don't want to stay present.

Parenting Steps for Entertainers

- Your perpetually upbeat energy may be jarring to your children, out of sync with their needs. Be skillful in how you use it. For instance, encourage others with your optimism and energy; don't overwhelm them. Support your family through your buoyancy and enthusiasm.

- Your preference is to equalize authority. Your children need an authority figure. Learn to role-model benevolent authority for them, however counterintuitive it feels. Continually work with issues of boundaries and limits. Be an authority figure to yourself. Develop the self-discipline to meet deadlines and see a process through. Sometimes your sense of entitlement causes you to ignore or belittle others. This can be devastating to your children.

- Parenting places limits and constraints on your time and options. Find ways to make mundane parenting tasks interesting, so you see them through. Here's where your imaginative and creative gifts can free you to enjoy your time with your children. Ground yourself and be present in the proceedings of the moment. Notice when you've escaped into a future fantasy world.

- Don't avoid painful emotions and situations. Getting acquainted with your pain will make you a more rounded, more understanding parent. Ask for help from your family to be in touch with your emotions. Practice saying, "This is what I'm feeling," not "This is what I'm thinking."

- Know when you're reframing facts—get a reality check. If you're reframing more than usual, you may want to ask yourself if something painful is going on with you or your children. It's your escape hatch to deal with pain.

- Get out of your head and ground your vision. Make use of your energy through structuring ideas into tasks and interesting, diverse projects for your family.

- Planning is your forte. Once you have the plan, commit yourself to a course of action as well. Be aware of when planning and fantasizing replace doing. Slow your racing mind and stay in the present. Be respectful of your children. Give them your full attention and be present in each moment. Find a safe place to bounce around the many ideas racing in your mind, without impinging on the boundaries of others (by monopolizing their time and energy). Be physically demonstrative in expressing your love to your children.

- Be aware that you try to keep your options open. Make yourself accountable. Don't try to slip through the cracks.

- Parenting can be fun. This is a lifelong commitment, so make it an adventure for yourself and your family. Support your children's dreams and imaginings. Find fascination in their development into independent adults.

SUMMARY: THE ENTERTAINER PARENT

Positives to Build On	*Negatives to Overcome*
Optimism and upbeat attitude	Trouble with commitment, seeks other options
Entertaining storyteller	Escapes from difficult personal interactions
Plans, visions, dreams	
Multioptional thinker	Evasive, skates over the hard parts
Upbeat energy and fun	Feels immune to others' pain and conflict
Egalitarian	
Renaissance thinker	Addicted to change for change's sake
Interconnective conceptual ability	Feels entitled by own mental gifts
Sparks energy and excitement	Tends to live in a future fantasy world of many options
	Overly creative imagination, charms and disarms, smooth talker
	Avoids (emotional and mental) pain

CHAPTER 8

The Protector

I Am Your Sanctuary:
Nothing Threatens You Here

Brad—Larger Than Life

Brad was an unmistakable presence. When he walked into a room, he seemed to take up a good deal of space. This had little to do with his physical stature, and much with the forcefulness of his personality. Brad understood his strength of character: "When I'm behind something, I'm a force—energetic, loud, certainly pushy, and maybe obnoxious, but I'm present, a hundred and ten percent. If I don't believe in something, I can't pretend. I have no interest in putting energy into something that is not meaningful to me."

Brad's family held a good deal of meaning for him. He loved them fiercely, protectively. He took on the role of guardian, first to his wife, but then especially to his children. He delighted in his three daughters. When they were little, their vulnerability touched him deeply; he knew he was capable of tearing the world asunder if anything happened to them.

The force of his conviction regarding this response registered firmly with him. He would exert all the control he could on the circumstances of their lives so he wouldn't have to do what he was fully prepared to do if need be; he'd be a buffer between his children and the dangers of the troubled world.

The girls' laughter, their trust in him, their joy of discovery, the disarming way their small hands nestled so innocently in his own—he felt his love for them as a fiery energy in his belly. Sometimes this feeling was so strong it choked him. Each child in her own way managed to penetrate his usual barrier of combative defensiveness; he took care of them with loving protection. Brad did not want to be held accountable for tainting their innocence, destroying their vulnerability with his natural bent to confrontation. This behavior was different from his usual mode of operation, but it was also a way of loving his babies that seemed quite natural to him.

His children's vulnerability, their lack of defenses, struck a basic chord in Brad. Being vulnerable was an intrinsic part of their childhood, but for him it was an Achilles' heel, an area approached only with great caution. (There were few people with whom he would let down his guard enough to let himself be vulnerable.) When he felt secure, he did open up to others; he showed that he was needy, hungry for affection and understanding, often teary-eyed, emotional, and sentimental. Like other Protectors, Brad *knew* that the world was a threatening place, that he'd be jumped if he were dumb enough not to protect himself. Opening up to his daughters' love was a joy: "I'm much more unguarded with them, I can let out the tenderness I never knew was in me."

Brad was not a pushover as a parent. An inherent part of protecting his children was to teach them a sense of the rules of the game of life. The first rule was to establish who was in control; if it couldn't be you, you'd do well to find out if the authority was fair and just. Protectors establish rules, tangible evidence of their power and control, but often the rules are there for others to follow, not for themselves. Brad held the line with his children: "You come when I call, or else there'll be consequences. Such as I'll leave without you." Or "You won't get to eat dinner. But don't question me if I'm late." Or "You can't use swear words around the house, but it's okay if I do."

Sometimes Brad was deliberately provocative. He wanted his children to learn to stand firm and hold their ground. From the Protector perspective this question always arises: "If you can't or won't stand up for yourself, how can I trust you to stand up for me?"

If in the moment when Protectors choose to mount their challenge, one can meet it, this stand will earn their respect. As they grew older, Brad's daughters learned how to deflect and parry his provocation and confrontations; they were secure in his love. He was a warm, dependable presence. Protectors have an innate ability to take charge and make sure that all those harbored safely around them have what they need and are where they need to be.

Brad's high energy powered his interactive parenting. For instance, on any given Saturday he would manage to attend all three of his daughters' sports activities, often driving long distances to do so. As they grew older, they had mixed feelings about his presence at their practices and games; they liked having him there for support but disliked his loud commentary from the sidelines and his fairly regular run-ins with other parents, coaches, refs, and umpires. *They* (the girls) knew that this was just part of his personality and that he was only expressing his opinion—he didn't mean to be pushy or rude—but other people shied away from him or felt embarrassed by encounters with him.

On that same Saturday he'd also run errands for his wife, do chores around the yard, work out at the gym, help set up a dinner party, and be a lively and entertaining host through the evening. His daughters, like many people caught up in his presence, learned to draw a good deal of their energy from his overabundant supply.

Protectors have a gift for harnessing their energy to empower those they love and care for, those they consider to fall within their territory. There can be few more empowering personalities than people who have their energetic strength under control. Another way to understand this personality is to liken the Protector to a crashing wave, always moving forward onto the beach. The forward momentum is positive; it helps to keep others in motion. But it can be overwhelming and sweep people away. This momentum is different from that of other powerful personalities; for instance, the implosive power of the passive-aggressive stance of the Peacekeeper, or the retracted power of the Observer. Both the latter are as forceful as the Protector, but they drain energy negatively out of situations, while Protectors share their gift of positive energy with others. Brad's daughters have learned to rely on his larger-than-life presence.

When the children were young adolescents, the family went on a ski trip. One afternoon Brad watched a group of boys playing with bicycles on the slippery, snow-covered road at the condos where they were staying. They were having so much fun that he couldn't restrain himself from joining them. His wife and daughters watched from the window as he engaged the boys, commandeered a bicycle, and disappeared down the frozen road. He was way too big for the bike, and he soon lost control of it on the ice. He crashed into a tree and landed in a six-foot pile of snow. He suffered a broken collarbone and a severely sprained ankle. But when his family reached him, he was grinning with enthusiasm at his helter-skelter ride down the hill.

Rose—the Freedom to Do It My Way

Rose was a rebel growing up. She remembered her mother's phrases, repeated endlessly: "You're giving me gray hair." "You're driving me to an early grave." "You'll be the death of me." Rose resisted these castigations, because she knew she wasn't responsible for her mother's responses; she was simply living her life the only way she knew how: to the max.

Rose was thrown out of kindergarten, a rare feat. The pattern

continued, as Rose explains: "Unfortunately, I wasn't quick to figure out that you did what the teacher wanted, so I got thrown out
right through high school. Along the way, in grade school, I tried
to burn down the whole place. Of course that stayed on my
record—'troublemaker.' There were a few good guys, teachers
who made a difference. But it wasn't until college that I figured out
a way to be successful as a student."

She was hyperactive. She hated being told she was in the
wrong, because she *knew* she was right. Rose simply didn't have
trust in authority figures at school (or at home), so she didn't listen to them. She believed in her own power: "I might not have the
power to get the teacher to like me or my mother not to fight with
me, but I have the power to be the way I need to be." Rose ran
with a fast crowd, other kids who liked to live on the edge. After
high school she drifted from place to place, from casual job to
casual job, until she got bored and decided to try some courses at
a community college.

In college Rose could create her own curriculum. After the first
six months she was on the dean's list and had won a full scholar-
ship, and years later graduated second in her class from her mas-
ter's program, primarily because she had the freedom to do it her
way. She also got pregnant around the same time. And as she
didn't particularly like the baby's father, she decided to become a
single mother.

When Rose held her baby daughter in her arms for the first
time, she felt such a rush of protective love that she knew she'd
been waiting all along for this person to share her life: "It's you
and me, kiddo, for life. Nothing comes between you and me."

Rose became a social worker who specialized in working with
parolees. She'd been given second and third chances in her life,
and she wanted to help others fight for another chance for themselves. She chose tough neighborhoods to live in, because she
believed that you had to walk the walk; there was no way she
could work in halfway houses with ex-cons during the day and
retire to the suburbs at night. Besides, Rose loved the excitement

of an urban environment; the pulse of energy and danger in the air made her feel on high alert, truly alive. When her mother protested that it was too dangerous for her to visit her granddaughter, that for the child's sake she should move, Rose's heartfelt response was that life in the suburbs for them would be a slow death. But she did make an effort to bring the little girl often to visit her grandparents. As Rose grew older, she saw her mother through more compassionate eyes, no longer the symbolic authority figure she'd spent her first eighteen years pushing up against.

Anyway, why should they move when her daughter thrived in their city neighborhood? She was always able to find children to play with on the street. And Rose was protectively vigilant behind her nonchalant demeanor. She made sure that her daughter and the other neighborhood children had a strong support system, conscientious eyes to watch over them. She organized the neighborhood parents into care groups, and together they developed a high degree of communal responsibility. If something happened to any one child, in any family, the neighborhood rallied to that child's aid. The local police chief was sympathetic and lent his support to Rose's efforts.

Rose's battles started in earnest once her daughter enrolled in school. It was simply not fair or just, she believed, that "her" neighborhood children put up with an education inferior to that of their suburban peers. Armed with vigor and passion and most often with her daughter and a couple of other moms and their kids in tow, Rose began a relentless reform campaign aimed at the school board.

Protectors need a large theater of operation—they're territorial—and Rose's neighborhood became *her* neighborhood, the children *her* children. Protectors are gifted in their ability to be protective of those who form part of their territory. Rose could yell at a neglectful mother or a negligent child, but then she'd go to bat for them when the need arose.

Like the animosity of other Protectors, Rose's anger could often come across as abusive. Confrontation was not frightening to her; she used it as a way of stirring up others. Often she pushed too far and then realized that she had to engage in damage control. Not with her daughter, though. With the child Rose was a firm, gentle, patient, compassionate mother, capable of expressing profound tenderness and love. Her daughter flourished in her mother's warmth and devotion. She knew a side of Rose not many other people ever saw, for Rose relished her tough-woman persona.

As confrontation didn't scare Rose, it was hard for her to understand how she could devastate a whole roomful of school-board officials with her anger. She was used to feeling excesses of energy, belly energy available to her in a split second. She never counted to ten before moving into action or speaking out—she seldom counted to one! The react response was combative and almost involuntary.

Rose's great motivational drive on behalf of both the parolees she worked with and her daughter and her daughter's peers was her demand for justice. Like Perfectionists, Protectors have a moral sense of right and wrong, but in their case it's based on what's fair, not on avoiding error. Situations, decisions, issues are either just or unjust; there is no middle ground. Fairness for what's right is a passion. Rose was not angry with anybody in the room. Her passion was directed at the board's policies. But the board members found it hard to regroup after her outbursts. The charge of energy was still present, as well as the ruffled feathers.

It is critically important to remember that Protectors are passionate about a cause or an idea; their anger is usually not directed personally. They're defending a belief system or what's fair—or perceived of as fair by the Protector. But when someone is standing six inches from your face and bellowing at you, it can be hard to remember this. Rose knew that the bull-in-the-china-shop effect was something she needed to work on; finesse in presenting an argument would be helpful.

Like other Protectors, Rose saw the world as she believed it should be—and she believed fervently that all children *should* have equal educational opportunities. Neither illness, weakness, disappointment, nor setbacks would stop her juggernaut energy and passion. She always simply assumed that her sheer power of will would carry the day.

Ten years later Rose and her committee of neighborhood parents for educational reform could point to a number of successes in improved local schooling. In her very early years her daughter, besides her formal education, had received an education in how to organize others, persevere, conduct local politics, and have fun while being so involved. She was proud that Rose was her mother.

Rose married the local police chief when her daughter was six. A year later father, mother, and daughter welcomed a baby boy into their circle of love.

PERSONAL ACCOUNT

Donna, a stepmother of four children, gives this account

I like the nurturing and support that I'm able to give, emotionally, intellectually, and spiritually, and then seeing and experiencing the development of independent, strong, caring younger adults. I can look at my stepchildren in their careers, relationships, and parenting and feel good that I contributed to their becoming people I'm proud of. I've always enjoyed being able to laugh and play with the children, and now with the young adults. Also, I like that my children push me (although usually after the fact) to come up against my edges and the personal areas where I need to grow and go beyond my limiting beliefs and rigidities.

When they were younger, I disliked setting and maintaining limits and enforcing rules. At times I also disliked the strength and forthrightness I embodied, coming right back at me. Some of the lessons that I've needed to learn the most have come from having my personality limitations staring me in the face. I also disliked the infringement upon my time and space, my privacy. I wanted them to respect my space and needs, as I attempted to do with them; often it felt like I was fighting a losing battle.

Some of this was due to my being the "stepmother." This is a large part of what I disliked about parenting: being a step-mother with different standards, expectations, and philoso-phies about parenting from their biological mother.

I'm a direct person; they know where I stand about most issues. I don't stay mad or hold grudges, so I'm soon available to listen and understand where they're coming from. If, after I've thought over a situation, I see that I'm wrong or that I've meted out too heavy a consequence, I'm comfortable in admitting this to the child involved and altering my earlier decision.

For instance, I had discussed the problems of underage drinking (perhaps ad nauseam) with the son who lived with us; if he was caught, he had already chosen the consequences because he knew he was breaking the law and our standards. One cold winter night the parents of a group of boys near us called and asked if he could spend the night, as they were cel-ebrating their eighteen-year-old's birthday. The next morning we were sitting at the table, and he came in, mumbled good morning, and went downstairs. The next thing I knew the washer was going. He seemed somewhat sullen and then looked at us with a funny grin and said, "If I drink too much again, I'll know just what consequences I'm choosing." We asked what other consequences, and he suggested grounding. We thought that being sick for two days and recognizing his folly was punishment enough. He didn't drink alcohol again until he was in his early twenties.

My most glaring weakness is being quick to anger and at times too protective of the children from other people's criti-cism. I can also be judgmental and think that I have the truth in a situation, forgetting that I have only my perspective and can also learn from them.

For example, when two of the kids were about eleven and thirteen, they were drying dishes after lunch. I was having a bad day and told the kids that I was upset about things that had nothing to do with them. They began to snap dish towels at one another while one was drying some expensive glasses. After I'd told them several times to stop and gotten angrier each time, one of the glasses broke. I lost it and yelled loudly, threatened to ground them for the rest of the day, insisting that they would have to pay for the glass. My anger and tone were quite unreasonable, and I remember the fear on their faces. I froze, and when I got control of myself again, I apologized, but it was already too late to undo the fear I had instilled. When the eleven-year-old was twenty-four and in therapy, she told me how much the incident had frightened her. Of course, because of her fear, she doesn't remember my apology and remorse; the damage was done.

My children know that they can count on me when they need me: emotionally, physically, or financially. Also the two boys have thanked me for "putting up with all of their high jinks and anger and not turning my back on them." They've all said they know how much I love them and that when I've disapproved of their choices or behaviors, I wasn't withholding love. They say that I was too quick to anger, an observation I agree with. Also that I could be unbending or rigid about decisions that I'd made about their responsibility; at times I expected too much from them.

Be there for your children, be aware of the subtle cues, ask questions from love and curiosity. Be a parent, a responsible role model for them, not primarily a friend. Tell them you love them with words and with behavior. Support their strengths and encourage their natural curiosity, playfulness, and growth into conscientious, caring human beings. ❧

The Best Strategy and Action Program for Protectors

Protective Empowerment

Protectors are forceful, influential parents when they harness their gifts of energy, vision, and leadership for the empowerment of their families. They're excellent motivators. They like to set up family rules that suit their own style. Protector parents feel empowered themselves when their children respond to their energy. But the obverse is also true: they feel challenged when their children defy or ignore their well-intentioned guidelines and procedures.

ACTION: *Be careful not to fudge the line between control and protective empowerment.* Be aware that the way you structure your authority may be too rigid for some of your children, especially as they grow older. Allow for their input into how the cogs of the family wheels should move. Encourage innovation and alternative ways to perceive and do things. You are able to sense shifts of energy in your body; you like to push at the edges. Empower your children in the same way. Learn what they want to become, how they see themselves. Let them unfold and develop in a way that is inherently their own.

Don't Discomfort Your Children

Protectors chafe under the illusion that life itself is an authority. Since they're motivated by their defense mechanisms to root out threats, there is a constant testing of limits that may result in excessive behavior. Protectors lock horns with life, with authority (in its myriad forms) in order to establish who has control and if that person will be fair—in other words, if the Protector and his or her family are safe. Protectors don't want to be controlled: "Don't let down your guard, don't trust easily, don't show any vulnerability—

otherwise you're a deluded fool, and threats will manifest themselves like self-fulfilling prophecies. You'll be controlled, and you and your family deserve whatever is coming to you."

The following Protector enlightens us on the inner workings of this dynamic. She accurately states how authority is acceptable if she shares the same values as the authority; otherwise she assumes her confrontation mode: "If the values and the ideas of the authority are not in sync with me, I have a difficult time. I will continually confront the authority in hopes that it will change. This has been a downfall for me all my life, because I realize that some authority, no matter what it is, isn't going to change; it's going to stay the way it is. Rather than asking it to change—tilting at windmills—what's important for me is to find a place where I fit, where my children can fit, so I'm not hitting up against authority all the time."

ACTION: *Be aware that you may be imposing your worldview on your children.* Many personalities shy away from confrontation, while others accommodate to authority. You feel that you are protecting them with your vigilance and challenge to authority, but in fact you may be making them uncomfortable, even embarrassed, by your behavior. Try to learn to see the world through other viewfinders in addition to your own. Ask your children how they perceive situations, and let them teach you.

Try to Find Ambiguity

Protectors tend to paint the world black or white. A Protector mother reports, "I went to a parent/teacher meeting for my youngest child. Her midterm report did not have good enough grades, but all through the meeting the teacher smiled at me and told me how well my daughter was doing. I was getting a mixed message, so I pulled out the report card and said, 'You're not working honestly with me or my daughter. Here's her report card, and you're giving me information that contradicts what's written here.' She proceeded to tell me she was being 'diplomatic'—in other words, lying. She said she didn't want to hurt my feelings or discourage my daughter, but there were all kinds of learning problems. I said, 'I don't accept that. She's never had problems before. There's only one problem here—you. You don't know how to be truthful.' She got defensive. I asked her to bring in her principal, and I told him what was going on. They ended up firing her. To me that was perfectly appropriate; she was not doing her job with honesty. In life either you're doing your job truthfully or you're not. It's not my fault. It's your problem, your choice. To me that's pretty simple."

ACTION: *Be aware that you can come across as overzealous and vindictive, as in the above example.* The outcome of your actions may be appropriate, but you can come off smelling bad. Make an effort to see ambiguity in the world. Everything seems so clear-cut to you, but you may be missing many subtleties and nuances, many important shadings of gray. Think of alternative ways you might have handled the above scenario and others like it.

You are passionate around issues of truth. You know immediately when people are lying to you, people who try to smooth the waters, find subtler ways to deliver their news, be diplomatic—all these forms of expression raise your level of suspicion. Let your family know this. Try to teach them that they should be direct and straightforward in dealing with you. Explain why you don't do well with ambiguity: you don't want to have anything to do with hidden agendas. Nonetheless be willing to try to learn about subtleties and ambiguities.

Try to Be Less Blunt, Not Less Truthful

This Protector father reports that he welcomes feedback and can adjust his behavior when the results of his style are pointed out to him. He sheds light on how to get Protectors on board—don't tell them they're wrong, tell them of someone else's need: "You can always turn me around if you point out your own or someone else's vulnerability, rather than trying to power back at me. If you say to me, like my wife does about our eldest son, 'He needs to express himself, and he doesn't get the opportunity because of how forceful you are. I'm wondering if there's any other way you can be with him?' I will hear that message. If you try to put me in the wrong, I'm going to come right back at you. But if you go to my protective side, I'll hear the need. Of course I'm interested in my son's needs and in having him come forward, too."

ACTION: *Don't wait to be told of how your force and power are adversely affecting relationships, especially those you care about the most.* Learn to observe your behavior and the effect it's having on others. Listen to your words and reflect on whether there's a less direct or blunt way to express yourself. I'm not asking you to be less honest or truthful, but to try to find another way to say the same thing.

Carry Your Share of Responsibility, Even Blame

Protectors blame others for personal setbacks. It's part of their personality strategy that directs them to always appear powerful and forceful, to ignore limiting factors that will take away from that stance. Protectors deny their own deficiencies or their own role in an argument in order to protect the space their self-defenses have created for them to appear strong in the world. Obviously this can have repercussions in parenting situations when the logistics of an arrangement go awry or the Protector parent won't take responsibility for his or her part in an argument or clash within the family.

This Protector highlights an interesting take on blaming others to get herself off the hook: "People say to me, 'Well, you intimidate me.' Actually I'm not doing anything to you. I can't intimidate you—you're letting yourself be intimidated. I've learned to get over that behavior a little, because it might not win me friends. But that's how I feel: why are you being a wimp? I don't like wimps. Wimps are wishy-washy. It's one of the worst names I can call you. I would rather you came at me with your own energy. Then I'll respect you. If you wimp out, I won't even want to annihilate you—I'll dismiss you like a little fly: 'Go away.' You've got to meet my energy. There's the wimp and there's the under-dog. They're two different things. Underdogs are people who need my help (like all little children), and I'll do anything for them, I will. But the wimp is someone who has no backbone. There's a dis-tinction: whereas the underdog needs help, a wimp is just a wimp."

While it's essentially true that the recipients of Protector anger and confrontation are allowing themselves to be intimidated, Pro-tectors aren't blameless in their habit of going after people. All relationships are two-way streets. Each person has to shoulder responsibility for the conduct of the interaction.

ACTION: *Be aware that when you're angry, confrontational, and blaming others, you may be in denial about your own role in whatever it is you're angry about.* Like the previous Protector, you tend to be dismissive of others, even those closest to you. Remember that when you're pointing one finger of blame at someone, three fingers are pointing back at you. Whenever this feeling comes up, try to examine your role in the situation. The more you deny your responsibility, the more you may regard your partner, children, or others as wimps. Think about the fact that *you* may be a wimp for not carrying your share of responsibility, even blame. While your anger release may feel good to you, it can feel abusive, even annihilating, to the recipients. You do tremen-dous damage to your parenting relationships in inflicting your anger on your children. Try to *protect* them from your anger rather than dumping on them. Remember, there are many different ways people handle difficult situations. Get a reality check about your own behavior.

Learn to Contain Your Energy

A lust for life is characteristic of Protectors; more is never enough. Protectors are aware of their energy as a high-voltage charge. They're constantly seeking ways of release: food, drugs, sex, sports, play, work, laughter, troublemaking, and so on. A Protector father tells us, "I have such energy it can drive everybody crazy. I notice at home I'm moving all the time, I can't stay still. My wife says, 'Where are you? What are you doing?' There's just so much energy. I tell you, I feel like I have to get right out of my skin—I can't sit any longer. As far as being with my children, I have to be aware of my energy, because my energy is big, overwhelming. People say they feel me coming before I enter a room, and I believe them. I feel energy in my body strongly. It can be a problem sometimes. I'm intense with my children. They complain that I never give them any downtime. My thinking is that we've only got one life to live—let's live it. It's my obligation as a parent to get as much done as we can together, to give them as many experiences as I can."

ACTION: *Learn how to become quieter inside yourself.* This last father tells us he's aware that his energy may be overwhelming to his children, but he can't hold back on the intensity of his parenting interactions. If you learn to hold back, you give your partner, your children, and other people a sense of being able to *come toward you,* so that you *meet* their energy rather than push at it.

It's important that you work at building a container for your energy. You need to embody the idea of containment, of not allowing your energy to spill over and consume everyone and everything around you. Practice holding back rather than letting your energy overpower others. This way you'll allow space for your children's personalities to flourish in their own way and at their own pace.

Realize That Not Only Those Who Engage in Confrontation Are Trustworthy

Simply put, an intrinsic part of the Protector personality is to use confrontation as a strategy to flush out threats, to find safety zones. Confrontation is not scary to Protectors; it's a way of life. In any parenting situation, Protectors look forward to, even assume, that there's going to be confrontation. It doesn't disturb them that it's going to happen. In fact, they value it. They find people who stand up for themselves trustworthy. They encourage their children to be confrontational.

ACTION: *Reexamine your belief that only people who will confront you are worthy, more trustworthy than those who withdraw from you.* If one of your children is reserved or withdrawn and doesn't come toward you, your inclination may be to keep pushing at him to try to provoke a response. *This may be entirely the wrong strategy to engage that child.*

Try to observe your behavior, how you are coming across, from that child's point of view. Ask him for input and help in how to interact. Open a dialogue, and be honest about your sense of frustration that you can't seem to get through to him. At first this may be difficult for you, because you're allowing yourself to be vulnerable. But it may be an interesting learning process for both of you.

Count to Ten

For Protectors, anger is tied in to their passionate belief in truth telling: "I speak directly, don't mince words, let others feel the full force of my truth." When Protectors see the effect of their anger, they're often remorseful. This perception is echoed by another Protector mother: "I think my anger is often read by my children as harsh. Actually they are correct—it is. There were times when I should not have gone to where I did with them. I get too carried away emotionally. Also I don't realize that for most people, including my children, confrontation is a problem, because for me it's not. It's not meant to be. When I'm angry, confrontational, it's because I'm defending what I believe, not because I want to hurt any person, especially not those closest to me. Yet I can come across sometimes as hurtful, even to my own children. So I say I'm sorry—too often."

ACTION: *Instead of learning to say you're sorry, why not learn to count to ten before you lash out?* Often in dealing with children the subliminal damage is already done. It's too late to mend fences even if you apologize. When you're a parent, dealing with the developing personalities of children and adolescents, your direct anger can be damaging—their emerging egos are fragile. It's imperative that you teach your children to tell you when they think you are going overboard with your passion. Learn to stop and consider what they are telling you. Asking for a time-out, pausing to regroup (go hit a punching bag), or reflecting on the situation may save you from being involved in constant damage control.

Rachet Down Your Delight in Revenge

Plotting and executing revenge ties in with the Protector defense mechanism of being strong and infallible in the eyes of the world. If, from the Protector's point of view, someone has let her down, bettered her, caught her off guard, taken advantage of her, and she plots revenge, she can keep the dynamic going *in her own mind,* she *can* have the last word. Most often revenge is played out internally, and even partners and children are not exempt. This Protector father reported, "I told my wife, my children, 'Never go behind my back. If you have an issue, come to me, and we'll settle it.' One time my wife did something that involved the family without telling me. I was angry at her for three months—*three months*—we barely spoke for three months. All the time she's asking me, 'What's wrong with you?' but I cut her off. I wouldn't go along with her efforts to end the standoff till much later."

ACTION: *Realize that if you don't feel appreciated, or if you feel betrayed, or if you sense you're not being heard or listened to, your energy can go underground in a way that's undermining and damaging.* Your energy goes into bringing down the person who has made you feel unappreciated. Before the situation reaches a point where things are untenable, take some time to see if you're not overreacting or if perhaps *you* have played a role in setting up the standoff. Are you plotting and executing revenge because you enjoy it or because you believe you have legitimate reasons? Remember that it's hard for you to forget a slight or a betrayal—again it goes back to the justice issue. Practice taking energy away from the affront. Maybe you're keeping it alive because you relish a sense of being vengeful. Don't taint family relationships without legitimate cause. Talk to the people involved. Reality checks can be useful.

Trust Your Intuition

Protectors fall into the instinctual triad. Like the other members of this triad—the Peacekeepers, who are able to "feel into" their children's needs, or Moralizers, who say, "I can't explain it, it's all sensing and feeling. It's reliable"—Protectors have an intuitive ability, too. Protectors speak of how they can "sense what the other person needs." This Protector mother knows instinctively what will work with her children: "As far as my parenting style is concerned, I think it's intuitive. Sometimes I take a risk and try something, and it will work. Usually I sense what my children need, and I try to see what it is that excites them, what it is they want from me, and how they want it. As an example, I used to teach my son in a home-schooling setup. I didn't trust he'd get the right guidance elsewhere. We made a bargain: if he worked hard in the mornings at the basic skills, he could choose whatever learning experience he wanted for the afternoon. This worked well. I had a feeling *that* particular motivating ploy would work for him, and it did."

ACTION: *Learn to trust your intuition with your children; it's one of your gifts.* You'll be wrong some of the time, but most of the time you'll be right.

Be Aware of Burnout

Protectors can be hard on themselves. They forget the cost of continually putting out energy, often excessive energy, on behalf of others or of advocating for others. There is a cost in terms of their own well-being for their directness, forcefulness, confrontational encounters, dealing with other highly charged situations. They forget to take care of themselves, to allow time to recharge. Here is a report from a Protector father: "I hear a lot about abuse that I do to others, and I don't talk about the abuse I do to myself. I'm harder on myself than I could ever be about anybody else, and it's difficult. Even with all my energy, I will burn myself out. Now I've learned to actually block off time in the day, quiet times for me, because otherwise I will keep going until I drop, and I won't even know I was in that state of exhaustion. The pattern for me is always to go to self-abuse, always go to excess. I often feel sad. Part of the sadness I feel is for myself."

ACTION: *Learn to take care of yourself before you reach an abyss of self-abuse.* When everything is going well and you're in control of yourself, you're happy, your family is happy. When an unforeseen problem arises, you have enough energy in reserve so you can keep it in perspective and deal with it without running on empty and then fighting back overzealously. Learn to avoid those painful places and times when you're devoid of any energy.

Become aware that it's okay to sit back and be still, to learn the passive stance; patience has its own rewards. One of the hardest and greatest lessons for you to learn is patience. As a parent you tend to push, push, push, push, and with some children you can't do that—you'll roll over them. *You have to give them space to come toward you.* Try different techniques for yourself to learn how to create that space. You need to have energy in reserve for your children. Try not to expend yourself on other projects and then interact with your family while you're running on empty.

Adjust Your Energy to Your Child's Pace

Protectors are powerful parents and role models. We've discussed some of the disadvantages of their take-charge parenting style and overabundant energy. But, with some adjustments, both of these can be positive factors in parenting. Here's what a Protector parent has to say on her parenting style: "I think that what makes me effective as a parent is that I can describe and enroll my children in a vision of what we are as a family and what we can accomplish, and then not move in any other direction. Regardless of what happens, I'm still moving toward the vision with energy and enthusiasm, and I hope I'm bringing them with me. I've had to learn to temper my energy so I don't exhaust them along the way. I don't think I'd be half as good a parent as I know I am if I didn't learn some adjustments to my parenting style."

And this Protector parent who is also self-aware admits that her energy may be hard to take: "One of my strengths as a parent is that I'm willing to try anything if I think it will be of value to my family. I'll throw all my energy at it to prove whether it's valuable. I embroil my children in all these ventures, and I know that sometimes my energy is hard to take. So I've learned to ask them for feedback and to go at their pace. I'm also willing to accommodate the underdog—for instance, my youngest or the slowest child. In general, I'm willing to work with and support in any way I can a person who I feel has not been given an equal opportunity. You can always count on me in that regard."

ACTION: *Learn from the realizations articulated above by Protector parents. As they have done, practice how to temper your energy, ask for feedback from your children.* Perhaps find another pace and rhythm in which to operate, and so make a place for the underdog in your family to feel part of the adventure, instead of feeling dragged along.

Parenting Steps for Protectors

- Structure your authority so it's not too rigid and controlling. Allow for your children's input into the dynamic. Use your energy and take-charge leadership style to build and maintain the dynamic of family life and values you can all buy into. Together set up a framework of rules for your family life, and don't deviate from them. Make sure you also respect the rules.

- Your constant challenges to authority may discomfort your children. Be aware that your passion about your belief system can be intimidating to most other people. Encourage your children to come back at you when you violate their boundaries with excessive challenges. Otherwise you'll never know how they view the world.

- Make an effort to see ambiguity. Things are not all black-and-white justice issues. Be aware of when the instinct for revenge becomes powerful. Cut the intrigue—you can damage yourself and others. If you think someone in your family acted behind your back (betrayed you), ask before you start plotting revenge (whether you act on your revenge impulse or not). Constantly keep your family informed of your position.

- Try to be less blunt, not less truthful. Count to ten. There are many ways of saying the same thing. Learn to trust and be open and vulnerable, and you will find that others can approach you more easily, especially within your own family.

- Be aware that when you're blaming others, you're usually in denial of your own responsibility. When you point a finger at someone, three other fingers are pointing back at you. Be aware that your energy is overwhelming to most people. Structure a feedback process with your family to help you see when you're in the wrong, and then shoulder your part of the blame.

- Embody the idea of containment, of not allowing your energy to spill over and consume everyone and everything around you. More is often too much. Curtail your excesses in whatever form they take; don't you (and your family) be at their mercy. Often, when your all-or-nothing behavior becomes a compulsion, you're usually in denial about something that's on your mind.

- Not everyone has to operate the way you do in order to be trustworthy. Some of the quietest, least confrontational personalities are steady, reliable, and trustworthy. Try to develop patience and passivity; let your children come toward you. You'll learn more about them and receive more from them that way.

- Learn to trust your intuition with your children; it's one of your gifts. You'll be wrong some of the time, but most of the time you'll be right. Try to be a team player, and support the ideas of other people. Your leadership can be invaluable to them.

- Adjust your energy to your children's pace. Your presence looms larger than life, and that stance is attractive but also formidable. Your children are underdogs when it comes to interacting with your energy. Take opportunities to champion their growth and development.

SUMMARY: THE PROTECTOR PARENT

Positives to Build On	*Negatives to Overcome*
Take-charge leadership	Excessive behavior, can't maintain stability
Forges a path for others to follow	Authoritarian, controlling, rigid
Ability to confront	Blames others for own miscalculations
Directness	
Protective of underdogs	Denial of limitations, seen as weaknesses
Shares intimacy when it's "safe"	Damaging, direct anger, tests limits
Seeks justice and upholds truth	Keeps a lid on vulnerability, controls being hurt
Loyal to trusted people	Being vengeful wards off vulnerability and hurt
Empowers others, uses force on behalf of others	Extreme—no middle ground
	Lag time in acknowledging own feelings

CHAPTER 9

The Peacekeeper
Living Life through Others

Susan—Mother Earth

Susan was an attractive young woman, and she married a designer, but it could easily have been a farmer. The farmer didn't mind the extra weight she carried on her hips, the denims and T-shirts she enjoyed wearing, the beat-up Volkswagen she drove. But the designer wanted a showpiece wife—and she bought his agenda with equanimity. She haunted the weight-loss salon, the manicurist, the chic dress shops. She grew confident on stiletto heels, draped long silk scarves over her shoulders, loved the speedy convertible he bought her. Then the babies came, four babies in quick succession, and for the first time in her life Susan felt truly happy, truly herself: Mother Earth.

Those years passed in a wash of breast milk, laundry, home-baked bread, puppies. There were tears, tantrums, exhaustion, tenderness. There was nothing to plan, nothing to anticipate, simply living fully each day as it came, all her energy devoted to caring for her four lovely children and their dapper father. Susan never before felt that life had fitted her so well.

Summers found them at the home of his family in Maine. She stayed for two months with the children and dogs and clutter; he came and went. She missed him, but she would never ask that he change his routine to spend more time with them. Besides, she was on amiable good terms with her in-laws; she relished harmony and peace. Susan loved the long hours of daylight, the slow turn of the day into evening. She carried the youngest baby to the rocky beach in the woven straw Ndebele tote her husband had brought back from South Africa. The two older children and the toddler raced down the path mowed between swaths of tall grasses. Watching them, Susan felt proud, lucky, and happy.

As the children grew older and began school, the designer wanted a bigger house, so they moved to the newer suburbs. Susan had time on her hands, and she missed the intimate warmth she had shared with her babies. But the designer had a project in mind: a landscaped yard with a fountain, a rock pool, paths, a gazebo. Susan became an enthusiastic landscape gardener, her abundant energy going into every herb and shrub, every flagstone. The garden flourished. Susan was a soccer mom, Susan was the chairperson of the PTA, Susan ran the spring yard sale.

Then the children grew older, and Susan lost all those agendas. She felt adrift and was sucked into depression. What Susan needed to do was remember the feeling of inner wholeness she'd experienced when she was a young mother and bring it to other areas of her life, in order for her to be awake to the potential of what she wanted for herself. Claiming right action on her own behalf, setting up and maintaining boundaries also meant she was taking right action in relationship to her intimates.

It's difficult work for Peacekeepers to find their own agenda— and all too easy to find someone else's. When Peacekeepers feel secure, it's usually because they've taken on the agenda of someone else, or a job-related goal, or a hobby. They can access great energy and drive to achieve goals, and they can demonstrate an ability to prioritize and perform. Peacekeepers report that they function in high gear in total-immersion experiences for a long time. Even though this energy is generally a comfortable behavioral mode for them, if Peacekeepers cannot fulfill the agenda they've taken on (e.g., the PTA loses money for the first time ever under Susan's tenure), they can become aware of self-deceit and rationalizing in an effort to explain the failure to themselves and others.

When Susan's children were adolescents and she was at a loss as to what to do with herself, the designer, now well known, wanted to entertain in his home. Susan dutifully went to cooking lessons and became a competent hostess. She didn't outshine him, as she knew she could do; rather, she went along with his show. But she was never on board with home entertaining. She disliked the feeling of being on display, of performing; she didn't feel comfortable with small talk, and she resented the false intimacy of strangers. She didn't exactly tell her husband of her discomfort, but he knew from her strained appearance that she wasn't enjoying herself. There were fewer and fewer parties at home; now he entertained clients and business acquaintances at the office, or in restaurants, and he asked her to join him less and less often.

Susan didn't like being the society hostess, but she didn't *tell* her husband so. By her retracted actions she made it obvious that entertaining was a strain for her and that she resented doing it. In an inadvertent way the instinctual energy of Peacekeepers can be a charge to help them take right action on their own behalf, to put up boundaries, albeit—like Susan—in a passive-aggressive way.

There was trouble with one of their sons. He got into the drug scene and became violent, and they had to put him into a rehab center. Susan visited him whenever she was allowed to and ignored his snarling invective, smiling at him as he poured insults at her, mocking her passivity, her compliance. Then their daughter dyed her hair pink, ran away, and hitchhiked from Boston to Arizona before the police caught up with her. Susan folded her into her arms when they brought her back, told her what a good baby she'd been, said she'd be okay.

Among Susan's gifts as a mother is her ability to love unconditionally. This universal love provided a safe haven for her children. They knew that whatever they did—fail at school, get caught illegally consuming alcohol—and whatever the consequences, her love was constant.

Peacekeepers see how individual scenarios fit into a big picture. This is a great asset for a parent, since they don't get mired in petty arguments and the crosscurrents of resentments and upsets—they go with the flow. No one has to earn their love; it is noncensorial, nonjudgmental. Susan kept her heart and arms open to both her drug-addicted son and her runaway daughter. Her love was constant, *and* she helped them accept the consequences of their actions.

All the children survived adolescence, somehow or other. Over the ensuing years first one, then another was married, and eventually all four moved away. When Susan turned fifty, her husband left her for a younger woman, an architect. He gave her a large settlement and, in a moment of remorse perhaps, a retriever puppy, a reminder of better times. Susan was deeply angry at him, and in what she felt was a gesture of grand defiance, she gave the dog away. Then she felt guilty, because she knew she could have provided the puppy with a good home.

Susan helped in an inner-city AIDS hospice until the grandchildren came, and then she became the most accommodating of grandmothers. Susan loved being a grandmother. She easily entered a child's world—life was so essentially uncomplicated there.

Scott—Losing Your Agenda

Scott loved his family. He felt a jolt of happiness in his body when he looked at his two girls. He would give them anything, do anything for them. His wife remarked to him with a smile of sympathy that they had him twisted around their little fingers. But then, didn't *she* have him that way, too? When had he refused her anything? Scott avoided conflict. He knew this truth about himself: he'd go to great lengths to ensure that everyone was happy, everyone got along.

When they were little, seven days a week Scott was up at 5:00 A.M. as the youngest awoke, waking her sister. He knew how much the extra hours of sleep meant to his wife. He would dress them both, give them a snack, and in fine weather wheel them in a stroller (the elder with great delight riding shotgun on the back axle) around the suburban streets, long before even the most ardent jogger ventured out. His only company was the newspaper deliveryperson pulling in and out of driveways. Scott would quietly tell the girls stories or hum snatches of the Beatles and Mozart. When it was cold, he'd bundle them into the car and drive to the nearest airport, where they loved to ride up and down the escalators, with no passengers to disturb so early in the morning. He'd be back home by 7:00 A.M., and after breakfast he'd set off to work. Scott loved routine, and he looked back with satisfaction on those early years when he shared the rigors of their baby days. Time was like a river then, a mature river, meandering over the lowlands in great horseshoe curves, slow-moving, reliable, no surprises. Day followed day, and each day embraced the same flow of children, work, children. That pace suited his inner rhythm.

When his daughters were babies, Scott assumed the agenda of taking care of them not only in the early mornings but whenever else he could find time to do so. He did this with great love, selfless devotion, and no ulterior motive. His wife, on the other hand, was clearly frustrated during those years. She resented being tied to the babies, to their routine, to having to snatch time for herself when they napped or at night when they were asleep. Scott felt her frustration as if it were his own, and he did all he could with the girls so she could have time for herself. He hated the inner conflict he knew motherhood engendered in her. She never articulated the depth of her conflict to him: that along with maternal love was the guilt she felt at being trapped and not in control of her time, or that she wasn't a good mom because she resented being so housebound. She didn't *have* to speak. He could have told her about those feelings. Often he knew her feelings better than she knew them herself, better certainly than he knew his *own* feelings.

Peacekeepers are the most supportive of the personality types. Words like "competition" or "ego" don't have the same charge for them as they do for other personalities. Look how Scott knew the intricacies and depths of his wife's frustration at being a full-time mom. Peacekeepers act on behalf of others without much concern for their own sense of achievement or success. It's fair to say that as a parent (or a spouse) they live through their children (or spouse): their success is the Peacekeeper's success. Peacekeepers can be dynamic parents *because* they take on the wholeness of being a parent. Their children motivate them, get them going; they are the spark that fuels Peacekeepers' activity. Taking on the agenda of others is the Peacekeeper's focus of attention.

Scott was present at the births of both his daughters, saw them even before their mother did, held them gently; they fitted into his hands like little miracles. He was awed that he was part of the process, that he'd fathered two human beings. This achievement seemed so at odds with the rest of his life, where things happened *to* him; he wasn't the sort of person who went out and grabbed life. He had energy, but it was for others. He could make decisions and take action, but it was on behalf of others. He couldn't easily tell his family what restaurant he wanted to eat at, what gifts he wanted for his birthday or Christmas; what *they* wanted was always more important to him.

Peacekeeper parents' strengths play out in the arena of loving unconditionally, exercising energy on behalf of others, and being supportive and predictable. Their weaknesses point to passivity, difficulty in personal decision making, and at times a pattern of passive-aggressive (obstinate) behavior that can underlie their inertia. This pattern needs explanation.

Scott lost part of his life's agenda when his daughters grew older and didn't need his energy and attention anymore. He spent longer and longer hours in front of the TV, not watching attentively but passively. His wife and girls nagged at him for being lazy, for not finding a hobby. Partially his vegging out in front of the TV can be seen as passive-aggressive behavior: "You don't need me anymore, so I'll sit here by myself, and you can nag away." Scott was asleep to the fact that he felt life passing him by while he sat for long periods ostensibly watching TV, but in truth he was on automatic pilot; *he* was not there. Scott needed to pay attention to his inner self, to find a way of knowing when he was asleep to himself.

Although Peacekeepers can be stubborn and obstinate, it's not a confrontational stance, because they avoid conflict. There is a seeming paradox here: how can someone who promotes harmony and peace and avoids conflict as a survival strategy also exert control through obstinacy and the retractive force of passive-aggressive behavior? We know, for instance, that Scott was aware that in life things happened to him, that he didn't go out and grab life. His unconscious anger (resentment) at this reality can take a diffuse form that drains energy out of many interactions (for example, going on automatic in front of the TV). A major blind spot for Peacekeepers is that they deny being angry.

If Scott's children were to ask him if he was angry because they didn't spend Saturday mornings together at museums the way they used to, he would be absolutely astonished. "I'm not angry at you," he'd reply. "I'm not angry at all." If they persisted, the denial escalated. Scott didn't even know that his anger had built up over a long time, yet once he finally lost his temper, he felt wonderfully energized. He found it hard to believe that his daughters took his anger personally. He certainly didn't love *them* any differently because *they* were in a different phase of their lives.

PERSONAL ACCOUNT

Franklin, a Peacekeeper father of two sons, gives this account

I like knowing that my participation and contribution have played a part in the ongoing process of my children's development into increasingly autonomous, mature, and humane individuals. I like our sharing experiences together, and I also like sharing with them my own and their independent experiences.

I don't like the fact that I can empathize with and understand my children's painful experiences at times when I'm powerless to assist them. I always feel that I should never be powerless to act, but I've often been in that position. One example that comes to mind is when a child wants to go on vacation and I can't afford to fund it for him. I don't have this response if the source of the pain is intrinsic to the nature of living. What I mean is, for example, if a child believes he's unable to find the soul mate of his dreams. In this situation my actions turn to positive understanding and rational analysis to help him work through the situation.

My strengths as a parent are good empathy with each of my children. I have a clear determination to see and treat them first and foremost as individuals. I believe that my function as a parent is to do all in my power to support their development into the most complete individuals they're capable of becoming. A good example of this is when they were two and three years old I would encourage them to crawl all over a large rock (about eighteen feet high) without their being aware that I was right behind them ready to stop them from falling. This is a metaphor that I use to remind myself of my role, which is that of unseen protector and growth agent.

The strong tendency I have to live through my children's lives rather than living my own life is probably my greatest weakness as a parent. Another weakness is appearing dishonest and devious by agreeing with each in turn about a situation in which they're opposed. This comes from two opposite tendencies. The positive one is the genuine capability of seeing the virtues in both sides of an argument. The negative comes from the inclination to be deviously loose with what I say in order to be liked by all parties.

There have been times in my life where I've avoided dealing with my own agenda (needs, wants, and desires) and found solace in the success of my children. For example, during a period when my job wasn't going well, instead of focusing on that issue I spent a disproportionate amount of time watching my children playing sports. I responded in an exaggerated manner to their success or failure on the field. My happiness came to depend on their success: a totally unfair burden to lay on them.

I think my children have a remarkable degree of equanimity about me as a parent. Soon after he finished college, my son and I spent an evening watching a poor baseball game. Our conversation turned to how people interact with each other and whether there's any psychological truth in the biblical quote that "the sins of the fathers shall be visited unto their children, yea even until the seventh generation." His conclusion at the bottom of the fifth inning was "You're a better father than *your* father was." This was said in the context of a brutally frank conversation about the times I'd failed him, but also about when I had been credible, direct, and supportive. Another complimentary observation was offered by my other child, then a young adult: "We *both* have issues. Let's talk about them."

I see these comments as tributes to my success in having built a close understanding with them based on mutual appreciation and the knowledge that there's no such thing as a perfect parent or a perfect child.

Obviously there's another side to this, too. They've been quite honest with me about the fact that I come across as deceitful, that I've made promises and prophecies of what I would do, both for myself and for them, that haven't come about. Specifically, one child told me, "You've lied to yourself and to us about what was happening in your life." The other expressed a similar sentiment: "We can't trust what you say, because in the past you've pretended to us that all was well when it wasn't."

My advice to other parents is to know that each child is a special and different individual. Each child starts out totally dependent on you but must (and will) grow to be totally independent. You're also an independent individual. Recognize that your interactions with each of your children should be different. ❧

The Best Strategy and Action Program for Peacekeepers

Prioritizing Can Be Valuable

The idea of highs and lows, or periods of greater or lesser intensity, is not part of the inner framework of the Peacekeeper. Inherent to this pattern, in the Peacekeeper's personal or professional life, and often in the role of parent, is a reluctance to prioritize, to give more importance to one project over another. In our culture, with its emphasis on prioritization and deadlines, Peacekeepers run headlong into societal problems. Since everything they do seems equally important to them—their job, driving the kids to school, taking out the garbage, jogging for half an hour, washing the dog—they tend not to plan and execute activities in methodical order. Sometimes Peacekeepers forget to do what they say, and other times they haven't forgotten—they still intend to do it— but the timeline they've committed to has come and gone. Often their desk or closet looks a mess to others, but, as a Peacekeeper parent said, "*I* know where everything is. I tell my family, 'Please don't tidy up or move anything.' There's little point in putting things away if you're only going to use them again." Yet family members they live with may not see eye to eye with them on this.

ACTION: *Find a space in the house that is your own, and follow your natural tendencies there.* In common areas avoid causing unnecessary tension with your practice of least-effort housekeeping. And try to accept that some tasks *are* more important than others. For instance, don't keep your child waiting at the bus stop (when you said you'd be there at a certain time), because you also told your spouse you'd wash the outside windows, and somehow you mixed up the time. Your children will quickly label you as unreliable, and you'll lose their respect.

Claim Pieces of Yourself

As we've seen with Susan and Scott, others' agendas replace being awake to oneself, having one's own agenda. Peacekeeper parents can utilize enormous energy, be decisive and forceful, and show passion for their children. If one of their children is seriously ill, they can keep going almost twenty-four hours a day on that child's behalf (without a thought to the Peacekeeper's own welfare). They use others' agendas as a filter, because they want to avoid conflict by not drawing attention to themselves. A Peacekeeper reports, "I don't know how to present to others (even my family) that I need something. I feel it's almost a crime to say, 'I need this.' How can I ask for something for myself, when they need so much time and attention?"

A Peacekeeper mother was so angry at her husband one morning that before she knew what she was doing, she started throwing objects at the glass doors of his golf trophy case in the den. When she turned around, her husband and children, drawn by the noise, applauded and laughed. Her eldest daughter said, "You should do that more often. Then we'll know there's someone alive in there." She admitted to herself that it felt good to vent her anger. She says she's beginning to claim "pieces of herself." When she told this story, she also said that she'd never had agendas of her own; personal agendas weren't something that she knew about at all. But she added that now, even though she's finding some of the personal pieces of her own self, she still doesn't know how to fight for them. She can claim them, but if somebody attacks her, then her position no longer has any traction.

ACTION: *Realize that your family is fully aware of when you're not present (although you think no one has noticed).* Try to get in touch with what *you* want, or feel, or desire to express. Try saying it out loud in private, and share your desires with a buddy. Then talk to your spouse, or your child, or your boss. Take small steps. Give yourself some of the love you pour into others. Be aware that the very strategy you employ to *avoid* conflict *generates* conflict. For example, Susan's son in the rehab facility berates her for her passivity, and still she doesn't react. Instead she calmly takes on the agenda of being the easy target for his anger.

Strive to Establish Your Autonomy

Spouses/partners and children of Peacekeepers should be aware that Peacekeepers will often take on their whole agenda and then blend into that agenda. It may seem that Peacekeepers have lost their boundaries, but the fact is that because their self is so laid back, or asleep, it's simply that *their inner self is not present.* Peacekeepers are on automatic pilot, and the self is replaced by the agenda they've adopted. It's up to others to draw boundaries for them, to anticipate the consequences of certain (in)actions.

One suggestion to help Peacekeepers is for them to develop a powerful buddy system, preferably with someone other than their partner. A friend they trust to help them with reality checks, to see the consequences of a course of action or a decision, to make sure they're on track. Typically Peacekeepers are numbered among those people who have trouble paying their bills on time, or reserving theater tickets in a timely fashion, or remembering to go to the dry cleaner or pick up the wine before the dinner party. This behavior can drive the whole family crazy. Here's an instance when a buddy system comes in handy, asking someone to remind them when something important is at hand.

Peacekeepers describe how they can unify with another person, literally lose their boundaries so that they feel as if they become that person—adopting the other person's moods, energy level—they can even anticipate thought and speech patterns, and know what the other person is going to say before it's said. Peacekeeper parents take on the whole agenda of their child. Their interaction with one child can be quite different from that with another. Peacekeeper parents do tend to live life through their children: the child's dreams become their dreams, the child's successes their successes. Is this fair to the child?

ACTION: *Be aware that merging with your children is a double-edged sword.* On the one hand, this ability can be remarkably supportive for children; on the other hand, it can be smothering and rob them of independence when they're young or force them to push up against you when they're older, in order to establish autonomy. Above all you need to be aware that you should establish and maintain boundaries for yourself, especially when you feel all your merging octopus arms about to encircle your children. They need *you* intact, not the other way around.

Practice Occasionally Saying No

It is a truism that Peacekeepers are reluctant self-starters. As parents they're motivated by the expectations of their children and their desire to promote harmony in the family. If their children need a ride to school early for a special outing, everyone knows that the Peacekeeper will drive them. The family falls easily into the expectation that the Peacekeeper will pick up the slack (because for years now she or he has). It may be difficult for

Peacekeepers to rouse themselves in the morning—they'd rather lie in bed and be comfortable—but it's easy if they have to do it to accommodate someone else.

ACTION: *Practice occasionally saying no.* Saying no doesn't mean, "No, I don't love you." Your children understand this, even if you have qualms. You need to build boundaries for yourself. Your children will respect you for doing so. Think of it this way: how are you going to teach them the value of self-esteem if it's so hard for you to take a stand for yourself? You're doing them a favor when you say no.

Procrastination Is Deadening

In our society, with its institutions that place such importance on being able to set priorities and keep deadlines as a way of reaching goals, most Peacekeepers are out of step. Procrastination can become a charged issue in the parenting dynamic as well, particularly when the Peacekeeper's spouse or partner thinks he's shirking his responsibilities because of his tendency to procrastinate. The Peacekeeper *knows* he'll get it done, but it doesn't appear that way to the significant other, and often to their children.

So how do Peacekeepers meet deadlines? They operate in a world where there are institutional rules, societal rules, family rules and expectations, so there are consequences for procrastination. As one Peacekeeper parent said, "I know how to prioritize and meet deadlines on behalf of my children, and their agenda presents no problems for me. It's my own agenda that's a struggle." They complete the task in their head in good time; the problem arises in actualizing it in the world.

If Peacekeepers have a sense that there is a deadline or a task has to be done in a specific order, it disturbs their inner sense of wanting to keep everything even and flat, of not giving more importance to any one thing over another. Peacekeepers write lists, adding to lists that grow ever longer. The longer they become, the harder it is to cross off the top item, so the lists often collapse of their own weight and inertia. Peacekeepers keep deadlines by becoming champions at the last-minute save. They kick into an amazing energy level and work twenty-four hours straight to meet the ultimatum that's been given, often after the deadline has passed.

ACTION: *Learn strategies to help minimize the effects of your procrastination.* Perhaps you can get your family to cooperate. Tell them that you rely on them to remind you of things you've said you'll do. And give them permission to nag you about those things. Remember when this happens that they're not *telling* you what to do (don't adopt your obstinacy mode), they're trying to help you as you requested them to do.

Lists are a great help to plan and impose structure on your life, as long as making the list is not the end of your commitment. It's not easy for you to impose a sequential pattern of importance and priorities on outside commitments and events, but as long as bits and pieces of all the things on the list do get done all the time, you'll keep moving forward and work against that deadening procrastination.

Reflect the Multiple Facets of the World

Part of the Peacekeeper parenting style is linked to teaching children the value of choices: they believe strongly in choices. The idea of deadlines and consequences runs contrary to choice making. Peacekeepers feel that their child's opinions, choices, thoughts, failures, and attempts matter more than their being told what to do and then doing it. This parenting principle rests on their perception of a diffuse, global view of life. They find it difficult and of little value to impose a rigid structure of steps and priorities or to build a framework that can sufficiently reflect the multiplicity of the nature of the world.

ACTION: *Be aware that your child may not be a Peacekeeper and that the conceptual mode you live by may seem counterintuitive and wishy-washy to her.* However, if your child *is* a Peacekeeper, or another personality style that is risk-averse, you will give her a great gift: a safe place to try all her ideas without constraints or consequences.

Practice Speaking with More Animation

Peacekeepers want the reassurance that they're being listened to, that what they have to say is heard. (They're excellent listeners by the way.) If they sense someone tuning out, this arouses great anxiety, because if their spouse, child, or someone else doesn't listen and understand them, the situation has potential for conflict. They will relentlessly pursue that person until they sense that the potential for conflict is past or that a resolution has been found. Little else makes Peacekeepers as uncomfortable as having unresolved issues dangling in front of them. A Peacekeeper said, "Someone pointed out to me that often I speak in a flat, even tone, that I meander as I make my point in a saga-like description—and people tune out." Many Peacekeepers report that they can sense this happening. They agree that it's a primary sin in their book if people don't listen, and they can become quite angry (although one may not see that anger immediately).

Interestingly, Peacekeeper speech patterns mirror their interior world. A Peacekeeper father said, "I live in a world that has the appearances of a level landscape. Time spreads out. There's no urgency: if it doesn't get done today, it will tomorrow. Nothing is of more importance than anything else." We also saw this with Scott, who loves the predictability of the days of his early fatherhood, when time moved in slow, gentle curves. Susan loved the summer months at her parents-in-laws' house, the flow of long, sunlit days one into the other. Peacekeepers convince themselves that time is part of this terrain, that events are that way, people are that way, that the gestalt is flat and even, diffuse. There's always enough time, there's always another event, there are always other people. There's always another saga to spin.

ACTION: *Communication is another example of where a buddy system can come in handy; get a reality check.* Ask your spouse, children, friends to check with you about the point of what you're saying, something like "This is what I'm hearing—is this what you are saying?" Taking these sorts of steps can clear up many misperceptions.

Being listened to is connected with your style of communication. Often your meandering anecdotes threaten to lose contact with the main thread of what you're trying to say. It simply does not occur to you that you can get through to others without all the minute detail. Many people tune out on this long-winded, indirect style, especially children. They find it hard to sit still and listen while you unfold what you want to say. Practice speaking in more precise detail. Try not to repeat yourself or what someone else has just said to you.

Step Up to the Plate

A major psychological driver among Peacekeepers is the avoidance of conflict. It is sensible strategy to maintain an even tenor to all that is happening around them, to view the world through a diffuse lens. By not paying more attention to any one feature of the interior or exterior landscape, they can keep their environment flat, even, and uncontentious.

In Peacekeepers' perceptual lens, conflict invariably brings up anger (someone else's or their own). If they become angry, they wake up to themselves and other people take notice of them, which can lead to more conflict. So part of their instinct is to contain the anger, and the energy, by avoiding conflict if at all possible. Not only do Peacekeeper parents avoid conflict for themselves, but they also try to quash it down in the family and work to promote harmony. They try to convince the family of how unreasonable it is to create unpleasantness.

ACTION: *Some people regard conflict as a way of clearing the air, and they welcome it. Your dislike of conflict can be seen as avoiding central issues.* You need to take the extra step of ensuring that somehow everyone gets to the root of the conflict even though you prefer that they discuss it quietly rather than yell and perform. Often this latter option is not available in dealing with younger children; you have to take (often conflictual) action and address the consequences of *their actions,* although your preference may be to take a path of least resistance.

Why You're Stubborn

As explained above, Peacekeepers are often disconcerted by the energy that arises when they become angry. If they express anger directly, it's sure to lead to conflict, so the Peacekeeper strategy directs them to express their anger indirectly, in passive-aggressive (stubborn) behavior that drains energy out of the situation. This way they won't have to do what they don't want to do, *and* they gain the moral upper hand by making the other party frustrated and angry.

ACTION: *Try to put yourself into situations where you can (safely) engage in conflict, however difficult it is for you to find the strength to willingly face the discomfort of coming up against someone else, especially someone you love.* This person may be your spouse or your child, someone who you know loves you *and* (you may be surprised to learn) who may be pleased that you're engaging in this manner. Several personalities do not shy away from conflict. Releasing your anger (or other emotions) will help you begin to find your own position, your own self.

Don't Agree to Do Something Unless You're Committed

Peacekeepers like to do things for people, but they don't like to be *told* what to do—they like to be *asked.* (Spouses, partners, and children should be aware that this is key in interactions with their Peacekeeper.) The first approach is all-important; otherwise the obstinacy dynamic kicks in, and they'll say, "I'll do this for you," while thinking, "But that doesn't mean I've agreed." Later the Peacekeeper starts to feel, "Why am I here, and why am I doing this? I don't want to do this. I never agreed to it." A passive-aggressive pattern can take hold. By ostensibly buying your agenda but then holding up everything because they don't want to be on board, Peacekeepers can adopt a retractive and controlling stance.

The passive-aggressive response is a tendency to obstinacy. Peacekeepers know that simply because they've said they're going to do something, or because they've agreed that it's a good thing to do, that doesn't necessarily mean they've bought into it. Says a Peacekeeper mother, "Many times I'll tell my children that I'll do things with them because they seem like such great things to do, but when it comes time to do them, I'm not committed to them. I do them anyway, but my children can sense my foot dragging." It's so hard for Peacekeepers to figure out when this is *their* commitment, *their* passion. They struggle with other people's seeing them as lazy or as not keeping the commitments they make.

ACTION: *Don't agree to do something unless you're committed.* Learn to test your own boundaries inwardly. Ask yourself if you want to do what you're being asked to do. Learn to trust your first instinctive response. Tell people what you're thinking and feeling about their request. You want to avoid conflict, but if you don't speak up at the outset, the potential for conflict expands exponentially.

Try to become more aware of what you're saying in these situations, to speak with integrity. For instance, practice asking yourself, "Do I really want to do this?" If the answer is negative, practice saying, "No, I don't want to do that because . . ." Another strategy is to ask for a reality check, teach your children to ask you, "Are you sure you'll still be willing to do this when the time comes?" (or some such question). Make certain that you and everyone around you understands the concept of commitment and is held accountable.

One Foot on the Brake, One Foot on the Gas

Peacekeepers sit on reserves of energy. If that energy is released on their own behalf, it can explode like a firecracker, blowing others away in a blast. (At least this is how it feels to Peacekeepers, for instance, when they lose their tempers.) It can create conflict, involve them in all sorts of unpredictable, uncomfortable, and unwelcome consequences. Some Peacekeepers will admit that they suffer more from fear of success (putting that energy to work for themselves) than fear of failure (comfortably tamping it down). Another Peacekeeper reports, "Success tends to raise expectations, demands more energy, and sets people up for disappointment when I can't deliver again. The world expects more from successful people. It's safer and more comfortable to coast." The Peacekeeper strategy directs them to sit on the energy on their own behalf and use it only on behalf of others. This is why many Peacekeepers appear highly energetic and enthusiastic. The form this tamping down takes when it comes to their own agenda is inertia, going to sleep to oneself, not being present.

When Peacekeepers are stressed, their tendency to inertia is exacerbated by worst-case-scenario thinking, and often fear and paranoia kick in. If they allow this scenario to build, the effect can be paralyzing. They find it harder and harder to take any action, and they feel powerless, like the walls are closing in. And because they don't take action, the consequences of their inaction indeed become more and more serious: a self-fulfilling prophecy.

ACTION: *Be aware of the push/pull you exert on your own energy—one foot on the brake and one on the gas—when it comes to your own needs.* There's so much energy coming through your system, and (as a parent, for instance) you use it so well for others that you don't need to be scared of it for yourself. Practice claiming it in small amounts; *you* make the decision about the family movie this week, the family dinner out next week. Each step after that will be even easier to take.

Avoid the pattern of procrastination/paralysis. Get things done on time, even if it's stressful. Sometimes stress is good for you. Often when you are stressed, you're aware that your mind is clear, that you can think logically and clearly. Stress can also give you courage to take right action on your own behalf.

Stay Present for Your Children

The reason for maintaining a level inner tenor is that it allows Peacekeepers to go to sleep to themselves. The Peacekeeper lens *sees* no conflict, so there *is* no conflict. On the other hand, they perceive anything and everything as having *potential for conflict:* querying bills, wanting to change an appointment with the children's doctor, a teacher's asking for a conference. Procrastination starts up; the more they avoid the situation, the more potential for conflict there is. By the time they actually grab the bull by the horns, in their heads the conflict has already escalated. Often they're surprised: "Oh, the teacher was so nice."

When they sit on the fence, if they try to mediate, try to find the smooth spots in a choppy situation, they are indeed keepers of the peace. In the family dynamic they have the ability to sense intuitively where there is resistance, and they can get everybody working together to create harmony, so there is no conflict. Like Franklin, the father we met earlier in this chapter, they're easily able to take on the position and perspective of each family member, to see a problem from many points of view. This helps in mediation, but it can be a handicap when they need to make a decision on their own behalf. Also, as they can agree with two conflicting points of view, their children (and others) may regard them as deceitful.

Peacekeepers are sometimes jolted into an awareness that they're asleep to themselves, and it's not a comforting realization. They're particularly aware of this when they suddenly stop doing whatever it was they were doing for someone else, and the dead stop feels to them as if they may never be able to move again. Real terror comes when they have no clue as to how to find a way to force themselves to do something. A typical Peacekeeper says, "I don't know where the energy is. I know it's in there all right—I simply don't know how to find it. As a parent I have people relying on me. I have to get moving, or else I'll scare them, too."

Being unaware of their impact on others can play out in another area. Peacekeepers often don't know how they're coming across to people, their children included. The same speaker again: "I'm not that aware of when I'm speaking sharply to someone and have hurt their feelings, which I had no intention of doing. I see myself as a peaceful, loving person, and it startles me when others tell me that they're getting anger or sharpness from me. It startles me when someone says, 'You didn't have to say it like that.'"

Action: *It's not easy to cope with the realization that you are asleep to yourself* and *that this is such a fundamental part of your psychology. Take a deep breath when the terror comes on, and try and deal in small increments with what's in front of you.* Try to break down that big picture into manageable pieces. Stop thinking, "I have to be able to do it all, or I won't be able to do any of it." Once again a buddy system will be of great strength and comfort in getting you going. Try not to let your children see that you're in a funk. Stay present for them. You don't want to add their fear to your own.

Parenting Steps for Peacekeepers

- Accept that some tasks *are* more important than others. Be aware of when nonessential activities replace fulfilling your commitments to your family. Above all honor your commitments to your children. Remember, you have desires, needs, and rights, too. You lose sight of these too easily.

- Get in touch with what *you* want, or feel, or desire to express. Claim your*self.* Learn to make decisions for yourself, voice your own opinion, notice when you defer to others. Your children are aware that you don't take the lead.

- Keep a constant check on merging with your children's agendas. You find this a pleasant path, one of little resistance, but you may be smothering them in your (over)attention, robbing them of their independence. Practice saying no. No does not necessarily mean conflict. Insist on limits and consequences. Even though you can associate with their points of view, it's essential for their development that you do not avoid conflict, that you keep boundaries in place, and have expectations for their behavior. You have excellent conflict-resolution skills; make use of them to help mediate family conflicts.

- Develop strategies to minimize the effects on your family of your procrastination. Give them permission to jolt you about commitments. Make sure you listen when they point out that you're on automatic pilot. It will help you see how easily inertia comes on and energy drains away. Ask for help to structure a framework of short-term objectives, and discover more of your own needs and identity. Try to finish projects. Be aware of when your energy and attention are siphoned off. Know that an urge to gather more and more information is a cover-up for procrastination in making decisions. When you find this happening, take a deep breath and uncover the decision you're putting off.

- Uncork your energy by doing some form of physical exercise. Perhaps you want to try to coordinate your running or swimming program with activities your children are doing at the community center. Learn to handle anger better; go off and punch a pillow or dig in the garden to lessen the charge. Don't bury the anger, because it will explode later and can be damaging, especially with children.

- Life is not an all-or-nothing proposition. There are many different and incremental ways to achieve desired outcomes. Let your children teach you how they undertake a project or task. In all areas of your life try to structure manageable, short-term steps and goals for yourself. Have a fallback plan if you can't keep to the program. Remember what Mother Teresa said: "Small steps with great love."

- Try to speak with energy and intonation in your voice; this will help mitigate the dullness you feel and others hear. Be aware of when you're talking in sagas and meandering.

- Be aware of when you dig in your heels and become stubborn. The stubbornness will lead to conflict and negativity. Try to nip it in the bud.

- Receive the unconditional love your family gives you. It's okay for you to believe them when they say they love you and believe in you. Build a buddy system involving several people in different relationships to you. Reality checks with more than one person are extremely beneficial.

SUMMARY: THE PEACEKEEPER PARENT

Positives to Build On	*Negatives to Overcome*
Loves unconditionally	Stubborn, avoids anger and conflict
Energy on behalf of others	Procrastination
Accepts others	Asleep to him- or herself, runs in neutral
Good listener	
Fair—sees all points of view	Contains own energy by inertia
Able to help others access feelings	
Tries to keep family dynamic nonconflictual	Loses own position, passive, not an initiator
Supportive	Slow to express anger, to know own feelings
Predictable	Difficulty coming to personal decisions
	Obstinate, tamps down emotions, drains energy
	Prefers the familiar, problems with prioritizing

CHAPTER 10

The Moralizer
Aways Striving for Perfection

Richard—the Moral Compass

Richard was a fastidious man: in his attitudes, his mannerisms, his clothes. He liked being a father, relished the responsibility of shaping his children to live ethical lives. A moral tone underscored most of his interactions with his son and daughter; it was almost as if he willed them to see the world through his eyes: "You *will* see things this way." Perhaps he was overzealous in his insistence on their accord with him, but he firmly believed that he was right and it was for their own good that they saw things that way, too. Richard tended to have a preachy tone to his conversation. He was not aware of this and became mortified when someone (usually his wife) pointed it out to him. Richard interpreted others' observations, innocent comments—any remark—either as direct or implied criticism; in other words, *his error*. Moralizers avoid error. Richard's perceptions regarding error were in a way responsible for his preachy tone. He wanted to make sure others heard him and understood him correctly: "You're not getting this right. I *do* get this, and I can teach you the right way."

A gift of Moralizer parents like Richard is to be a moral compass; he can guide his children to an ethical life. Most often Richard did have an intuitive sense of what was right; he felt it in his body. But his focus on error was a drawback. For instance, Richard could walk into the kitchen (he was a gourmet cook), and even if the room was perfectly neat and tidy, except for a dusting of sugar where someone forgot to clean up a spill, his attention would fixate on the sugar, and immediately the room was imperfect. Not only did his focus of attention go only to what was wrong, but invariably the next step kicked in: "How can I correct this?" Avoiding error was a two-step process: "What's wrong here, and how can I correct it?"

Richard took on the burden of responsibility for correcting error, because he believed (it was part of this worldview) that he could see how to *perfect* things that were in error. This belief was annoying to his family; they were always being told how to correct things. Doing it right was not a particular concern of theirs—they had other personality preoccupations. Often his children felt resentment toward their father's unrelenting quest to perfect them.

Richard was oblivious about coming across as critical or preachy; he was single-mindedly trying to make life as perfect for his family as it could be. Often he felt burdened by his sense of responsibility (but he knew he could be depended on to fulfill it). Sometimes he felt that he alone was aware of a responsibility to keep the world on track. In a family effort like planning a vacation, Richard would say to himself, "Okay, I'll go along with the family's plans, as long as ultimately I can have a chance to check them out one last time."

Richard saw himself as a moral standard-bearer, and his internalized motto was "I see the world as perfect." Richard got angry, often, because he could not shape the world into the perfect state he saw in his head, and he took that on as his responsibility, too: "I'm the only one who sees perfection, and I can never make it as perfect as I see it, so I get angry." Imperfection was all around him: the world was filled with polluters, cruel pet owners, criminals. People in his neighborhood didn't comply with the recycling program. Pets were abused and left to suffer and starve on the streets. Criminals broke in to houses and violated all sorts of moral codes. Pedestrians jaywalked, motorists didn't obey traffic lights.

Often his anger at abusers, criminals, jaywalkers, and the like devolved not on the perpetrators, but on his closest and safest targets, his children. He was not aware of this. He didn't yell at his children—that would be bad behavior—but the more anger he felt, the sharper and more intense was the criticism leveled at them.

Richard's tense body language—clenched jaw, stiff neck, rigidity around the shoulders, and staccato walking—broadcast his level of discontent. His wife and children knew when to steer clear, to keep away from him. Resentment, judgmental thoughts, and comparisons of himself with others occurred internally. If Richard ever stopped to think about it, he'd realize that these judgmental comparisons were a continuous process: "I work twice as hard as my neighbor, but he lives on trust funds, so he gets the cars, vacations, clothes that I can't give my kids."

If Richard was critical of his family (for their own good), his chiding did not compare to the criticism he aimed internally at himself. Moralizers live with a judging inner voice that directs a constant commentary on the way they *should* conduct their lives. This voice peppers the commentary with "oughts," "shoulds," "musts." This sometimes censorious, sometimes disparaging voice (a mental construct of their own consciousness) is the inner standard, the inner measure by which Moralizers weigh the rightness of every facet of their lives.

Part of the purpose of this inner voice is to conduct an ongoing comparison to others. It's always strikingly poignant to me when Moralizers realize that other personalities don't have this inner critic. Another internal conversation for Richard ran along the lines of "I'm putting out all this effort, *she* [his wife!] isn't putting out nearly as much, yet *she* gets all the kudos. Nobody appreciates how much *I'm* doing."

No one asked Richard to go the extra mile—he made the effort to satisfy his inner naysayer—yet nonetheless he often felt underappreciated. If this feeling of lack of appreciation continued, a cycle of resentment and indirect anger against his family could kick in.

Richard was an amateur botanist; his field: wildflowers. Among his happiest moments were the times he spent on forested mountainsides photographing and collecting specimens for his growing collection. He was gratified when his daughter showed a similar interest and joined him on field trips. At these times Richard felt at peace, at one with nature. He sensed a perfection in the nonstriving "beingness" of the natural world, perfection in and of itself. Flora and fauna, photosynthesis and evaporation, the food chain, the ecosystem—no one was responsible for the trees and the flowers and the birds and the clouds; they all worked on their own.

Over time his appreciation of natural perfection began to lessen the impact of inflexibility on his own way of being in the world: "I see now that I've tried to manipulate my life, my choices, into some sort of conformity that is not perfection at all but an expectation of the ways things should be. Sometimes now I can see perfection as an ever-expanding awareness of the way things are. There's an inherent perfection in that. It's not about interacting with my family in a perfect way, or cooking the perfect meal, or creating the perfect life. It's about accepting the perfection of all the chaos, the mess. It's hard for me, and I can't always stick with this understanding that life is perfect just the way it is."

Molly—Heeding the Inner Critic

In the bathroom shared by two boys, aged fourteen and eleven, the combs, brushes, toothbrushes, hair gels and braces paraphernalia on the vanity top were in perfect order, lined up with surprising neatness. Morning and night Molly, the boys' mother, glanced into the bathroom and their bedrooms and smiled approvingly to herself; everything was as it should be. By now tidiness and orderliness were second nature to both children. Molly had regimented order in their psyches from infancy on. The behavior was now habitual.

Molly believed that this trait would continue throughout their lives, and it was a good thing. She felt it a worthwhile effort that she'd taught her children to value orderliness as she did. Regimenting life into neat order made sense to her, a way to ward off the chaos of the world around her, to impose control on reality. Her husband teased her that phrases like "unharnessed energy," "spiraling out of control," "unfathomable depths," "impromptu parties or dates," and "spur-of-the-moment decisions" had a negative charge for her, whereas phrases like "law and order," "just desserts," "flawless design," "in the right order," and "predictable outcome" made her feel much more comfortable.

Molly loved her children fiercely, and they knew that, but lately they—in particular the elder boy—had started to chafe against her rules and regulations; often he was rude and surly. The other day he had called her "a bloody liar"—*and* with company in the house. It was wrong to subject company to that kind of outburst, but she didn't want to escalate the argument, so she let that accusation, however injudicious, go by. Internally she justified his rudeness as unusual hormonal activity. Yet she was disturbed enough by the incident to discuss it with her best friend, although even with her friend it was hard for Molly to admit that there was something wrong in her household: "We were all deciding where to go for lunch. The others suggested a Mexican place we'd been to before. I knew that the boys had not eaten all they'd ordered that time. I reminded them of this, that we shouldn't go there if they didn't like the food. That's when he called me a 'bloody liar.' Maybe I'm not remembering correctly, maybe he did clean his plate last time as he said he did. It *was* a while back. I told the boys that they knew it was wasteful to order food and not eat it. I don't mind spending money on a meal, but they should eat what they order. Waste is not something I encourage."

Molly's friend repeated what she'd told her on other occasions when similar situations of minor rebellion had occurred: Molly was too strict and controlling, and the boys would increasingly push up against her and grow to resent her regime. She had to find ways to adapt to their growing older, to give them more autonomy, more control of their lives. By virtue of her rigid grip on all their attitudes, activities, homework, and friends, she was infantilizing them. She was too tense. She should try to relax, to enjoy them and herself more.

Molly tried to let the advice sink in this time, for she knew she had to change something now that her sons were growing older. Previously she'd dismissed her friend's observations as arising from the fact that she was not a hands-on or, in Molly's judgment, a "good" mother. Molly kept her opinion to herself, but on an inner scale of comparison, she felt that "good" parents were involved, even overinvolved, in their children's lives, and "not-good-enough" or "poor" parents gave their children way too much freedom. And as far as enjoyment went, where would she find permission to enjoy herself?

But she'd been taken aback by the intensity of her son's outburst. She was concerned about the possibility that one day he might rebel against her, walk away from her. As she could not begin to grapple with the implications of that idea, she pushed it aside. She was self-aware enough to know that what guided her parenting was her fear of making an error, screwing up. (Truth to tell, this motivation powered almost *every* facet of her life!) They were human beings, after all. She was responsible for their *lives*. There was little margin for error in that responsibility; that's why she was hypervigilant, totally involved in their day-to-day activities, constantly hovering at the edges of their interactions, ready to swoop in and protect them from harm. The consequences of error could be catastrophic; a familiar, critical inner voice had told her this from before they were born. Molly heeded that voice.

She would say to people, "When they were little, I didn't know if I'd get them through to preschool. Now one's about to start high school and the other middle school, and I don't know if I'll survive their adolescence. Then they'll go off to college. Already I don't like that idea. You put in all this time and effort, and then they leave you. It doesn't seem right."

Moralizers like Molly belong in the Defender triad. As with Protectors and Peacekeepers, they interact in an interspace that exists between themselves and others. For Moralizers the interspace is problematic, for when they brush up against others, there's potential for error; this is where Molly gets hung up. There was a wariness, an edginess, a scratchiness to her interactions even with her dearly beloved sons. Potentially they represented a flaw, or a mistake, for which she'd be responsible, blamed. This realization was so strong for her that until they went to preschool, she wouldn't let them out of her sight, not even into the care of her mother.

Molly, like other Moralizers, spends a good deal of energy on avoiding error. While Questioners live with the illusion that outside influences, even life, are authorities, and Protectors live with the illusion that life must be challenged in order to establish their own power and control, and Organizers *do* life as a task instead of living it, for Moralizers all of life is potential for error. Each personality type is conditioned to cope with its compulsions and defenses, and most Moralizers function positively in the world. But internally there are stark patterns. As Molly rationalized to herself, "I *have* to keep a sense of distance from my children. This takes the form of my having control. Through this control I can try to keep them safe."

There was another side of Molly that emerged when the family was on vacation. It was almost as if shifting locales gave her permission to have fun, be playful, enjoy herself. She still felt responsible for the children, but vacation meant she could leave behind the rigors of their daily routine and relax into a week or two of being somewhere different, doing different activities;

generally speaking, she could let her hair down. Her major responsibility on vacation was to ensure that no one was bored; she made certain that, like herself, the children had fun, were carefree, kept their options open. Being anonymous in a strange place gave Molly enough of a safety zone to tell her inner critical voice to take a walk.

PERSONAL ACCOUNT

Terry, a Moralizer mother of four sons, gives this account

Raising my children was the most wonderful time of my life, in spite of the pressure I felt to do the job the right way. I actually liked the responsibility I had for their well-being. I welcomed the opportunity to teach them to bring goodness to the world. Knowing that they've been kind to others along the way gives me a tremendous sense of satisfaction, for I tend to give myself credit for making that a priority in their upbringing. They've described me as the kindest person they know, and it's gratifying to be thought of that way. They were fun to be with, so innocent and good. I felt responsible for keeping them that way somehow, although I doubted that I could. I always tried to love unconditionally, but it was hard to do. Only now, at midlife, do I seem capable of doing it. My children remind me that I'm critical and lecture a lot. This hurts me, for I want to be a good, good parent, not one who makes them unhappy.

I tended to blame myself for their flaws and shortcomings, like poor manners, rudeness. I couldn't stand being legally responsible for their behavior, especially during the high-school years. I would actually lose sleep at night worrying about all the things they could do wrong, involving drinking and so on. I carried a tremendous sense of concern that some-day I would be held accountable for the parenting job I'd done.

Character development was probably my highest priority

as a parent. I loved to discuss issues of the day with them at dinner, events happening on the news at night, the right and wrong of them. When they seemed interested, I was eager to explain my reasons to them for my involvement in volunteer work. My children have taken action, too, such as volunteering as a Big Brother, serving in homeless shelters and the like. This makes me feel as if I've done a good job as a parent.

I've always stressed the need for spirituality in our lives, and I think that they understand this at a deep level. I taught them to love and respect one another. I referred to each as a "prince" in our home, a place where they will always be loved for themselves. This message seems to have taken hold, and I'm grateful for it. Our house was full of pets, too (mostly strays that needed homes), and the children learned to care for other living things in this way. I was willing to have a houseful of friends over (for that way I knew what they were doing). Also I was always actively involved in their school lives. I loved being in their classrooms, it was like reliving my own childhood. I thrived on it.

When one of my sons was in the third grade, he and a friend wrote graffiti on the school walls, and I was called in by the principal. He said that my son had been honest in admitting the deed and had dismissed his friend as not responsible, confessing, "It was my idea." That evening I told him how happy I was that he was able to tell the truth and take responsibility for his actions. This was evidence of the good person he was. I said I would always remember that about him and not the mistake in judgment he made about the graffiti. I asked *him* to remember the shame he felt about his poor choice and to promise himself to avoid that sense of shame as he grew older. He fell asleep knowing that he was much loved and respected by his mother.

On the other hand, I berated myself mercilessly with the message that if I were a better parent they would not act like that. Also, it was hard to cut the umbilical cord connected to their moral development. I still take their faults much too personally. When they were young, I felt that I never had enough energy to do all that I should be doing for and with them, like not decorating their rooms well enough, not making good enough meals, and so on. It seems that I apologized to them too much. I work hard on not feeling guilty for all the things I *could* have done but didn't.

My weaknesses could fill volumes. One example comes to mind, a time when my sons were all happy—my husband as well—laughing and enjoying a football game on TV in the family room. I looked around the room and saw only mess. I wondered why I was distressed and judged that they were inconsiderate slobs. It was difficult for me to appreciate their company in such a situation. Then I felt bad that I'd even mentioned the mess. Guilt. Awful. This is the story of my life. I was capable of thinking that they were guilty of every offense ever committed by a teenager; it was hard to trust them. My mind always thought of the bad things they were probably doing. And these were good kids.

Trust your instincts. *Loosen up.* Avoid obsessing about all that can go wrong, such as the poor choices children invariably make. Be a "good enough" parent, and be gentle with yourself. Play with your kids (I did that a lot), and experience childhood a second time. Remind yourself that at any given moment you did the best you knew how to do. ❧

The Best Strategy and Action Program for Moralizers

Avoid the Pitfalls of Trying to Create a Perfect World

Of all the personality types, Moralizers are perhaps those most easily recognized. We call them perfectionists, and we (and they) know that they can be obsessive in their drive to do things right, to be perfect. They can make excellent role models, inspirational parents with their passion for excellence, their sense of right and wrong, and the enthusiasm with which they try to impart moral standards and life lessons. Note how convinced this Moralizer parent is of the rightness of her message (many Moralizers share this belief): "There's never been any doubt that I immerse myself genuinely in whatever it is I'm doing with my children. I value what we're doing, and find great satisfaction when I sense them coming along to the way I see things."

Another parent tells us of the downside of the passionate intensity for perfection, shooting for the ideal: "When I'm convinced about the way things should be, and I spend tremendous energy in a positive direction toward that end, *and* still I can't accomplish the great things I set out to achieve, it's like coming up against a brick wall. I feel the anger inside. Then a phrase comes to my mind that someone shared with me a long time ago: 'Be careful of sacrificing the real for the ideal.'"

A Moralizer mother told me that if she if feels she can't get through to her children right away or they don't feel comfortable with what she's asking for, she won't leave them alone. She feels so confident that even if they are determined not to see things her way, she knows eventually they will come around: "I don't give up. I want my children to be like me, for their own good."

ACTION: *Be careful of the diligence with which you may go about trying to convince your children of the rightness of your approach.* Try not to work so hard at it. Some children (because they're such different personalities from you) may not be able, however hard they try, to appreciate your viewpoint, the way you see the world. To a reluctant child it's almost as if you're shaking them and saying, "You *will* see this is the right way." This methodology may work, but it may also cause lasting damage to their self-esteem and your relationship.

You may evoke a response of resentment toward yourself if you insist on living in a world of perfectionism. *You* may find it wonderfully energizing to aspire to the ideal, but unless this desire is grounded in reality *and* a sense of incorporating many points of view, the result may not be what you hoped to achieve. If you want recognition for your efforts in trying to make things the best they can be, back off a little.

Know that you are an idealistic, moral, and inspiring parent. The messages of virtuous living you try to teach your children are important and worthy. If you want each of them to understand what you're saying in their individual ways, try to tailor the message to them, so they can hear it according to their differing personalities. Try to lessen the impression that you are *the* moral authority, that only you know what's right. Let them know you love them unconditionally despite the fact that you're often picking on them for errors and misdemeanors. Enter into a dialogue with your children on issues of morality. You may be surprised (and pleased) at what you learn.

Beware of Self-Righteousness

Moralizers have a central preoccupation with rightness, and they often feel they have a monopoly on knowing what's correct. This is different from Protectors, who ask, "Is it just? Is it fair?" Moralizers ask, "Is it right?" Everything is either right or wrong. This is a primary Moralizer blind spot, because the world simply is as it is. The right/wrong construct exists only in their heads. We see that the Moralizers' strategy is highly internalized. This personality takes subtle forms: anger is *indirect,* Moralizers contend with an *internal* critic, and they judge themselves and others by an *internalized* yardstick.

ACTION: *Be aware of how your gut instinct translates into conviction about being right. (Your instinct may be off.)* You are an excellent guide for your children in the ethics and morals of a good life, but this is also the root of your characteristic of coming across as self-righteous. Other personalities (for other reasons) may believe that *they* are right. Learn to respect other points of view. Try to see the world through the eyes of your children. They may be right, too, however wrongheaded they appear to you at first glance.

Know That You Are a "Good Enough" Parent

We all talk to ourselves to some degree, but Moralizers live with an inner critic who is constantly commenting on their lives. This Moralizer shares her thoughts: "Whatever I'm doing, an inner voice always goads me to perfection. It's painful, and yet it pushes me to a high level of achievement. But in the long run I don't think it's worth all the excessive efforts I undertake. I would like to do things with a lot more spontaneity, to feel less burdened by responsibility, but there's that inner critic telling me, 'Do it right, do it now, do it thoroughly, or don't do it at all.'"

When Moralizers identify their personality type and learn of the concept of the inner critic, many are shocked that not everyone has this internal feature of consciousness. Then comes anger that they have to live with this phenomenon. Says another Moralizer parent, "Often you're absolutely sure that the inner voice is absolute truth. It helps to question it, to state simply when it gets going, "Okay, but that isn't God. It isn't absolute truth or absolute authority.'"

This next Moralizer echoes the first: he knows that following his "path of shoulds" is a mental process. But he's aware also that the "something" he trusts deep down is fundamental and life-sustaining, a source of good: "There's always something that I trust deep down and that seems to operate in spite of all of the other 'shoulds' on top of that. That's one of the things that helped me to build a base of self-esteem, because despite having all of this self-imposed pressure to behave in a certain way, and the conviction that it is important to do so, nevertheless I do have that more basic sense that there's something right about me. There's a contradiction here, because to this day I still operate with a pretty strong sense of how things *should* be for myself. I couldn't tell you what the consequences might be if I didn't do that. I'm not going to hell, life isn't going to turn awful, but there's a sense I have that in order to be authentic and true, I have to follow that path of 'shoulds.'"

ACTION: *Be skeptical of the inner voice, the inner critic, but don't fight it.* Accept that it's there, but train yourself to make a choice about heeding it. A personal-growth teacher once said "Don't 'should' on your life." This is good advice for Moralizers. The best technique to use to counter the influence of the inner critic with your children is to ask for reality checks from your family: "Is this good enough?" "Do you like it done this way or another way?" And so on. Explain to them about your inner critic. They'll help you keep it in check.

Learn to Recognize the Source of Your Anger

Many Moralizers can be found in the ranks of those who work on behalf of social and political causes, from the local grassroots level to national office. As Terry, the mother we heard from earlier, said, from a young age she tried to politicize her children in relation to the world around them. Teaching others about issues, communicating the rights and wrongs of political decisions, taking action on behalf of victims of wars and natural disasters, fighting cruelty to animals—Moralizers find legitimate outlets for both their rage and anger and their sense of morals and ethics. A Moralizer mother says, "I have to make the world better. That's my mantra. You *need* to know that we are the world, and we have a responsibility to do things better."

ACTION: *The sense of responsibility that comes to you about being the exemplar of perfection carries commensurate resentment: "Why should I be the only one who seems responsible?" Learn to recognize when you feel diffuse and indirect anger that takes the form of criticality and judging.* This indirect anger focuses on error and is driven by the "shoulds" and "oughts" of your inner critic. Try to shift to a type of serenity that essentially encompasses a sense of letting go, of allowing the world to take responsibility for itself. Try to learn to let go of your anger. Express your irritation and feelings in the moment, so that anger doesn't build. You'll be less tense, and your family will find it more relaxing to be around you. Serenity, an acceptance of how things are, is a growth path for you.

Practice Expressing Legitimate Anger

As we've seen, the personalities in the Defender triad embody variants of the self-forgetting theme. Protectors guard themselves against vulnerability and openness, the self kept under powerful lock and key. Peacekeepers lose their own agenda in the agendas of others, and Moralizers tamp down their emotional energy, mainly anger, lest it burst forth and they be seen as badly behaved.

The denial and repression of anger take a toll on the Moralizer's energy. When your personality motivation directs you to good behavior, you cannot risk the consequences of out-of-control anger. This Moralizer father makes a clear distinction between good and bad anger: "I've come to the conclusion that the problem I have with anger is that it always ends up hurting someone else, and for me the ultimate wrong is causing somebody else distress. I can immediately see when I've hurt somebody, and I just die—that's bad anger. Especially when it's a member of my family. The anger is so instinctual, and *boom*, before you know it, somebody's hurting there, and I had no idea that that was going to happen. It just did. Good anger is anger on behalf of someone who's being treated unjustly, that's righteous anger."

ACTION: *Learn to express anger calmly and rationally.* You feel unbelievably bad when you've expressed your anger in an outburst at your family because, indeed, you've hurt people you love and you've lost your control. What lies behind the motivation of control for you is the overriding principle that you must be good, well behaved. Try to come to terms with the fact that anger is an emotion, and emotions need expression. If you're angry, you don't need to have a tantrum with it. Express legitimate anger, but in a way that doesn't assault others. Don't deny your anger, but handle the energy with calm and serenity, and you won't be afraid of your anger anymore. Your family will find you more predictable, more direct, and easier to get along with.

Take Time Off and Have Fun

This Moralizer parent is good-humoredly aware of her own intensity and how its effect on her children needs to be ameliorated: "I have the good fortune to have a husband who teases me when I get too intense, too rigid, too structured. I can always rely on him to lighten things up. I notice that when he's not around, I try conscientiously to move myself to a place where I can be more relaxed with my children, have fun myself, and let them have fun. It's as if my husband has given me permission to do this, shown me how to have fun."

ACTION: *Be aware of a need to suppress spontaneity, and anything else that is associated with what's not under control or in order.* The motivation for this is a defense against the details spinning out of your control. Try to be flexible, even if that feels risky. You seek permission from external authority figures; try to internalize this by becoming your own authority.

For your own sake and the sake of your children, try not to postpone having fun. If you've got an inner conviction that you have a moral responsibility to save the world from itself, it's hard to justify taking time off. Learn to give yourself permission to take time off. Life goes by, and you don't want to be plagued by so many missed opportunities. Before you know it, your children are in high school and college, and you still haven't had much fun with them.

Try Not to See Fun as a Temptation for "Wrong" Behavior

For Moralizers life can often seem overwhelmingly grim and rigid. When the tensions become too high, many Moralizers develop a "trapdoor" mechanism, a way to release that pent-up anger, self-criticism, and judging. They do find a way to have fun, usually at a physical distance from the place where they conduct their daily lives, such as at a favorite vacation spot where no one knows them, where they can dress casually and behave spontaneously, going with the flow wherever it leads them. As we saw earlier in the chapter, Molly is a good example of this.

However, Moralizers can also shift to fun-loving energy mode in activities and situations where they feel secure. Finding that trapdoor to release tensions and the sense of a divided self are interrelated: both are a rebellion against the rigidity of the inner critic. Essentially Moralizers live with a divided consciousness. On the one side the punitive inner critic pushes down emotions, stamps on anger, sexuality, permissiveness—all of which get translated as temptations to "wrong" behavior. The other side is a private consciousness that evolves in which these forbidden emotions are acted out as fantasies or, at times, in reality.

ACTION: *Remember, you may be alone in your family in manifesting this consciousness.* Your parenting partner and your children may have no idea of how your inner world operates. Choose an appropriate time to tell them about the inner critic and about the way you often see having fun as a temptation for bad behavior. Ask for their help and support in giving you a reality check when you feel tension concerning these issues. Nothing breaks the grip of these prohibitions as effectively as talking about them with others and seeing that they are unconcerned and unaffected by whatever behavior is of such concern to you.

Try Not to Obsess Over the Details

It's not surprising that a personality based on precision and correctness also has a need for accuracy, which translates into thinking in terms of details. For instance, Moralizers often insist on helping their elementary-school children with the details of homework, or they meticulously detail a gardening project or a dinner party. Moralizers have a gift of critical thinking: analytical ability. Details allow all the pieces to be put in place, and they deliberately complete all the steps of a process. Attention is more focused on breaking down the task into manageable pieces than on putting it together in a mental construct, as we saw with Observers (big-picture thinkers) and Entertainers (multioptional thinkers). This need for, and emphasis on, details (along with fear of error) is among the root motivations for the Moralizer pattern of procrastination. They believe (another blind spot), "I can never have enough detail." Or "If I've amassed all the details, that's even a worse dilemma, because what's the right order and selection to put them in? If I make those decisions and complete a plan, I'm going to have to proceed to put it into action. Then there's no chance of my being able to redo it yet again, and I know some of it is bound to be wrong." Moralizers wrestle with that final moment of decision and will often procrastinate while grappling with the question "Is this error-free enough?"

ACTION: *Remember, righteously adhering to the steps of a process does not easily translate to various areas of parenting.* Children are full of joy, spontaneity, surprises—try not to channel their life force into your preconceived pipelines. By all means ease the family schedule into manageable details by using your gift to accurately make fine judgments and distinctions. Acknowledge that your secret for success at juggling all the pieces of your life and the life of the family lies in the details. However, don't get stuck there. As an understanding parent you now know that there are many different personality styles, so your family members are going to interact with you, show appreciation, and so on in different ways. Try to be less rigid in how you handle the details. Allow for spontaneity. Give yourself and them a wider field of operation, more freedom; try to keep from getting too narrowly focused because you're obsessing over the details.

Handle Criticism Gracefully

When Moralizers are criticized, a painful process occurs as they try to rationalize the criticism, to remove its powerful charge. Since they've already been beaten up by their inner critic, external criticism is mortifying. The pain arises from their having caused the error in the first place that brings on the criticism. Moralizers assume that they're responsible, if only indirectly, for the criticism they receive. The following parent sheds light on an important facet of this personality; criticism is internalized as a feature of her own psyche: "When criticism comes my way, I want to respond rationally; to change myself, because I want to be good, or perfect, or please in some way. But the shame is so huge that I absolutely go into a black hole and disappear, completely withdraw, and that pain follows me often for years, cumulatively adding to all the other pain and shame."

ACTION: *Your children are going to criticize you. It goes with the territory of being a parent. Try to find a place within yourself where you can ride out the criticism, see it as something external.* Especially with those closest to you, don't build resentments and hold judgments and grudges. Most often your children are making comments to you and about you in an attempt to be funny, witty, and clever and also to take a dig at your self-righteousness. (This could be a self-defense maneuver on their part.) Their intention is not to hurt you deliberately, to cause you pain. The same applies to parenting partners and others. Learn to build appropriate containers for what appears to you as criticism. Learn to tell people of the effect their words are having on you; this action can be healing for you. And in the process you also help others to be more sensitive about what they say and how they say it.

Break the Cycle of Judgment, Criticality, and Internalized Anger

One of the functions of the inner critic is to offer a constant commentary comparing Moralizers to others around them. As a consequence, Moralizers carry around the internal judgments of others, even those closest to them. Most often the judgments stay in their minds, are never articulated. Judgment helps to fuel the inflammatory anger that has no place to go. This Moralizer father gives a clear articulation of this process: "I've noticed I'm often in this position of being torn between wanting to be the good parent, wanting to be the one who's there in a supportive way, who's identifying with the goals of my children, and knowing how I should behave, while at the same time needing to deal with anger that comes up, especially in situations where I feel that my child is not doing something right. If I have a sense that people's action is well intentioned, I can stand behind them. But if there's a problem in attitude or behavior, that's where I find judgment in me that stays inside in the form of anger."

ACTION: *Whenever the criticism, judgment, and anger arise, talk to yourself.* Tell yourself that the other person, maybe your child, is not deliberately setting out to challenge you. Ask yourself what it is about that child and that situation that makes it so hard for you to accept what's being said or done. It's a three-step process: learn to become aware of the judgment, learn to be able to express the anger rather than simply sitting on it, and learn to discuss your reaction with the other person.

Parenting Steps for Moralizers

- Know that you are an idealistic, moral, and inspiring parent. The messages of virtuous living you try to teach your children are important and worthy. If you want each of them to understand what you're saying in their individual ways, try to tailor the message to them, so they each can hear it according to their differing personalities. Avoid the pitfalls of trying to create a perfect world.

- Be aware that you can come across as self-righteous or morally superior. Curb judgment and criticism of yourself and others. Especially with your children, state your criticism gently, repeating that it's constructive feedback and that you love them unconditionally.

- Accept that your inner critic is there, but train yourself to make a choice about heeding it. A personal-growth teacher once said, "Don't 'should' on your life." Find ways to lessen the internal critic's grip on how you conduct your life. Accept that you are a "good enough" parent.

- Recognize that the source of your anger is your feeling responsible for making the world "right." Try to shift to a type of serenity that essentially encompasses a sense of letting go, of allowing the world to take responsibility for itself. Find a way to release your anger when it first starts to build. Internal judging and comparing are signs that you're angry. When you undertake responsibilities, make sure you (and everyone around you) understands the limits. Otherwise you'll feel personally responsible (and burdened) for the whole project.

- Learn to give yourself permission to take time off. Have fun—life is short. Your life is not a rehearsal, but the real thing. Build in body work or exercise to release the tension that accumulates, especially in your neck and shoulders.

- Don't get stuck in the details. Try to be less rigid in the way you handle them. Sometimes your attention to details is overkill. Remember, 100 percent is enough.

- Practice letting go; a mistake is simply what it is, a mistake. Practice being imperfect, deliberately make mistakes in front of your children. That will be fun for all of you.

- Try to find a balance between outer expectations and your own internal standards. Short-circuit judgment, criticality, and internalized anger. Your children want to know why you always seem mad at them (by the evidence of your attitude and behavior) but seldom say anything. Ask for feedback, but then don't feel defensive and criticized. Accept their genuine praise for your striving for or achieving excellence.

- Trust your intuitive responses. You can be a moral compass for your family.

SUMMARY: THE MORALIZER PARENT

Positives to Build On	*Negatives to Overcome*
Moral compass, trusts instincts	Focuses on what's wrong
Analytic ability	One-track thinking, it's either right or wrong
Detail orientation	Overpreparation, avoids error
Honorable	Inflexible, rigid, tends to self-righteousness
Continual self-improvement	Moral superiority masks real emotions
Can envision perfection	Procrastination from fear of error
Takes on causes; upholds justice, ethics, and moral principles	Indirect anger at being responsible for making the world "right"
Helps others see error	Lives with harsh inner critic commenting on performance
Strives for excellence	Burdened by self-criticism about not meeting internal standards of perfection

Epilogue
Taking the Next Step

What Do I Do Now?

This is the most frequently asked question after people work with this material, conclude that they know their personality type, and understand their parenting strategy. When you first encounter a family situation in which it is clear to you how your motivation and behavior are affecting your parenting, you'll want to try out the steps in the program. This process is like learning to drive a car. At first, thinking simultaneously about applying the accelerator, braking, handling the steering wheel, gauging your distance from the side of the road and from the vehicles in front of and behind you is overwhelming. But after a few months of practice, driving becomes second nature.

Don't give up, back off, or fall back into previous habits of communication and interaction. Through trial and error you'll begin to find edges where you can push your parenting relationship into a much more satisfactory shape. Remember, you're not trying to transform your child; you're trying to put your newfound understanding of your personality into positive action.

Your parenting situation is fluid; you are changing as you mature, grow, and learn from life. Your child is changing as he matures, grows, and learns from life. You can't change your personality, but you can learn how to maximize the positives and minimize the negatives.

Typing and Stereotyping: A Cautionary Note

This material is powerful; there is great potency in understanding your personality. By reading this book, you have gained the tools to understand not only your own motivational patterns but also the behavior patterns of other people. I believe that this understanding gives us great responsibility. We can learn all we want about ourselves, but let others take the same journey for themselves. Please don't try to type other people. It's almost impossible, once you have this material in your hands, not to try to type those closest to you, but don't tell them what you suspect. Let that moment of discovery belong to them, as yours did to you. There is no greater turnoff to this study than having someone tell you, "Well, you did X because your personality is Y, and you always do Z, so I can't expect anything different from you." You can be wrong. You can do great harm by labeling others, especially your children. That is stereotyping. Simply put, you cannot know others as they know themselves. The more important work is to understand yourself, to feel comfortable with who *you* are. For the rest, now that you know that there are eight other personality patterns, it's your responsibility to figure out how *you* interact with them, to put to use your informed understanding of how *you* are affecting others.

We need to keep the spotlight of inquiry on ourselves. Let's make the means of self-discovery available but leave the gift of that discovery to each individual.

Taking This Practice to Another Level

Basically the overriding principle behind activating any of the personality strategies is cultivating a sense of self-awareness. This sense is what gives us the space to become proactive and not reactive. There are many different attention practices that lead to self-awareness, so that when our old habits kick in, as we do with a record that's stuck in one groove and going around and around on the turntable, we can stop the cycle. Our self-awareness allows us to step back, find (increasing) levels of objectivity, and give ourselves choices as to how to respond. With that level of self-awareness, we provide an empathic, supportive space for our children, for all the people in our lives. Eventually the practice can take hold so strongly that stepping back, the "counting to ten" routine, becomes automatic. Some personalities need this space because they are up and out too quickly, others because they want to withdraw, and yet others because their habit is to sit on the fence, anyway. Self-awareness can be seen as a safety zone.

Finding a safety zone is as easy as breathing—literally. Breath is life. If we don't breathe, we die. The breath is a neutral reference point, always present. We can come back to it again and again. It is the most basic safety zone. In different practices of the martial arts, in athletic training, in yoga and meditation exercises, awareness of how we breathe, how we can train the breath, is common to all.

Here is a the simplest breathing exercise: Sit comfortably in a chair or cross-legged on the floor. Put your hands on your knees. Close your eyes. Breathe in, breathe out. You don't have to do anything else but be aware of your breath as it enters your nostrils and leaves your nostrils. Your breath breathes you. Concentrate on the flow of the breath. Become so quiet inside that you can hear your heartbeat. When thoughts come, let them go without judgment, and then return to concentrate on the breath. Do this exercise over and over and over. Start with practicing for two minutes, five minutes, ten minutes. After a few weeks the practice will begin to take hold. If you can remember to concentrate on the breath, find your reference point, you can short-circuit your habitual behavior, give yourself space to put in place your new understanding. And you can learn to do it instantaneously, with your eyes open, walking, driving, eating. Just drop in to the safety zone. It's that simple.

Of course, breathing exercises can become much more elaborate, such as imagining the turn of the breath as occurring in the belly. Or visualizing the breath as a jeweled cloud moving through the body. Do whatever works for you to find the breath, the constant reference point, the safety zone.

Another common practice that helps our self-awareness and our ability to stay in the safety zone (objectivity) is to align our sense of inner balance. Again, this is a simple exercise. Stand up, making sure your weight is evenly balanced on both feet. Lift your head so it sits comfortably on your neck and is not drooping forward. Most of us stand with our heads pointing forward. In our society we tend to rely on our intellect to power our lives, and so we lead with our heads. Put your head back about an inch or two more than feels comfortable. If you can see yourself in a mirror, you'll realize that you are now standing with much more natural alignment. Stand still, and imagine that you have a line, a piece of string, running from the ceiling, through the middle of your head, down your throat, through the center of your body, and into the ground. The line of string aligns your head, heart, and belly. This exercise helps you achieve inner balance.

Concluding Thoughts

Parenting is a dynamic process. Family situations are fluid. There is nothing mechanistic about the process, no blueprint to help build your parenting. But understanding your personality, activating your parenting strategy, developing this step now and then that one, being aware of how each step affects each child (because each child is a different personality), slowly you gain confidence. Truly, now that you see with new eyes, you can cut through personality differences.

Cultivate self-awareness. This gives you space for sustained personal effort, so that the implementation of the strategies in this book is realistic and rational. Working gradually with yourself in these ways and refining your understanding of personality are guides that console you and nourish your parenting wisdom.

APPENDIX

History, Research, and Theory on Personality Studies

The E-model below provides a framework and conceptual vocabulary for understanding people and behavior.

The Peacekeeper
Calm, seeks consensus, takes on others' position at expense of own agenda, obstinate and stubborn

The Protector
Take-charge, protective of turf (family), combative, likes control

The Moralizer
Conscientious, preoccupied with correcting error, inflexible, judgmental

The Entertainer
Mercurial, hard to pin down, childlike charm, backs away from commitment

The Helper
Devoted, empathic, needs approval, can be manipulative

The Questioner
Prone to doubt, scans for danger, loyal, questioning, excellent troubleshooter

The Organizer
High achiever, efficient, competitive, obsessed with image

The Dreamer
Creative, emotionally charged, melancholic, attracted to the unavailable

The Observer
Privacy is paramount, rational, detached

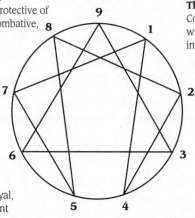

In the above diagram of the E-model there are numbers placed around the circle. Different E-model authors (myself included) choose their own names to refer to these numbers, but we all call them "Points." Thus, if we are speaking generically about the E-model, we refer to Point One, Point Two, and so on. In this book the following points align with the names I've used.

Point One—Moralizer

Point Two—Helper

Point Three—Organizer

Point Four—Dreamer

Point Five—Observer

Point Six—Questioner

Point Seven—Entertainer

Point Eight—Protector

Point Nine—Peacekeeper

A Brief History

What is the history of the Enneagram (E-model)? In 1972, a group of psychologists, psychiatrists, and students gathered in the living room of a house in Berkeley, California, to learn from Claudio Naranjo, a prominent University of California at Berkeley psychiatrist, about a psychological system called the E-model. Naranjo had recently returned from Arica, Chile, where he'd spent time studying with a spiritual teacher named Oscar Ichazo. Ichazo gave Naranjo fragments of insights into this tantalizing psychological model.

Week after week, the group met in Berkeley and painstakingly tried to align the central features of the E-model type with descriptions from the 1952 *Diagnostic and Statistical Manual of Mental Disorders,* volume one *(DSM-I).* They made hypotheses and drew conclusions through a hit-and-miss process of discussion and by careful interviewing of individuals on panels by Naranjo to elicit their inner psychological worlds. Putting together the two templates—the E-model's central fixations and the *DSM-I* categories—Naranjo provided the Rosetta Stone for understanding and presenting the E-model of personality in its modern form.

While the *DSM* describes pathologies, the E-model describes the broadly correlating features of ordinary people: Point One's *anger* at the world not being perfect lines up with the *compulsive* pathology; Point Two's *pride* in acting out with other people and repressing their needs lines up with the *histrionic;* Point Three's *identification* with what they do and *self-deceit* lines up with the secondary *narcissist;* Point Four's *envy* for what is unavailable, leading to self-attack and capitulation, lines up with the *depressive;* Point Five's *avarice* in withholding and retractive behavior lines up with the *avoidant;* Point Six's constant *fear* and vigilance lines up with the *paranoid;* Point Seven's *gluttony,* the escape into enjoyment and pleasure away from darkness and pain, lines up with the true *narcissist;* Point Eight's *lust* in excessive behavior and action without thought lines up with the *sociopath;* Point Nine's *sloth* in being asleep to themselves and caught up in others' agendas lines up with the (passive aggressive) *obsessive-compulsive.*

Unfortunately, the historical picture is not as simple and clear as the Berkeley living-room explorations imply. There is another strand of E-model influence in this century. In fact, the first person to bring the diagram to the West was the Russian mystic and charismatic teacher George Ivanovitch Gurdjieff, who settled in Paris after the Russian Revolution in the late 1920s and established a spiritual school there. Gurdjieff painted a huge E-model on the floor of the Institute for the Harmonious Development of Man, the name of his school where students practiced dance and movement on the diagram. Much of Gurdjieff's teachings centered on what he called Chief Feature, personality characteristics akin to the central features Naranjo describes in *Ennea-type Structures* (1990). Gurdjieff purportedly attributed the E-model diagram to Sufi sources. It's interesting to note that Oscar Ichazo, Naranjo's teacher, studied in Gurdjieffian Fourth Way schools in South America before starting a spiritual school of his own.

Following Gurdjieff's lead, many of the first wave of E-model authors in the mid-eighties declared that the model has its source in Sufism. They are correct up to a point. Central to Islamic esotericism is a system of psychoethics based on a version of the E-model diagram. A well-known Sufi scholar and writer, Laleh Bakhtiar, notably in her book *Traditional Psychoethics and Personality Paradigm* (1993), exhaustively explores the dynamics of this paradigm. But it appears that the E-model may be even older than its Sufi version. Sufi adepts kept the diagram and the psychoethical system alive through the dawn of Islam, in much the same way as medieval monks kept Latin and Greek alive in the early Middle (Dark) Ages in Europe.

Rabbi Howard Addison *(The Enneagram and Kabbalah: Reading your Soul,* 1998), in groundbreaking research on the overlay of the kabbalah, the Tree of Life of Jewish mysticism (geometric diagrams of the Sefirot, the kabbalah's manifestations of the divine personality that are also understood as a symbolic representation of traits that make up the human psyche), and the E-model, states that the two personality systems share numerous common sources that derive from antiquity. These include Pythagoreanism, Neoplatonism, Gnosticism, and Sufism. He makes the point that while Gurdjieff credits the E-model to the secret Samoun brotherhood that lived near Mesopotamia around the end of the third millennium B.C.E., clearly predating Sufism, the kabbalah views the Old Testament figure Abraham as its founder and claims that his sons, born of his concubines, brought this secret knowledge east to the same region at approximately the same time.

Addison builds a convincing argument for recognizing connections between the E-model and the kabbalah. Without going into the details of his argument here, he correlates the nine Sefirot with the E-model in the following way: Point One aligns with *Hochma* (All-knowing, correct, internalized father, Abba), Point Two with *Bina* (understanding, controlling, supernal mother, Ima), Point Three with *Gedula* (Impetus to Be Great), Point Four with *Tiferet* (beauty, romantic longing), Point Five with *Din* (bound, enclosed, limited), Point Six with *Nezeh* (enduring, seeking authority), Point Seven with *Hod* (splendor), Point Eight with *Yesod* (seminal force), and Point Nine with *Shechina* (accepting presence).

The psychological profiles of the E-types constellate around a central feature. Other E-model authors describe in detail how these features approximate the psychological states described in many major religious traditions (as we have seen): the seven deadly sins of Christianity, the mind-states of Buddhism, the sacred psychology of Sufism, and the kabbalah. The fact that ancient personality systems are contained in variants of the E-model in esoteric Christianity, Sufism, and Judaism implies an even older common source.

It is apparent that there is a "missing link" in the history of the E-model, as there are other strands that lead into the modern-day E-model. For instance, the Platonic tradition describes a philosophy that resonates with the E-model—Plato's ideal forms: nine perfect essential states and a tenth called unity.

CORRELATIONS BETWEEN E-MODEL TYPE, THE KABBALAH'S SEFIROT, CHRISTIANITY'S CAPITAL SINS, AND *DSM-I* CATEGORIES

E-Model	Kabbalah	Capital Sins	DSM-I
Point One—Moralizer	*Hochma*—All-knowing, correct	Anger	Compulsive
Point Two—Helper	*Bina*—Understanding, supernal mother	Pride	Histrionic
Point Three—Organizer	*Gedula*—Impetus to be great	Deceit (Self)	Narcissist (Secondary)
Point Four—Dreamer	*Tiferet*—Romantic longing	Envy	Depressive
Point Five—Observer	*Din*—Bound, enclosed	Avarice	Avoidant
Point Six—Questioner	*Nezeh*—Seeking authority	Fear	Paranoid
Point Seven—Entertainer	*Hod*—Splendor	Gluttony	Narcissist (Primary)
Point Eight—Protector	*Yesod*—Seminal force	Lust	Sociopath
Point Nine—Peacekeeper	*Shechina*—Accepting presence	Sloth	Obsessive-compulsive

The Hermetic schools of Egypt with their links to ancient cosmology are surfacing as another possible source for the diagram. Whatever that source may be, what is certain is that deep in the human psyche is an impulse to understand the personality of others, and the leaders, initiates, and adepts of many sacred traditions over many centuries used a form of secret knowledge to gratify this impulse, including the twenty-five-hundred-year tradition of Buddhism. "Even Buddhism," as Mark Epstein points out in his 1995 book *Thoughts Without a Thinker,* "is, in its psychological form, a depth psychology. It is able to describe, in terms that would make any psychoanalyst proud, the full range of the human emotional experience." Depth psychology, too, the full range of human emotional experience, is the territory of the E-model.

How can it be that a contemporary psychological system has its roots in these sacred traditions? Is it possible that there's a link between personality type and spirituality? Not only does the E-model posit that understanding personality type can be accomplished without first accessing pathologies, but also it takes another revolutionary leap in viewing psychology and spirituality as two sides of the same coin. Finding one's E-type is only the initial step; learning how to work with one's strategy, to grow in understanding, compassion, and acceptance of oneself and others is the journey. To this end the technology of the sacred traditions—such as training awareness, using the practices of breathing and meditation, developing a sense of ground and presence by employing principles of, for instance, the martial arts—becomes viable and within reach of ordinary people, many of whom do not necessarily consider themselves spiritual seekers.

Theory and Research—What Is Type?

What is type? There is a large body of literature in psychology on personality type. Essentially it says that people have to survive in the world and need to organize traits and characteristics that will enable them to make their way and form relationships, with both themselves and others. Personality is about defense mechanisms, characteristic habits of thought, emotions that underpin thoughts, interpersonal aptitudes and abilities, and a way of handling the body to manage energy. While all people have access to all these areas, in many instances one area predominates, and the literature describes people as falling broadly into body, mental, and emotional types. The E-model is dead on in recognizing these distinctions. The E-model is organized into triads that are made up of these distinct energies. Points Two, Three, and Four are the emotional triad; Points Five, Six, and Seven are the mental triad; and Points Eight, Nine, and One are the body-based triad.

Enneagram types (E-types) are powerful habits kept in place to help normal and high-functioning people manage their existential fears that can range from mild anxiety to outright nihilism. Ordinary people spend great energy in keeping these habits intact. Going on automatic, reproducing the psychological conditions that keep panic at bay—these feel like sensible activities, life-preserving instead of life-dulling. In an E-model frame these energetic habits can be described as the narrowed attentional focus that underpins the survival strategy of each individual and becomes his or her view of the world. They are the inner behaviors of normal and high-functioning people, people who do not relate their personality habits to descriptions of pathologies. Yet these same people in E-model classes—listening to others like themselves who have developed some degree of self-awareness and can describe their inner world—resonate with what they are hearing as the familiar patterning of their own lives. Having panels of self-observers talking about themselves is a potent methodology for E-model public education.

Personality type has traditionally been identified through pathology. The psychological world has found pathology helpful, because if people can be brought to see how their personalities disintegrated, they can be helped to reintegrate themselves. Psychotherapists are trained to find how the personality defense mechanisms have broken down, rather than to concentrate on what's working. The E-model provides a format for normal, non-pathological people to examine through close self-observation what component of anxiety their habitual behavior papers over. E-model psychology pinpoints nine patterns of avoidance—error, emotional needs, failure, ordinariness, connection, deviance (being different), pain, vulnerability, and conflict. Our sense of self is manufactured largely out of one of these avoidances in our emotional experience. When we face up to, process, and integrate those aspects of ourselves we've been denying, the self can emerge as a whole, and the grace of compassion for self and others becomes possible.

The E-model offers the choice for proactive, rather than reactive, behavior and the opportunity to cease going on automatic without realizing what one is doing. Knowledge of their E-type frees people to expand the way they think about themselves, to find compassion for themselves and others, to manage emotional energy with more skill, and to begin to end habitual behavior.

E-Model Specifics

This section explains the theoretical terms used in the chapters in this book that describe the personality types. These explanations give added depth and perspective to the type descriptions.

Triads

As we've seen in psychological literature, many authors have different ways of observing what they call body, mental, and emotional types. These are three distinct modalities of being, three broad patterns of behavior, three primal, intuitive motivations driving how people operate in the world. The E-model accounts for these three basic ways of behavior in the E-triads, which I call Attachers (emotional triad), Detachers (mental triad), and Defenders (instinctual triad). (See the illustration on page 259.) My nomenclature is based on the work of the pioneering psychologist

Karen Horney, who in *Our Inner Conflicts* (1945) describes the three broad personality patterns as those of moving toward people, moving away from people, and moving against people. (See chapter 1, "Discovering Your Parenting Personality.")

One modality—that of the Attachers—can be described as outer-directed attention, *moving toward people,* a way of making sense of and operating in the world through connection to people and relationships. The emotional context is the Attachers' environment. Points Two, Three, and Four are Attachers.

Another modality—that of the Detachers—can be described as inner-directed attention, *moving away from people,* a way of making sense of and operating in the world from inside one's head. The mental context is the Detachers' environment. Points Five, Six, and Seven are Detachers.

The third modality—that of the Defenders—can be described

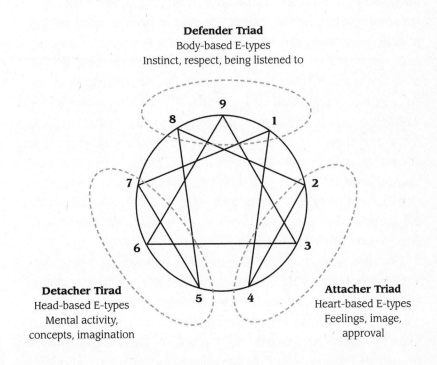

Defender Triad
Body-based E-types
Instinct, respect, being listened to

Detacher Tirad
Head-based E-types
Mental activity,
concepts, imagination

Attacher Triad
Heart-based E-types
Feelings, image,
approval

The E-Model with the Triads

as self-protective attention, *moving (brushing up) against people,* a way of making sense of and operating in the world with an awareness of intrapersonal space and boundaries. The body-based context is the Defenders' environment. Points Eight, Nine, and One are Defenders.

Attentional Focus

Much of what makes the E-model such a powerful model of personality is its ability to pinpoint an unconscious, characteristic narrowing of attention in each strategy. Helen Palmer is a leading author and teacher of the E-model. Palmer's (*The Enneagram: Understanding Yourself and the Others in Your Life,* 1988) original contribution to the field is the classification of the foci of attention of the E-types. This attentional focus directly affects behavior in all its forms, including motivation, learning, communication, leadership, relationships with others, and so on. The narrowing of attention ordinarily operates as an involuntary response, until we become aware of its grip on our lives. The narrowing lens of attention through which we perceive the world most often looms so large in our unconscious awareness that it becomes our entire worldview: "My attention is on gaining approval for what I accomplish, and therefore so is everyone else's"—the Organizer (the Organizer parent). "My attention is on seeking safety and certainty in every situation, and therefore so is everyone else's"—the Questioner (the Questioner parent). "My attention is on taking on the agenda of others, and therefore so is everyone else's"—the Peacekeeper (the Peacekeeper parent).

Recognizing when attention narrows and the lens takes over allows people to see themselves anew and to work constructively with their perceptual bias. Once we understand its power, we can consciously use it in positive ways and modify its tendency to induce worldview myopia. An Organizer parent will always remain an Organizer, but the attentional narrowing to tasks and getting the job done regardless of human cost (his or her own and that to others) can be modified to take cognizance of personal feelings and the input and concerns of others.

We can understand and appreciate the intentions of those whose attentional focus makes them see the world differently from the way we do. Knowing their own strategy and learning about the eight others with whom they share the world incrementally increases understanding and compassion and vastly reduces misunderstandings and misapplied motives.

A frequent question I'm asked in workshops involves the nature/nurture dichotomy of developmental psychology. Both propositions are evident in E-type development. Most E-model authors and theorists currently agree that people are born with a disposition toward one of the nine strategies (nature). If a person's childhood was tense and stressful, the E-type characteristics go deep. If a person's childhood was secure, the E-type characteristics appear more lightly (nurture). In both instances the perception of the focus of attention is a key consideration of E-type.

- Point One—error/how corrected
- Point Two—needs of others
- Point Three—tasks
- Point Four—what's missing
- Point Five—acquiring knowledge
- Point Six—scanning for hidden dangers
- Point Seven—pleasant plans and future options
- Point Eight—power and control
- Point Nine—others' agenda

Gifts

It is a truism that people have low and high sides to their personalities: "This brings out the best (or worst) in me." The classification of the gifts of the E-types is another of my original contributions to the system. The gifts of the E-types come to the fore when people are feeling secure within themselves and managing their anxiety threshold. When they're not in the downside of their fixation, not avoiding their central preoccupation, they are in a sense more whole, more able to utilize the positive flow of their personality traits. Each description of the personality types in this book discusses these implications in depth.

- Point One—moral compass
- Point Two—true altruism
- Point Three—leadership on behalf of others
- Point Four—creativity and uniqueness
- Point Five—rationality
- Point Six—logic
- Point Seven—optimism
- Point Eight—harnessing energy to empower others
- Point Nine—universal love

Avoidances

E-model psychology pinpoints nine pivotal avoidances. These avoidances play a major role in our habitual, or unawakened, personality. Our sense of self and our very defense mechanisms are largely put in place around the avoidances. Much of what drives people to behave the way they do and much of how they experience their emotional world is a consequence of avoiding or denying these preoccupations. People become anxious over what they're avoiding and experience themselves through their anxiety.

A first step in self-awareness can be to begin examining what component of anxiety a person's compulsive behavior covers over. When those aspects of ourselves that have been avoided and denied are owned up to, processed, and integrated, the self can begin to emerge as a whole.

For example, an Observer parent avoids connection—to emotions and, to some degree, people. Observers are aware of a need to manage (hoard) their time, energy, and private space. Connections are unpredictable; they can lead to unexpected and unwanted drains on the Observer's reserves. Each day the Observer expends just so much energy and time. Surprises and unexpected demands can derail the Observer who is managing/avoiding connection with a mental control switch.

The Protector parent avoids vulnerability. Being vulnerable means not knowing who is in control or whether that person will be fair, and opening oneself to the risk of being jumped. This sounds like suicidal behavior to the Protector. So they make sure they're safe by taking control, seeking confrontation, and often moving into action without thinking. However, Protector parents will often let down their guard with their family and share the softer, more open side of their personality that not many other people know.

- Point One—error
- Point Two—own emotional needs
- Point Three—failure
- Point Four—ordinariness
- Point Five—connection
- Point Six—deviance (being seen as different)
- Point Seven—pain
- Point Eight—vulnerability
- Point Nine—conflict

Growth Path

The E-model describes nine ways of inner growth, each based on the central feature or fixation and moving toward its essential opposite. This has obvious implications for all who discover their E-type strategy and who, through self-awareness and attention practice, transform their core energy from the bondage of habitual behavior to the relief of freedom from its charge.

Parents encounter these fixations in their children daily. Good parents have probably already intervened in charged situations. In a sense they've indirectly enabled their children to think about working with their core energy (fixation) in a more constructive way. The E-model provides sophisticated interventions for what parents grope toward almost instinctively.

Questioner children may take a while to learn to ride a bicycle; they will continually look around to see if you're holding the seat as they pedal. If you're always there, they will forgo their preoccupation with falling off and begin to trust that their own balance and the forward momentum generated by their pedaling will allow them to ride. When they finally yell at you to let go, you've helped them find the courage to ride alone. Although you may feel that point was reached long before, because you were trustworthy and always there the Questioner children can now trust themselves more easily.

- Point One—from criticality and judging to serenity
- Point Two—from pride to humility
- Point Three—from self-deceit to honesty
- Point Four—from envy to equanimity
- Point Five—from hoarding (guarding) to allowing
- Point Six—from fear to courage
- Point Seven—from no limits to restraint
- Point Eight—from excess to trusting sufficiency
- Point Nine—from being asleep to oneself to right action

Essence

Essence is that quality of being that arises when people are totally present in the moment. No thoughts, memories, associations, emotions, or sensory perceptions interfere in the experience of being fully present. These moments are commonly known in our culture as "being in the flow" or "being in the zone" (see Csikszentmihalyi). In sports, athletes talk of being in the zone, a phenomenon that occurs when time and space take on a quality akin to slow motion. The real split-second timing to gather instinct, training, and reactivity to accomplish the athlete's goal seems to take place in a virtual pocket of enough time to do what has to be done. Essence qualities occur when people speak or act before they know they've spoken or acted. It's almost as if there is no sense of a dualistic self that can be observed. These are the peak moments of our life experience. The following list attempts to name the essence qualities, but these are only approximations. Our perceptual language does not have words for these qualities. Ephemeral, fleeting, they disappear the moment awareness of them arises.

- Point One—perfection
- Point Two—freedom/will
- Point Three—hope
- Point Four—universal belonging
- Point Five—omniscient awareness
- Point Six—faith
- Point Seven—commitment to work
- Point Eight—truth (fairness and justice)
- Point Nine—universal love

Arrows

While much of the psychological value of the E-model lies in its descriptions of the E-types, much of its predictive power lies in the patterns of interconnecting lines. These lines point away from and toward any one point on the diagram. In other words, every point is connected to two others with the arrows (see the illustration on page 266). The arrows' directions mirror predictable shifts in our E-type strategies, as when people feel personally secure or when they find themselves in stressful situations. For example, parents involved in an activity with their child where everything clicks relax their inner defenses. In that situation they may move against the arrows into behavior patterns of the E-type behind their own. Doing an activity where the chemistry is wrong is stressful. Following the flow pattern of the arrows, they are likely in this situation to move with the arrow and adopt the characteristics of the type ahead.

In these situations a task-driven Organizer parent can come across as almost a different person. In a secure mode the Organizer goes to the Questioner and reacts more slowly and thoughtfully and allows more time for process. In the shift to Peacekeeper under conditions of stress, the Organizer parent may come across as if acting in a daze—spinning his wheels, unable to prioritize, struggling to move into action. Once we know our basic strategy, we can connect the arrows to our stress and secure points. When people find their E-type strategy, they also discover these two other places they go to on the E-model, and they gravitate naturally into them.

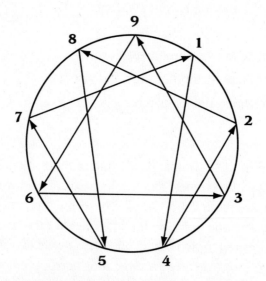

Secure point (move against the arrow, e.g., 3-6; 4-1).
Stress point (move with the arrow, e.g., 9-6; 8-5).

Basic E-Model with Arrows

Wings

People also have wings, the points on either side of their E-type. One wing may predominate, or both may be equally available, and these wings color or flavor the E-types. The Points Three-Six-Nine triangle have wings that can be seen as variants of the core preoccupations of that E-type triad, or even as a more inner-directed and outer-directed version of the core point. For example, Point Six with a Point Five wing (inner-directed) may be more private, withdrawn, and overtly fearful. Point Six with a Point Seven wing (outer-directed) may be more outgoing, friendly, less overtly suspicious and doubtful.

Similarly, a person with an E-type that falls on the hexagon (the figure formed by the other interconnecting lines) still acts out his or her preoccupations, but with a specific coloring. Point Eight with a Point Nine wing handles confrontation in a more stubborn, passive way, while Point Eight with a Point Seven wing is less overtly confrontational, more jocular, disarming the anger with a little charm.

Name Attribution

1. The name "Observer" is attributed to Helen Palmer. The name "Helper" is attributed to Don Riso and Russ Hudson. The names "Organizer, Dreamer, Questioner, Entertainer, Protector, Peacekeeper, and Moralizer" are attributed to Janet Levine.

2. The Parenting Personality questionnaire and profile in chapter 1 has been modified for parents. It is based on the Triads Personality Indicator (TPI) for educators that I developed from research and interviews, and tested initially in 1997 on over twelve hundred educators at all levels. Hundreds more workshop participants shared in the refinement of the instrument through their feedback.

REFERENCES

Addison, H. (1997). *The Enneagram and Kabbalah: Reading Your Soul.* Woodstock, Vt.: Jewish Lights Publishing.

American Psychiatric Association (1952). *Diagnostic and Statistical Manual of Mental Disorders (DSM-I).* Washington, D.C.: Mental Hospitals Service.

Bakhtiar, L. (1993). *Traditional Psychoethics and Personality Paradigm.* Chicago: Institute of Traditional Psychoethics and Guidance.

Csikszentmihalyi, M. (1991). *Flow: The Psychology of Optimal Experience.* New York: HarperCollins.

Epstein, M. (1995). *Thoughts Without a Thinker.* New York: Basic Books.

Horney, K. (1945). *Our Inner Conflicts.* New York: W. W. Norton.

Levine, J. (1999). *The Enneagram Intelligences: Understanding Personality for Effective Teaching and Learning.* Westport, Conn.: Greenwood Publishing Group.

Naranjo, C. (1990). *Ennea-type Structures.* Nevada City, Calif.: Gateways/ IDHHB.

Oldham, J. and Morris, L. B. (1995). *The New Personality Self-Portrait: Why You Think, Work, Love, and Act the Way You Do.* New York: Bantam Books.

Palmer, H. (1988). *The Enneagram: Understanding Yourself and the Others in Your Life.* New York: HarperCollins.

TOPICS FOR DISCUSSION

In your discussion group, you probably have many if not all of the parenting personalities described in the book. A proven way to discover more about each personality type is to hear each parent speak about his- or herself after reading this book.

Ask the Attachers (Helper, Organizer, Dreamer) to describe their inner emotional life, especially as it relates to their children. Ask for stories about how they react to their children's successes and failures and how they respond when their children challenge them. Let them describe what situations they find the most comfortable or the least comfortable when interacting with their children. Why was it comfortable or uncomfortable? By referring to relevant chapters, together you can help them figure out why they behave this way.

Ask Helpers to discuss what triggers their constant behavior pattern of wanting to help others. Ask them about how they get their own emotional needs met. What do the words willpower and freedom mean to them in their parenting role?

Ask Organizers to discuss what triggers their constant behavior pattern of doing tasks. Ask them why failure is such a no-no. What does the word hope mean to them in their parenting role?

Ask Dreamers to discuss what triggers their constant behavior pattern of seeing the glass half empty, of something missing. Ask them about uniqueness, authenticity, and being ordinary. What does the word connection mean to them in their parenting role?

Ask the Detachers (Observer, Questioner, Entertainer) to describe their inner mental life, especially as it relates to their children. Ask for stories about how they react to their children's successes and failures and how they respond when their children challenge them. Let them describe those situations that they find the most comfortable or the least comfortable when interacting with their children. Why was it comfortable or uncomfortable? By referring to relevant chapters, together you can help them determine why they behave this way.

Ask Observers to discuss what triggers their constant behavior pattern of standing back, of trying to ascertain the big picture, before moving into action. Ask them why they place so much emphasis on being rational and maintaining distance (objectivity). What does the word omniscience (all-knowingness) mean to them in their parenting role?

Ask Questioners to discuss what triggers their constant scanning for hidden dangers, their doubts and their fears. Ask them why they would rather not draw attention to themselves or become a target. What does the word faith mean to them in their parenting role?

Ask Entertainers to discuss what triggers their constant behavior pattern of seeking more and more options. Ask them what is so difficult about commitment. What does the word sacrifice mean to them in their parenting roles?

Ask the Defenders (Protector, Peacekeeper, Moralizer) to describe the way they view intra- and interpersonal boundaries, especially relative to their children. Ask for stories about how they react to their children's successes and failures and how they respond when their children challenge them. Let them describe situations where they are the most comfortable or the least comfortable when interacting with their children. Why was it comfortable or uncomfortable? By referring to relevant chapters, together you can help them find out why they behave this way.

Ask Protectors to discuss what triggers their constant behavior pattern of vigilance and confrontation, especially in threatening situations. Ask them why being vulnerable is such a charged concept for them. What do the words justice and truth mean to them in their parenting role?

Ask Peacekeepers to discuss what triggers their behavior pattern of going to sleep to themselves. Ask them why they avoid confrontation. What do the words universal love mean to them in their parenting role?

Ask Moralizers to discuss what triggers their constant behavior pattern to be right, to be correct. Ask them about their preoccupation with not making errors. What does the word serenity mean to them in their parenting role?

All parents in the group can discuss which of the key motivations and steps in the action program of parenting personality styles speak most directly to them. Discuss how you might implement the recommended actions in your role as a parent. Think of specific situations and stories where such knowledge will be/or would have been useful.

Discuss how you are going to introduce and share this new knowledge about your self and your personality with your family.

You can contact the author by email at jlevinegrp@aol.com. For more information check out her website: www.enneagram-edge. com.

INDEX

A

Addison, Howard, 253–254
altruism, 46–48
anger
  Moralizers and, 234–236, 240
  Protectors and, 187–188
approval
  Helpers and, 34, 50–52
  Organizers and, 73–75
Attachers
  description of, 16–17, 258–259
  discussion group topics for, 269
  key issues for, 17
  See also Dreamers; Helpers;
    Organizers
attentional focus, 260–261
author
  activism of, 5
  email and website of, 271
authority issues
  Entertainers and, 159
  Protectors and, 181–182
  Questioners and, 131, 137–139
avoidances, 262–263

B

Bakhtiar, Laleh, 253
balance, aligning inner, 248
"being in the zone," 264–265
blame, accepting, 184–185
boundaries, building
  Dreamers and, 92–94
  Helpers and, 34–35, 41–43, 45
  Peacekeepers and, 207
breathing exercise, 247–248

C

commitment
  Entertainers and, 160, 161
  Peacekeepers and, 213–214
communication
  deepening, with child, 3–5
  Helpers and, 51–52
  Peacekeepers and, 210–211
  Questioners and, 144–145
  See also conflict
compartmentalizing, 117
conflict
  Observers and, 114–115
  Peacekeepers and, 201, 206,
    210–212, 215–216
  Protectors and, 176–177, 184–185,
    187
connection with child, 2
control
  Moralizers and, 224–226, 227, 236
  Organizers and, 56, 57, 66–67, 72
  Protectors and, 171–173, 181
counting to ten, 247
criticism, 154–155, 239–240

D

Defenders
  description of, 27–28, 258–260
  discussion group topics for,
    270–271
  key issues for, 28
  See also Moralizers; Peacekeepers;
    Protectors
defense mechanism. *See* self-defense
    mechanism
Detachers
  description of, 22–23, 258–259
  discussion group topics for, 269–270
  fear and, 113–114
  key issues for, 22–23
  See also Entertainers; Observers;
    Questioners

Diagnostic and Statistical Manual of Mental Disorders, 1st edition (DSM-I), 252, 255
discussion group topics 269–271
Dreamers
  appreciation, believing in, 90–91
  authentic self, finding, 95–96
  boundaries, respecting, 92–93
  communication style of, 4
  description of, 20–22
  discussion group topics for, 269
  equanimity, developing, 83, 88–89
  feelings, supporting, 91–92
  gifts, positive use of, 94–95
  good enough parenting, 96–97
  interactions, taking personally, 93–94
  melancholia of, 80–81, 82–83
  mood and energy swings, evening out, 97–98
  opening self to others, 94
  ordinary, avoiding, 89–90
  parenting steps for, 98–99
  personal account, 85–88
  "something's missing" case study, 79–82
  "special parent" case study, 82–85
  strengths and weaknesses of, 100
  universal belonging concept, 108

E
email address of author, 271
E-model. *See* Enneagram (E-model) theory
emotions
  Dreamers and, 80, 81–82, 84, 93–94, 97–98
  Entertainers and, 160–162
  Moralizers and, 236
  Observers and, 101, 103, 106, 111–114
  Organizers and, 58, 62, 64–65, 75–77
  Questioners and, 129–130
empowering others, 48, 181
energy
  Dreamers and, 97–98
  Observers and, 116–118
  Peacekeepers and, 214–215
  Protectors and, 186, 191–192
Enneagram (E-model) theory
  arrows, 265–266
  attentional focus, 260–261
  avoidances, 262–263
  diagram of, 251
  essence, 264–265
  experience with, 7
  gifts, 261–262
  growth path, 263–264
  history of, 252–256
  name attribution, 267
  overview of, 1
  personality modes, 15–16, 256–258
  questions to determine personality mode, 9–15
  triads, 258–260
  wings, 267
Entertainers
  commitment and, 160, 161
  communication style of, 4
  criticism and, 154–155
  description of, 26–27
  discussion group topics for, 270
  "don't fence me in" case study, 152–155
  as entitled egalitarians, 159
  feelings, identifying and staying with, 160–162
  head, getting out of, 163–164
  lateness, pattern of, 154
  "magic circle of imagination" case study, 149–152
  mind, slowing racing, 165–166
  Observers compared to, 151
  optimism, responses to, 158
  parenting steps for, 167–168
  personal account, 155–157
  planning patterns of, 164–165
  positive spin on reality and, 162–163
  present, staying with, 166–167
  strengths and weaknesses of, 169
entitlement, sense of, 159

Epstein, Mark, 256
equanimity, 83, 88–89
essence, 264–265

F
facilitator, becoming, 6–7
failure
    Moralizers and, 226–227
    Organizers and, 57, 71–72
    Peacekeepers and, 197
fear, 135–137, 161
Feeling Mode. *See* Attachers;
    Dreamers; Helpers; Organizers

G
gifts
    identifying, 6
    overview of, 261–262
    using, 94–95
good enough parenting, 96–97,
    233–234
growth path
    for Observers, 104, 121
    overview of, 263–264
    for Questioners, 264
Gurdjieff, George Ivanovitch, 253,
    254

H
Helpers
    altruism, false, 47–48
    boundaries, building, 34–35,
        41–43, 45
    communication style of, 4
    confrontation and, 51–52
    description of, 17–18
    disapproval, dislike, and, 34,
        50–52
    discussion group topics for, 269
    help, giving judiciously, 45–46
    identity, building, 48–49
    "I'm here to help you" case study,
        36–39
    limits, setting, 46–47, 52
    needs, stating, 43–44
    "never say no" case study, 33–36
    others, empowering, 48

others, giving to, 37–38
    parenting steps for, 53–54
    personal account, 40–42
    self-identity, building and
        adhering to sense of, 44–45
    self-image, separating from
        achievements of others, 49–50
    strengths and weaknesses of,
        40–41, 54
honesty, practicing, 67–68
hope, 61
Horney, Karen, 258–259
Hudson, Russ, 267

I
Ichazo, Oscar, 252, 253
identification, 70–71
implementing program, 245–246
inner critic of Moralizers, 224–228,
    233–234, 236–237, 240
Instinctual Mode. *See* Defenders;
    Moralizers; Peacekeepers;
    Protectors
interspace between self and others,
    227

J
judgmentalism, 223, 240

K
kabbalah, 253–254, 255

L
labeling others, 246
limits, setting, 34–35, 41–43, 46–47,
    52. *See also* boundaries,
    building
love, unconditional, 72, 73, 198
loyalty, 139–140

M
Mental Mode. *See* Detachers;
    Entertainers; Observers;
    Questioners
momentum, 174
monkey-mind, 22, 152

Moralizers
    anger, expressing legitimate,
        235–236
    anger, recognizing source of,
        234–235
    communication style of, 4
    control and, 224–226, 227, 236
    criticism and, 155, 239–240
    description of, 31–32
    discussion group topics for, 271
    failure and, 226–227
    fun, having, 236–238
    good enough parenting, 233–234
    "heeding inner critic" case study,
        224–228
    inner critic and, 233–234, 236–237,
        240
    "moral compass" case study,
        221–224
    obsessing over details, 238–239
    parenting steps for, 241–242
    perfectionism and, 222–223, 224,
        230–232
    personal account, 228–230
    self-righteousness of, 232–233
    strengths and weaknesses of, 243

N
Naranjo, Claudio, 252
needs
    acknowledging, 38
    energy management and
        Observers, 116–118
    stating, 43–44

O
Observers
    avoidances of, 262–263
    big-picture thinking, managing,
        118–119
    communication style of, 4
    conflict and, 114–115
    description of, 23–24
    discussion group topics for, 270
    emotions, showing, 111–112
    energy management needs,
        116–118

    Entertainers compared to, 151
    growth path for, 104, 121
    "loving beyond words" case study,
        101–104
    parenting steps for, 122–123
    personal account, 108–111
    "puzzle pieces" case study,
        104–108
    self, sharing, 116
    self, trusting, 113–114
    social skills, practicing, 120–121
    spontaneity, role-modeling, 112
    strengths and weaknesses of, 123
    universal connection concept,
        107–108
Organizers
    approval and, 73–75
    Beaver vs. Peacock, 60
    communication style of, 4
    control and, 56, 57, 66–67, 72
    description of, 19–20
    discussion group topics for, 269
    "doing is great" case study, 55–59
    failure and, 57, 71–72
    honesty, practicing, 67–68
    identification and, 70–71
    image and, 72–73
    parenting steps for, 77–78
    personal account, 63–65
    "picture perfect" case study, 59–62
    self-worth, cultivating, 67
    slowing down, 65–66, 68–69
    staying present, 66, 75–76
    strengths and weaknesses of, 64,
        78
    stress and, 266
    task focus, altering, 69–70
    unconditional love and, 72, 73

P
pain, processing, 158
Palmer, Helen, 260, 267
parenting steps
    for Dreamers, 98–99
    for Entertainers, 167–168
    for Helpers, 53–54
    for Moralizers, 241–242

for Observers, 122–123
for Organizers, 77–78
for Peacekeepers, 217–218
practicing, 245–246
for Protectors, 192–193
for Questioners, 146–147
passive-aggressive behavior, 201,
212–214
Peacekeepers
autonomy, establishing, 206–207
choices and, 209–210
communication style of, 4
conflict and, 206, 210–212,
215–216
description of, 29–31
discussion group topics for, 271
energy, managing, 214–215
intuitive ability of, 189
"losing agenda" case study,
198–201
"Mother Earth" case study,
195–198
no, saying, 207–208
parenting steps for, 217–218
passive-aggressive behavior of,
201, 212–214
personal account, 202–204
prioritizing, value of, 204–205
procrastination and, 208–209
self, claiming pieces of, 205–206
speaking with animation,
210–211
staying present, 215–216
strengths and weaknesses of,
200–201, 219
perfectionism, 222–223, 224,
230–232
personality
as strength and weakness, 3
types of, 2, 256–258
typing and stereotyping, 246
See also Enneagram (E-model)
theory
present, staying with
Entertainers and, 166–167
Observers and, 116
Organizers and, 66, 75–76

Peacekeepers and, 215–216
pride, false sense of, 38, 39
privacy, 116, 117
problem solving, 119
procrastination
Moralizers and, 238
Peacekeepers and, 208–209
Questioners and, 144
Protectors
ambiguity, finding, 182–183
anger, managing, 187–188
authority issues and, 181–182
avoidances of, 263
blame, accepting, 184–185
bluntness and truthfulness,
183–184
burnout, awareness of, 190–191
communication style of, 4
confrontation and, 176–177,
184–185, 187
description of, 28–29
discussion group topics for,
270–271
empowerment and, 181
energy, containing, 186, 191–192
"freedom to do it my way" case
study, 174–178
intuition, trusting, 189–190
"larger than life" case study,
171–174
parenting steps for, 192–193
personal account, 178–180
revenge and, 188–189
slowing down, 191–192
strengths and weaknesses of, 194

Q
Questioners
authority issues and, 131, 137–139
communication style of, 4
description of, 24–26
devil's advocate role and, 143
discussion group topics for, 270
fear and, 135–137
goals, setting, 144
growth path, 264
loyalty and, 139–140

Questioners *(continued)*
"never let guard down" case study, 125–129
"nothing good or bad" case study, 129–132
parenting steps for, 146–147
personal account, 132–134
safety and, 126, 144–145
strengths and weaknesses of, 148
trust and, 138, 139–140
types of, 135–136
underdog, protecting, 141
vigilance of, 142

R
reframing, 162
Riso, Don, 267

S
safety
Peacekeepers and, 210
Questioners and, 126, 144–145
self-awareness and, 247–248
self
authentic, finding, 95–96
claiming pieces of, 205–206
interspace between others and, 227
pleasing, 50–51
sharing, 116
trusting, 113–114
self-awareness, gaining, 5–6, 247–249
self-deceit, 59, 60
self-defeating behavior pattern, changing, 2–3, 6–7
self-defense mechanism
Helpers and, 34
Moralizers and, 236

personality type and, 256–258
Protectors and, 188–189
self-forgetting, 27, 235
self-identity, building and adhering to sense of, 44–45
self-image, 49–50, 72–73
self-righteousness, 232–233
self-validation, 48
self-worth, 48–49, 67
silence, 119
sins, capital, of Christianity, 255
slowing down
Entertainers and, 165–166
Organizers and, 65–66, 68–69
Protectors and, 191–192
spontaneity, 112, 236–237
stereotyping people, 246
stress
Dreamers and, 80
Organizers and, 266
reducing, 5
Sufism, 253, 254

T
thinking patterns, 238
triads, 258–260
Triads Personality Indicator, 267
trust
Helpers and, 41–42
Observers and, 113–114
Protectors and, 187
Questioners and, 138, 139–140
typing people, 246

U
underdog, protecting, 141

W
website of author, 271